Living In

BALANCE

Living In
BALANCE

A DYNAMIC APPROACH FOR
CREATING HARMONY & WHOLENESS
IN A CHAOTIC WORLD

JOEL LEVEY AND MICHELLE LEVEY

FOREWORD BY THE DALAI LAMA

MJF BOOKS
NEW YORK

Published by MJF Books
Fine Communications
Two Lincoln Square
60 West 66th Street
New York, NY 10023

Living in Balance
LC Control Number 00-136522
ISBN 1-56731-433-3

This edition published by arrangement with Conari Press.
Cover Art Direction: Ame Beanland
Cover Design: Nita Ybarra
Cover photo: Kerama; Flash Photonica
Interior Design: Suzanne Albertson
Interior Diagrams: Sheila Hoffman
Authors' photo: jed & kaoru share

Manufactured in the United States of America on acid-free paper
MJF Books and the MJF colophon are trademarks of Fine Creative Media, Inc.

10   9   8   7   6   5   4   3   2

THIS BOOK IS DEDICATED TO ALL THOSE

WHO YEARN FOR BALANCE,

AND TO THE SPIRIT OF HARMONY AND WHOLENESS

AWAKENING WITHIN US ALL.

FOREWORD

Humankind has always been faced with problems, and in different parts of the world, at different times, people have come to varying conclusions about the nature of these problems and how to tackle them. One of Buddhism's most relevant lessons is the avoidance of extremes. It teaches that freedom and happiness will not be found in the extremes of either sensual indulgence or mortification: a middle way must be found.

Today there is an overemphasis on the external world. Science has rapidly extended our understanding of external phenomena, and technological advances have contributed to improved health and physical comfort. Yet even in the most developed countries we do not find a corresponding increase in peace and happiness; if anything, there is even greater anxiety and stress. Fear stimulates the need for terrifyingly destructive weapons systems, while greed gives rise to damage and pollution of the environment, putting the very existence of humanity at risk.

These trends are symptomatic of the dangers of pursuing external progress alone. What is missing is a corresponding inner development. To redeem the balance, our new frontier should be inner worlds, and not outer space. If the mind is explored with the same stringent scrutiny applied in other branches of science, it will certainly be of immense benefit not only to individuals but to society as a whole.

Within the world's contemplative traditions can be found numerous methods for investigating and training the mind. This book summarizes why the adoption of such "inner science" is necessary now, and how interest has grown in the search for compatibility between contemporary needs and ancient techniques. It presents an array of methods for transforming the mind. These methods may seem relatively simple, but to be effective they must be applied steadily in a rigorous, rational way—much as a physicist or a chemist conducts his experiments—so that the inner scientist may both test and become familiar with them.

This book will be of use to anyone interested in exploring and transforming the mind. As more people achieve some degree of mental calm, insight, or the ability to transform negative emotions into positive ones, there will be a natural reinforcement of basic human values and consequently a greater chance for peace and happiness for all.

—THE DALAI LAMA

STAYING CENTERED IN
CHALLENGING TIMES

As we sit down to write the introduction to this book on balance, we have to laugh as we are reminded of a cartoon we saw in *The New Yorker* some years ago. It showed two people talking at a crowded restaurant. One person leans over the menu and asks the other, "Have you read any good book reviews lately?" With humor and succinctness, the cartoonist had captured the predicament of our all-too-busy lives.

What does it mean to live in balance in our world today? Through the journey of writing this book we have been bringing this question into every day, in our work and travels, and into our meditations and our dreams at night. What we have discovered is that no realm of experience exists outside of this theme of "balance"! In fact, dynamic balance seems to be a central organizing principle of every living system in the universe. Is it any wonder, then, that as our lives become more complex, with increasing demands and less time to meet those demands, that the challenge and value of balance is looming large in our collective psyche? From boardrooms to bedrooms, in health care, education, and global forums, people are seeking to bring more of this elusive quality into their lives.

In our own lives, as a husband-and-wife consulting team to a wide spectrum of organizations, we witness, on a daily basis, the escalating longing for greater balance, emanating from people everywhere. Feeling this need resonating within ourselves as well, we wanted to respond to this general malaise of our time, to reach out to people's feelings of being overwhelmed and out of balance within themselves and with others. From our own experience, we have found many strategies and perspectives that can help restore and maintain a sense of inner and outer balance—even if you can't simplify your lifestyle, quit your job, or run away from home! We want to share this essential wisdom with you, and to offer you the knowledge and reassurance that balance can be cultivated and enjoyed.

"Balance—I've heard of it!"
—**Les Kurtz**

"We see that harmony does not mean a balance-at-rest but a vibrant, bi-polar energy force that urges on all other energy."
—**Matthew Fox**

Rather than try to write the definitive, exhaustive (and exhausting!) book about balance, we decided that the wisest course would be to acknowledge the immensity of the issue up front, and then focus on providing you with some practical, easy-to-integrate techniques to bring the living reality of balance and inner peace more alive for you, and for all whose lives you touch. We've been deeply inspired to see that the practices we ourselves use to keep balanced on the waves of our own busy lives work as reliably for the folks we've introduced them to. Those who have taken our approaches to heart and integrated them into their day-to-day lives have shown us that applying the wisdom of balance can truly save your health, your sanity, your relationships, your job, the quality of your life, and even your life itself!

Where Are You Right Now?

Pause for a moment now to appreciate where you are in the journey of your life, and to wonder at the miracle of your being. Some decades ago, through the merging of two cells in perfect harmony and balance, a doorway into life was opened to you. Myriad experiences, lessons, breakdowns, and breakthroughs later, you find yourself sitting here with this book in your hands, questioning, yearning, and wondering.

This book comes to you likely at just the right time, and at an appropriate stage of your pondering of your life with all its opportunities and challenges. In that spirit, we invite you to take the ideas and methods that you find here to heart. Listen deeply to the many voices that will speak to you through these pages; look for the value, meaning, and practical applications of what you discover here for enhancing the quality of your life and your influence in the lives of others. Much of what you find here will be new, and much will remind you again of things you once knew, but may have forgotten. Please take from these pages the inspiration you need to nourish and sustain yourself at this time in your journey.

"The spiritual gift on the inner journey is to know that creation comes out of chaos, and that even what has been created needs to be returned to chaos every now and then to get recreated in a more vital form. The spiritual gift on this inner journey is the knowledge that in chaos I can not only survive, but I can thrive, that there is vitality in that chaotic field of energy."

—**Parker J. Palmer**

Lessons of the Seasons

This morning we watched the spring equinox arrive with the rising sun. A new season filled with the joyful energies of bursting out, radiating, reaching, is blessing our hemisphere, bringing the pulsing vitality of awakening new life all around us.

As we've lived through the changing cycles of the seasons over the course of two years of writing this book and contemplating deeply the profound permutations, awesome implications, and vast dimensions of this mystery called balance, our lives, like the earth this morning, has been blessed and transformed.

We, too, feel like we are awakening into a new life as we put the final finishing touches on this work, and it feels so fitting that this book on balance is coming to completion at this time, ready to burst out with the tulips and the daffodils!

Through this deep immersion into the world of balance, we've seen that the lessons of balance abound everywhere when we begin to look for them, and like the fragrance of the cherry blossoms in the front yard, can always guide our way home. Our joined creativity has shown us the balance between structure and freedom, and the balance of our different styles. Through it all, we have grown in our appreciation and love for each other, and for this we are most grateful.

May the words on these pages help bring balance alive for you in new and meaningful ways, and may the turning of the seasons remind you that it is always the season for balance.

"Sitting quietly doing nothing spring comes and the grass grows by itself."
—**Zen poem**

An Inside-Out Approach
to Balanced Living

"To know how to wonder and question
is the first step of the mind
toward discovery."

—LOUIS PASTEUR

IT'S EASY TO SEE THAT MANY OF US
are living out of balance. People are working more and enjoying it less,
and the effects of such an unbalanced work life are manifesting everywhere. For example, numerous studies indicate that the majority of
Americans are suffering from a severe sleep deficit, and are currently getting 60 to 90 minutes less sleep per night than is necessary for optimal
health and performance. Many of us have no choice about where we
spend our time—or at least we feel we don't. As one young father said to
us recently, "Either I can spend time with my family or I can support
them—not both."

If you are reading this book, obviously you are feeling the need to examine this issue in your own life. So take a few minutes right now to consider these questions:

- What indications are there in your life that you are living more or less in balance?

- What indications are there in your life that your life is out of balance?

- What beliefs, values, and assumptions led you to your answers?

There will be time to examine your answers to these questions later. Right now, just hold onto what you learned as we look at some ways to begin thinking about balance itself.

The story of balance in our personal lives unfolds within a larger context of wholeness, but it begins from the inside out. That's why, in Section One, we begin by building the foundation for understanding this bigger picture. Here you will learn the number one skill for cultivating a balanced way of living. This indispensible skill is an inner awareness called mindfulness. Developing mindfulness gives you an internal guidance system that helps you know when you're heading off the course of balance, so you can self-correct and find your way back on track. It's like having an inner compass or radar, advising you of your present reality and the direction you're heading in, then lighting your way home. With this foundation to guide and support you, you are ready to begin the journey of turning toward balance—the most crucial journey of our time.

ONE

It's All About Balance

To everything there is a season, and a time to every purpose under
the heaven; A time to be born, and a time to die; A time to plant,
and a time to pluck up that which is planted; A time to kill, and a
time to heal; A time to break down, and a time to build up; A time
to weep, and a time to laugh; A time to mourn, and a time to dance;
A time to cast away stones, and a time to gather stones together; A
time to embrace, and a time to refrain from embracing; A time to
get, and a time to lose; A time to keep, and a time to cast away; A
time to rend, and a time to sew; A time to keep silence, and a time
to speak; A time to love, and a time to hate; A time of war, and a
time of peace.

—ECCLESIASTES 3:1-8

T hough our yearning for balance is a
deeply personal quest, it is truly a
journey of universal proportions.
While at an individual level, we may be feeling overwhelmed with trying to
juggle our jobs, family, and PTA, it is helpful to remember that every thing
at every level and dimension of the universe is constantly in search for balance. Indeed, it is the yearning for balance that keeps everything in our universe in motion, while the motion itself provides balance for the dimensions
of reality that dwell in stillness.

Science and spiritual teachings have converged to remind us that, in
truth, nothing is separate. Nothing can be sensibly studied in isolation from

its environment. Within seamless wholeness, the fields and flows of energy that we label as "living beings" or natural resources or "mysterious forces" all interact in perfect balance and harmony. In the dance of life, the currents of oppositely charged particles flow. Electrical, biochemical, chemical, and mind fields all interact and weave together. To truly understand anything, you must see it as a point of perfect balance, a reflection of everything else in the universe that converges in that moment and place to support the involvement of you, the observer and the observed. In the natural world, pressures build and are released, balance flows within natural limits that define the game of life. The earth spins, ever so steadily, moving through space at tens of thousands of miles per hour, yet nothing shakes apart and no one falls off!

In our own lives, balance emerges through the dynamic interplay of inner and outer forces. In order to get a feel for it, sense or imagine yourself sitting here now at the center of your universe, like an endless ocean of information and inspiration. Within you and around you myriad strong and subtle forces dance together in a movement of constant change to maintain the dynamic balance that weaves the amazing fabric of your life. Within you, each pulsing cell and organ maintains its integrity, form, and function by finding an active balance of energy and information flow within and across the permeable membranes that define the realms of "inner" and "outer." With the inhale and exhale of each breath, we affirm the life-giving flow of inside to outside and outside to inside. Breathing consciously with awareness, we begin to sense the flow and change that is at the heart of our experience of life, and in each moment, each interaction, each day well lived, we learn that balance is to be found in the flow of life.

As you approach this inquiry into the theme of balance in your life, you may discover, as we did, that everything will become a teacher for you. You will find lessons of balance in the rhythms of your breath and pulse, in the rising and setting of the sun, in the turning of the seasons, in the cycles of change that weave birth and death, activity and rest, work and play, and alone time and time with

"A human being is part of the whole called by us 'universe,' a part limited in time and space. We experience ourselves, our thoughts and feelings as something separate from the rest—a kind of optical delusion of consciousness. This delusion is a kind of prison for us, restricting us to our personal desires and to affection for a few persons nearest to us. Our task must be to free ourselves from this prison by widening our circle of compassion to embrace all living creatures and the whole of nature in its beauty."

—**Albert Einstein**

others into the wholeness of your existence. Viewed in this way, your whole life will become a wonder land in which the ongoing inquiry into the nature of balance unfolds.

By learning to be more fully present and aware of this process, your learning will increase and you will recognize many more possiblities and choices. As your insight deepens, you will see more clearly what paths in your life lead you toward and away from the balance you yearn for.

The Waves and the Ocean

Balance can also be sensed in terms of the waves and of the ocean. Just as waves have a beginning, development, culmination, disintegration, and end, balance in our life is found in the flow of periods of activity and rest, paying attention to others and to ourselves, work and play, wakefulness and sleep.

Yet at a deeper level, the changing tides of such "waves" are balanced by the profound reality of an unchanging "ocean" within you. Just as the ocean is the water that forms all waves, the ocean within you is the universal reality or essence that dwells within all beings. Its presence is so deep, clear, and transparent that, like a fish in the sea, your whole life may go by without ever really noticing it. Yet if for a moment you discover it, your life will never be quite the same. Discovering this ocean is vitally important for the discovery of balance because it provides a place of peace for you to return home to despite all the chaos of the day. You can discover the ocean within you right now.

Sit up and feel your feet touching the floor. As you breathe in, know you are breathing in. As you breathe out, know that you are breathing out. Just do that for one minute. Smile to yourself. Awareness of the Self is as simple as that. Just as waves rise out of and dissolve back into the water of the ocean, awareness pervades the changing flow of forms that weave the ever-unfolding patterns of your life. And the smile of balance keeps you from trying too hard, or getting too self-critical, or taking this marvelous discovery of yourself too seriously.

"The same stream of life that runs through the world runs through my veins night and day and dances in rhythmic measure. It is the same life that shoots in joy through the dust of the earth into the numberless blades of grass and breaks into tumultuous waves of flowers."

—Rabindranath Tagore

Walking the Tightrope of Daily Life

We find it helpful to view our journey through life as a walk on a tightrope stretched across the vastness of space. Life, in this sense, is a learning laboratory in which to learn how to walk in balance. Believing in a responsive, compassionate, and often playful universe, we notice that the width or narrowness of the rope appears to be adjusted to help each walker optimize his or her learning. For a real beginner, it might be ten feet wide with hand rails. As your skill and confidence grow, the rope narrows and becomes more challenging to walk. Ideally it is still just wide enough to keep you in the upper end of your "learning zone" rather than moving off into danger.

In thinking about balance in this way, there are a few helpful things to keep in mind:

- There are two primary states of being. One is walking in balance, i.e. staying on the rope. The other state is tumbling, i.e. mindless, fearful, and out of control. We are always either walking mindfully and fully present on our rope, or we are to some degree mindlessly tumbling.

- The moment you are mindful that you are tumbling, you are already moving back toward balance and you land back on the rope. Boing! People who have yet to learn this, tumble—and because they are tumbling, they get more stressed about being distressed, or become more anxious when they notice they are anxious, ad infinitum. These strategies, however, only lead to becoming more dangerously out of balance and feeling out of control.

- The name of the game is as much to know when you are tumbling as to know when you are in balance. That is, the real accomplishment—the deeper balance—is having the presence of mind to recognize when you are in balance and when you are not.

- The more you struggle to stay in control or in balance, the less you are. Real control, real balance, emerges as a state of

"Be patient with everyone, but above all with yourself. I mean, do not be disheartened by your imperfections, but always rise up with fresh courage. How are we to be patient in dealing with our neighbor's faults if we are impatient in dealing with our own? He who is fretted by his own failings will not correct them. All profitable correction comes from a calm, peaceful mind."

—St. Francis de Sales

naturalness. For people who play string instruments, this is easily understood by the anology of a well-tuned instrument. For the richest, most beautiful, most harmonious sounds, the strings must be neither too tight nor too loose. Learning to listen for when you are in or out of such a state of optimal tuning is in itself a fine art.

- Remember, it is all about learning, not about being perfect. The key is not to tumble about having tumbled, or to get more mindless about being mindless.

When we worked with the army we would often say, "Control follows awareness." In business settings we sometimes express this as "You can only manage what you monitor." Either way, it is only when you know that you are moving out of balance that you can take the necessary steps to move more toward balance—and remember, the recognition is in itself the first step of a return toward balance!

It's also important to recognize that walking on the rope means being more or less in balance. There are some of us who walk in a very tight, controlled way. These are the folks who are paranoid of falling, so afraid of the forces that might challenge them that they are easily knocked off balance. When they fall, they tumble for a long time, snarled in the net of frustration and blame. Though they tend to be very critical of others, they are especially hard on themselves. This attitude keeps them tumbling most of the time.

Fortunately, there is an alternative. Through awareness and practice, your confidence can grow to a point where your terror of falling fades away. For people in this league, the obstacles they encounter are viewed as welcome opportunities to further develop their skills and strengths. In those moments when they do fall, they pay more attention to how gracefully they can fall, and even learn how to glide through space with grace and ease. For these folks, falling ceases to be a "failure" and tumbling becomes an exercise in creative gliding.

You can learn to walk the tightrope of life this way. And the better you get, the more you will discover that walking and gliding

"Sometimes you reach a point of being so coordinated, so completely balanced, that you feel you can do anything—anything at all. At times like this I find I can run up to the front of the board and stand on the nose when pushing out through a broken wave; I can goof around, put myself in an impossible position and then pull out of it, simply because I feel happy. An extra bit of confidence like that can carry you through, and you can do things that are just about impossible."

—Midget Farrelly, champion surfer

become the same. As the tightrope gets finer and finer in response to your increasing skills, the more your walking begins to resemble flying. Each moment, each step, becomes one of joy, wonder, discovery, or creative expression. Are you ready to hop on the rope together now, and explore this balancing adventure further? Here we go!

"The most invisible creators I know of are those artists whose medium is life itself. The ones who express the inexpressible— without brush, hammer, clay or guitar. They neither paint nor sculpt—their medium is being. Whatever their presence touches has increased life. They see and don't have to draw. They are the artists of being alive."

—J. Stone

TWO

Glimpses of Wholeness

We are part of the earth and it is part of us...
The perfumed flowers are our sisters;
   the deer, the horse, the great eagle,
   these are our brothers.
The rocky crests, the juices of the meadows,
   the body heat of the pony, and human beings
   all belong to the same family...
The shining water that moves in the streams and rivers is not just water
   but the blood of our ancestors...
The rivers are our brothers, they quench our thirst...
   The air is precious to the red man, for all things share the same
   breath—the animal, the tree, the human, they all share the same breath...
   The air shares its spirit with all the life it supports. The wind that
   gave our grandfather his first breath also receives his last sigh...
What are people without animals?
   If all the animals were gone, humans would die from a great
loneliness of spirit.
For whatever happens to the animals soon happens to the people.
All things are connected. This we know.
The earth does not belong to human beings;
   human beings belong to the earth. This we know.
All things are connected
   like the blood which unites one family.
All things are connected.
Whatever befalls the earth
   befalls the children of the earth.
We do not weave the web of life,
   we are merely a strand in it.
Whatever we do to the web, we do to ourselves.

—ATTRIBUTED TO CHIEF SEALTH

To understand the deep yearning for balance in our own lives, let's take a giant step back and look at the search for balance from a more universal perspective. For millenia, a wealth of clues reminding us to live in balance have been offered in the sacred symbols of the world's great religious traditions. The balanced crossing of the lines of the Cross; the interpenetrating triangles of the Star of David; the complementarity of the swirling halves of the Tai Chi symbol; the harmony of the Islamic *kismet* of crescent moon and star; the Buddhist lotus or wheel of dharma; the ancient winged, double helical staff of the Greek *caduceus* used today as the symbol of the medical profession; the *shri yantra* of the Hindus; and the medicine wheels, mandalas, and sacred circles of many indigenous peoples of the world—reflect the marvelous sense of harmony, balance, and unification of complementary opposites that weave the fabric of the whole we call the universe. Through them we are continually reminded how to harmonize the forces of heaven and earth, the universal and the personal, in our everyday lives.

Properly understood, each of these sacred symbols serves as a beacon to help us find our way home to the center of all centers. By finding a balance between the personal and universal dimensions of ourselves, we can return to the harmony and balance of ourselves, inseparable from the whole of creation. In the realm of science, the equations of mathematicians and physicists can also be understood to symbolically represent this intrinsic balancing nature of the universe.

The Coincidence of Opposites

Balance is essentially about the wholeness in which all dualities, polarities, and complementary forces find their resolution. The wisdom traditions of the world, whether religious or scientific, remind us that the closer we come to truth, the more we encounter paradox. Nicholas de Cusa once described God as the "coincidence of opposites"—a description very much in keeping with the views of most scientists regarding the nature of the universe. Discovering wholeness and balance in our life brings us into an ongoing awareness of

> "There is in all visible things…a hidden wholeness."
>
> —Thomas Merton

> "The human mind recognizes things only in contrast to other things. We know "I" only in relation to "Thou," good only in relation to evil, right only in relation to left, up only in relation to down. The human mind rarely sees beyond these opposites to the Greater Unity that necessitates them. But the mind can awaken to Greater Unity, and in this lies the purpose of Creation and of humankind."
>
> —Reb Yerachmiel ben Yisrael

this coincidence of opposites. The ancient Hindu Upanishads puts it this way:"What is within us is also without.What is without us is also within." Or, as the ancient Greek sage Herakleitos puts it, "To live is to die, to be awake is to sleep, to be young is to be old, for the one flows into the other, and the process is capable of being reversed."

In search of balance, it is helpful to think of everything—every quality, action, or object—as inseparable from its opposite: male and female; night and day; inside and outside. No matter how much you might like to have only the positives in life—freedom, peace, love— if you are seeking that static state, you will always be disappointed. For every thing also contains its opposite and both sides must be balanced: form and space, creativity and receptivity, activity and rest, growth and decay, manifest creation and the unmanifest source of all creation. The good news is that, as your sense of balance grows, you'll find it easier to integrate the other side, "the negatives," into your life; you'll discover the clarity in the midst of confusion, the stillness at the center of motion, and the love that waits behind fear and anger. If you can learn to dance with the innumerable paradoxes of your life while staying anchored in an extraordinary suppleness and flexibility, you will create the stability necessary to actually find balance in your life.

"Almost every wise saying has an opposite one, no less wise, to balance it."

—Santayana

Stillness and Motion in Balance

Here's a practice to help you discover the exquisite balance that comes from holding a sense of both stillness and motion in your mind at the same time. Be aware that, while the ordinary mind tends to focus on objects in motion, the universal mind is rooted in the stillness that gives rise to all motion. As you observe stillness and motion you will learn that every motion begins with stillness and ends in stillness, and that at every moment along the way, stillness and movement interweave.

Begin by mindfully observing the world within and around you. Let your attention notice everything that is changing in the world

"When you make the two one, and when you make the inner as the outer and the outer as the inner, and the above as the below, and when you make the male and female into a single one—then shall you enter the Kingdom."

—Jesus in the Gospel of St. Thomas

around you: the breeze that comes and goes against your cheek, the dance of shadows against the roof of your house.

After a while, shift your attention inward and notice everything that is changing within you. Feel the myriad changing sensations and vibrations within you. Begin with the easily noticeable flow of your breathing. Then deepen your awareness to sense the more subtle beat of your pulse. Then shift your attention to sense the reverberations of the pulse as it echoes through even the tiniest part of your body. Notice the ebb and flow of vibrations and sensations as they constantly change.

Now ease your attention back to the world around you. In the midst of all of this noticeable change, search out stillness. Identify everything that is more or less unchanging. Notice how the buildings, lampposts, pavement, and fire hydrants remain still. Notice how the rocks, earth, and mountains are still, while the winds move the clouds and the trees. Notice the stillness of the space in which the trees sway.

Then, inwardly search out the stillness within you, even amid the million tiny changes. As you learn to find stillness in the midst of motion, a profound sense of balance, peace, and power can emerge for you. With practice, and with grace, you will learn how to discover this sublime sense of stillness even when you are actively moving through the world.

Balancing Sound and Silence

Our friend Rick is an inspired and compassionate teacher who works with inner city youth in Seattle. He was out on the playing field with the kids one day when suddenly he yelled out, "What was that?" The kids were silent, looking around and trying to figure out what he was talking about. Somewhat sheepishly Rick said, "I think that was a moment of silence. I don't know if we've ever had one of those in this class before."

Cultivating an integrated awareness of both silence and sound is another simple key to balance. Our ordinary habits of mind tend to

"The temple bell stops
But I still hear the
sound
coming out of the
flowers."
—**Basho**

pay attention to sounds and not pay much attention to the silence. But every sound arises out of silence, lasts a while, and then dissolves back into silence.

To notice this, sit and listen, really listen, to the world around you. Notice how many sounds you can hear. Notice how some are clear, close, and distinct, while other sounds are more faint and distant. Let your listening awareness reach out into the space around you. Sense yourself here at the center of your universe, bathed in sound vibrations, listening.

Next, turn your listening awareness inward, and listen for myriad often unnoticed, subtle, but present sounds: the inner gurgles in your belly, the sounds of your breathing and your pulse in your ears, the click of your jaw as you swallow. Hear also the conversations, inner mental voices, or sounds that you can "hear" as you listen. Smile to yourself, as you tune in to discover what is always going on.

Now, as you listen to these inner and outer sounds, try to feel the silence. Ah... Train your ear to listen to that space of silence that precedes every sound, surrounds every sound, absorbs every sound.

Notice how silence and sound dance together, and balance each other to weave the fabric of your experience. They are inseparable and make no sense without each other. Let your awareness open to the exquisite balance that can embrace both sounds and silence equally. In each moment they are inseparable from each other. Training your attention to embrace these two profound realities is another powerful way to find balance in every moment of your life.

"But if one listens a little harder and a little longer, one comes to hear silence... that silence is an integral part of life... Silence is not simply the absence of sounds. Rather it is the presence of the dimension of time. A realization of the instant and the situation. Furthermore, it is an expression of the completeness of the situation. In a very real way, silence is heard as an integral part of existence..."

—Howard Slusher

The Balance of Nature

We have seen how stillness is meaningless without motion and sound is meaningless without silence. Likewise male and female, light and dark, birth and death, summer and winter, full moon and new moon all have meaning only in their interdependence.

These and other complementary and inseparable realities unfold through four nodal phases of balance. For example, we see that from the darkness of midnight, light gradually grows until the dawn.

Dawn matures into the brilliance and warmth of noon time. The brightness and warmth of noon gradually diminishes until sunset. As light fades and darkness increases, we return again to the time of greatest darkness—midnight. In a similar way, the four seasons also exhibit the same waxing and waning. Following the dark, cold, starkness of winter, there is a time of warming, emergence and blossoming that we call springtime. And springtime matures into the fullness, warmth and brilliance of summer. The peaking of light, activity, and warmth in summer gradually diminishes into autumn, until once again we return to the darkness, stillness, and coldness of the winter solstice. The same theme is found in the lunar cycle, a human life, and mirrored throughout nature.

Miraculously, the balance and flow of the seasons is mirrored in the heavens. At the lightest, brightest time of summer, the summer solstice, the sun is farthest to the north in the northern hemisphere. At the winter solstice the sun is farthest to the south (or to the north if you live in the southern hemisphere). At spring and autumn equinoxes, the times of celestial balance, our sun is directly above the equator. For additional proof that balance is really an integral part of the larger cosmic dance, keep in mind that in the winter, when the days are short and dark and the sun is farthest from our part of the world, the moon is actually more directly overhead. So when we see the sun the least, the light of the moon is more available.

Though the moon is a thousand times smaller than the sun, it is a thousand times closer to us. And miraculously it is in orbit in such a way as to perfectly balance the sun, giving rise to the indescribable splendor of a full solar eclipse. When the moon perfectly covers the face of the sun, it reveals the true radiance of the sun's streaming corona, which is too bright to see at any other time.

Add to this the miracle of how steadily the light of the moon waxes and wanes, giving rise to an endless succession of full moons and new moons. Think also of the continuous rising and falling of the planetary tides, inseparably linked to the invisible pull of the moon's gravity, as the earth spins and the moon moves more slowly than the earth turns. Without these eternal rhythms, our ancestral forms of life would never have emerged from the sea to find dry land.

You and I, being physically composed of more than 70 percent water, are moved and touched by the same powerful and invisible forces of the moon. And we are also affected, more subtly of course and thus less noticeably, by the movements of the sun, the planets, and every heavenly body in the vastness of the universe.

In cultures where people live in tune with the natural world, people naturally rise and sleep with the changing cycles of the day. Women in these cultures often menstruate at the time of the full moon, so the women of a village will commonly have their monthly flow and times of fertility at the same time as each other. Even today with the hectic pace of our modern lives, most women have experienced how common it is for their periods to come at the same time as the other women in their dormitories or houses. This in turn sets up cycles and rhythms of interactions between men and women, and ripples out in natural ways into the formation and regulation of human societies.

And at our deepest core, we are connected and encoded in the most fundamental cyclic wisdom of the circadian rhythms that govern our waking and sleeping, our times of activity and rest, mental clarity and dullness. Thus our yearning for balance is completely natural, for our bodies seek only to live in harmony with the rhythms of the world around us.

"Sixty-six times these eyes beheld the changing scenes of Autumn.
I have said enough about moon light
Ask me no more.
Only listen to the voice of the pines and cedars
when no wind stirs."
—Ryo-Nen

Homeostasis: Balancing Inside and Outside, Self and Other

As we have begun to see, we are all *living systems,* complex interactions of energy-information which we freely and effectively exchange in relationship with our environment. As "open" living systems, we are also endowed with the capacity for *homeostasis,* which, like a thermostat, allows us to maintain balance within healthy limits. Derived from the Greek word meaning "to keep the same," the term encompasses the interplay of all the systems

"Beginning the day, I see that life is a miracle.
Attentive to each moment, I keep my mind clear like a calm river."
—Thich Nhat Hanh

necessary to preserve and maintain the constant conditions of life.

The principle of homeostasis is evident in our bodies, our minds, and in the world in which we live. For example, as long as you are alive, the internal temperature of your body will remain at approximately 98.6 degrees Fahrenheit, through a complex system of energy conservation and dissipation. Though you may be subject to environmental temperature changes of more than a hundred degrees, unless you are ill, it is unlikely that your internal temperature will vary more than a degree or two. When you are hot, your pores dilate, you perspire and cool off. When you are cold, your body warms itself by shivering and physical activity. Every system of your body is balanced with homeostatic wisdom: regulating the chemistry of your bloodstream, the functioning of your digestion, the repair and replacement of old or injured tissue. Neurological, biochemical, and energy systems function interdependently to maintain the dynamic balance that you call your life. The good news is that we are made for balance—it's our natural state!

Balance in the world around us is maintained in a similarly miraculous way. Like any other "living being," the earth has its own homeostatic mechanisms. The Gaia hypothesis, formulated through the painstaking research of James Lovelock, has helped many people come to look upon the earth itself as a self-regulating living system. By arranging a sensitive balance of atmosphere, oceans, and soil, and by absorbing and dissipating the energy of the sun, the intelligence of "Gaia" maintains the delicate planetary homeostasis necessary for life to thrive. A few examples will help us appreciate these exquisitely intricate balancing processes.

Though life can exist between the extreme ranges of 20 and 220 degrees Fahrenheit, it flourishes between 60 and 100 degrees. Gaia has managed to maintain this as an average temperature for hundreds of millions of years.

The mystery of balance upon the earth is also evident in Gaia's regulation of the amount of salt in the ocean. Despite eons of dramatic changes in weather patterns and sea levels, geological evidence indicates that the oceans have remained relatively constant at about

3.4 percent salinity. If this concentration were to rise to 4 percent, life as we know it would be much different. If it were to rise to 6 percent, even for a few minutes, all ocean life would be extinguished by the disintegration of cell walls at such a high concentration of salt. The oceans of the world would become as barren as the Dead Sea.

In physics, the second law of thermodynamics says that entropy tends to increase, so that ordered systems run down and become more chaotic and disorganized over time. Mountains wash to the sea, suns burn themselves out and explode, the energy potential of a rock at the top of a mountain exhausts itself as it rolls into the valley, buildings and bridges and books like this turn to dust over the ages. Though we might say that this entropic dissolution describes our life pretty well, the existence of life in the universe flies in the face of this "law." Living systems don't just run down. Entropy is not the only factor describing the evolution of systems in nature. Entropy and energy in the form of enthalpy together determine balance, which in chemical systems is called equilibrium. This balance is dynamic rather than static, as evidenced by a sugar crystal in water. A slight shift in temperature can favor dissolution or crystallization, but both processes are always occuring. Not all systems attain equilibrium because the approach to chemical balance is too slow at room temperature. This is a blessing because equilibrium for us would turn our marvelously complex body mainly into carbon dioxide, water, and a small pile of ashes!

Living systems are miraculous in that they continually renew themselves by reaching out beyond themselves to take in the stuff of the universe and transform themselves. Through photosynthesis, plants take in sunlight, carbon dioxide, and nutrients from the soil, and create new forms and structures through their growth. Animals take in food, water, and information, then grow, learn, and transform themselves and their world. For life to exist, a circle of unimaginable complexity and subtlety must remain unbroken. Countless factors within and between living beings and their environment must continually adjust to the changing flow on many levels within the whole.

"My own working assumption is that we are here as local Universe information gatherers. We are given access to the divine design principles so that from them we can invent the tools that qualify us as problem solvers in support of the integrity of an eternally regenerative Universe."

—Buckminster Fuller

As living beings, we too are subject to this same flow and our lives depend on learning ways to respond and adapt to the unrelenting challenges of our world. To live we must maintain ourselves—our general shape, form, functions, and identity—while all the time adapting, taking in, and releasing information from our environment to adjust to the changing flow of life. Our health and vitality reflect our ability to manage both the intensity of such change in our lives—and how we assimilate it. We tend to forget, however, that the true nature of life is based in fluidity, interconnectedness, and mystery. To the degree that we live or think in terms of a static, separate, controllable world, our confusion sets us up for frustration and suffering. Considerable evidence suggests that the rate of change in our work is rapidly speeding up, which may account for some of our frantic, panicked, out of control feelings. As the rate of change increases, our harmony, health, sanity, balance, and safety are not to be found in holding on more tightly, or by becoming more rigid or controlling. Our ability to control the environment is limited, and the wise ones among us have learned to stop exhausting themselves by trying to control the river of change. Rather, they focus their efforts on increasing their mental, emotional, and physical capacities to harmonize with the intensity offered by their encounters with the outer world. Have faith that with practice, you can learn to do this too.

"Nothing is finite which doesn't include the infinite. The finite is the mirror of the infinite, its external revealing image. Essence and form are inseparable. Essence is the eternal Being. But living form is its constantly ever new manifestation—everlasting revelation... I try to learn from the finite sciences the lessons of the infinite."

—Arthur Young

The Dance of Gaia and Chaos

Another way to look at the task ahead of us is to look at a Greek creation myth. Before time, at the very beginning, according to one story, was Chaos, the endless, yawning void empty of form or pattern, a state of complete unmanifest potential. The partner of Chaos was Gaia, the mother of the earth, who brought forth the form and stability of the earth and all manifest worlds. To the ancient Greeks, Gaia and Chaos were inseparable partners representing two primordial forces whose dynamic dance generates everything that we know in our world.

Our ability to live in balance in today's modern world depends on our ability to bring both Gaia and Chaos more consciously alive in our lives. In each moment that we give shape, form, and meaning to our world, Gaia is present, alive, and expressive. In each moment that we move in the powerful realm of potentials, Chaos surrounds us, embraces us. Finding the balance of Chaos and Gaia in our lives means learning to dwell in a lucid, clear, fully present quality of mind that can witness how we weave the limitless, unbroken wholeness of Chaos into the limited forms and ideas that allow us to live, work, and communicate effectively in the world.

Both Chaos and Gaia have their light and dark sides. We can be unconsciously lost and confused in Chaos. Or we can rest with an awake, appreciative, open mind in the ocean of Chaos and simply marvel at the presence of this profound reality in our lives. While the light side of Gaia is to manifest and express the potentials of Chaos by giving order and meaning to our experience, we are also in danger of slipping into the dark side of Gaia by holding our creations as being too rigid, too real, or by mistaking our wonderful ideas for being the absolute truth. A healthy balance is found in learning to live fluidly and to adapt where chaos and order meet.

This is hard enough, but it is even more of a challenge for those of us living in a culture with a longstanding fear of Chaos. We humans have a tendency to distrust the unknown and to believe in shallow and untested ideas. Many of us tend to believe that our concepts adequately describe the nature of reality; we ignore the raw intensity and uncertainty of our actual experience. We stubbornly fixate on things without recognizing that they are only relatively, not absolutely, the way things are.

As technology enables us to look ever more deeply into the mysterious foundations of our universe, a whole new science of complexity and chaos theory has arisen to describe what is observed. The deeper we look, it turns out, we find that even in the most subtle recesses of reality that are beyond our ability to adequately measure, there are exquisitely meaningful patterns and ordering principles at play. At the threshold where we are able to glimpse the emergence of these patterns into measurable forms, what we see is merely an

"By Chaord, I mean any self-organizing, adaptive, nonlinear, complex community or system, whether physical, biological or social, the behavior of which exhibits characteristics of both order and chaos... Chaordic systems... exist "on the edge of chaos"— between the ordered and the chaotic region. Living systems are drawn to the edge of chaos because that is where the capacity for information processing and learning and therefore, growth is maximized!"

—Dee Hock, Founder of Visa Card

extrapolation of an exquisite order that lies hidden in the heart of chaos. Properly understood, this profound insight tells us all, scientists and lay folks alike, that we can live with faith and trust and set aside our fear and anxiety, because we really do live in a universe that at the deepest level does make sense, even though we cannot fully fathom it.

Understanding the dance between Chaos and Gaia is essential in our lives, because to truly experience the quality of balance we seek, we must shift from focusing merely on the forms and structures in our lives—"If only I could figure out how to do my job, have time for my exercise class, and my husband and kids"—to becoming more aware of and sensitive to the flows of these energies as they present themselves in our lives. We have such trouble finding balance because we think it is about cleaning our desk or getting up an hour earlier in the morning. These may indeed be useful strategies, but not unless we first begin to have a deeper understanding of balance as an interplay of forces and energies. Balance is not a static state that we find once and for all by the perfect fine-tuning of our daily schedules.

Equilibrium is defined by Webster's as, "1. A condition in which all acting forces are canceled by others, resulting in a stable, balanced, or *unchanging* system [emphasis ours] 2. Physics. The condition of a system in which the resultant of all acting forces is zero..." The dynamically active quality of living balance presents a very different picture, in which we

- learn to listen to and trust our internal guidance system;
- notice whatever strong or subtle impressions are offered by our senses;
- observe the inner movements, attitudes, directions, and intentions of our hearts and minds;
- notice the dances and struggles at play in relationships;
- discover what feels right, true, and on purpose in living our life.

"Each day of human life contains joy and anger, pain and pleasure, darkness and light, growth and decay. Each moment is etched with nature's grand design—do not try to deny or oppose the cosmic order of things."
—**Morihei Ueshiba, O'Sensei**

"Try to develop models which are not arbitrary and man-made but organic and natural. The difference is in the intention. Arbitrary man-made models have as their intention manipulation and control. Natural organic models have as their intention resonance and reverence."
—**Margaret Mead**

Intention and Values: The "Strange Attractors" that Bring Balance to Our Lives

In modern times, scientific studies of chaos theory have revealed more of Chaos' mysterious qualities. Using computers to simulate the marvelous feedback loops that led to living systems emerging out of chaos, scientists can replicate and visually display in a very short time the trillions of moments of a system's evolution coming into form.

To get a feeling for this, imagine being able to take a composite photo of your journey through life from the moment of your conception until your death. Imagine that this sequence of images unfolds as a stream of light that traces pathways of light through space over time. Though at first the patterns may appear somewhat chaotic, as you watch over time meaningful patterns gradually begin to emerge. There would be the loops and patterns that you trace by getting up and going to bed, and to and from school or work. Your habits and values also organize the shape of your life as you weave in patterns of travel to shop at your favorite stores, visit your parents, or vacation at your summer home or ski lodge. Over time, an exquisite, complex, and beautiful image would appear, revealing an elaborate and meaningful tapestry of self-repeating patterns that offer a glimpse of some of the deep organizing principles and values that guide your life.

Like your own life, in the early stages of the computer simulations, it seems that only the unpredictability of chaos rules, with points lighting up on the screen as if at random. But, over time, these points weave into lines, and the lines weave themselves into webs and patterns of breathtaking beauty, revealing an order that emerges literally from the heart of chaos. No matter how chaotic the fluctuations begin, a strange ordering principle inevitably emerges, giving form, beauty, and meaning to the chaos. This invisible ordering principle defines what are called "strange attractors." Strange attractors are like guiding

"Until one is committed there is hesitance, the chance to draw back, always ineffectiveness. Concerning all acts of initiative there is one elementary truth, the ignorance of which kills countless ideas and splendid plans: That (the) moment one definitely commits oneself, then providence moves too. All sorts of things occur to help one that would otherwise never have occurred. A whole stream of events issues from the decision, raising in one's favor all manner of unforeseen incidents and meetings and material assistance, which no one could have dreamt would have come one's way."

**—W.N. Murray,
Scottish Himalayan
Expedition, 1951**

force-fields that define a basin of attraction within which the elements of a system are magnetically drawn into an observable and meaningful pattern.

One of the fascinating understandings from these computer simulations is that when even very tiny fluctuations are introduced into a system, especially early on in its evolution, dramatic changes in its evolving form will result. When the equation that gives form, meaning, and direction to the unfolding of chaos into order is changed even minutely—on the order of even a zillionth of a degree—the future of the pattern will be dramatically altered within a very short time. This is good news for us because it shows how we can influence the pattern of our lives by what we might consider to be a minor change. Thus, achieving the balance we are longing for is not as hard as it might first appear. It begins by looking at intention. For our intentions define the strange attractors that set the patterns for how our lives unfold.

The Power of Intention: Is My Life's Journey "On Purpose"?

Intention is a power that sets our trajectory as we initiate a path of action. If I set sail from Seattle in a boat, for example, my intention will determine where and how I go. (And if we set sail together, our shared intent will likewise determine the course that we take.) My intention may be to sail across the sound to visit friends on Vashon Island, or to sail to Orcas Island in the San Juan Islands, or to San Francisco, Honolulu, or Amsterdam. My intention may simply be to have the experience of a wonderful day on the water with my friends, and I may not be particularly concerned with making progress toward some outer destination. Or I can simply set sail for the pure joy and intent of discovering what the winds have in store for me, and be open to receiving and learning from the gifts of experience that I encounter along the way.

In life, if I "set sail" unclear of my intention, I tend to drift around, have pleasurable or frustrating experiences, driven by the

"Ask and it shall be given you;
Seek and you shall find;
Knock, and it shall be opened to you.
For whoever asks, receives;
and he who seeks, finds;
and to him who knocks, the door is opened."

—Jesus, in
Matthew 7:7:8

winds of my unconscious inclinations. If at some point along the way I am mindful enough to notice that my intention is not clear, I may stop to ask, "Why am I here? Where am I going? How do I want to make the journey?" When I am clear on the answers to these questions, I can take up the helm again and sail consciously and intentionally in the direction of my choosing. If the force of my habit is strong, it is likely that now and then I lapse into mindlessness, and that once again my freedom and control will be taken over by the force of my unconscious habit. Yet over time, if I am intent on becoming more in control of my journey, I quickly notice when old habits have asserted themselves, and I gently but firmly take the helm of my life again. With practice, I lose my intention less and less often, and if it is lost, I find it again quickly.

To the degree that I am clear on my intentions, I am more likely to stay on course in my journey, to travel "on purpose," and to be able to make healthy choices about how I want to spend my time. In this analogy, intention is the compass that I use to keep my life in balance. With intention, I will be more mindful of the direction that I am sailing and alert to when the winds and currents are supporting or challenging me in my journey. With clear intent in mind, I will check often to see if I am on course, on purpose, and will generate further intentions that lead to the actions that make subtle course corrections frequently along the way.

The more important my initial intention, the more likely I am to pay careful attention to how my journey unfolds. If I intend to move swiftly, I keep an eye on the sails and keep them filled to move me along. If I am intent on traveling in harmony and helpfulness with my crew members, I will likely have many moments to practice patience, and offer some helpful coaching or words of encouragement to them.

Or perhaps I'm just out sailing by myself, and my intent is to cultivate greater balance of mind, to stay alert, yet relaxed, or to cultivate a sense of the richness of my experience: the rudder in my hand, the cool breeze in my hair, the salt spray on my face, and my thoughts coming and going like so many clouds in the sky of my mind. If my

"The winds of grace are always blowing, but it is you that must raise your sails."

—Rabindranath Tagore

intent is to be fully present in each moment of my journey, I will be more aware of my mind wandering and I will gently bring it back into focus. I will also notice when I am tired: perhaps I need to drop anchor for a while, set the autopilot, or turn the helm over to a crew mate while I rest or nourish myself. As a fully present sailor, I am aware of the way I relate to my crew members and the quality of interaction that I have with them.

So in the search for balance, whenever you begin to feel off track or overwhelmed, the first step is to stop and rediscover your deepest intention for what you are doing. You may discover you are right on track, or you may find it necessary to change course in order to keep to your purpose.

It's also important to recognize the state of being your intention is rooted in. We all know from experience what can happen when we act out of fear or caring, greed or self-less service. Not only are the outcomes often different, but our own inner experience during the process is also deeply affected. We may sow the seeds of satisfaction, gratitude, or we may sow the seeds of frustration, sadness, or guilt that may grow like weeds and plague us for a lifetime. Checking our intentions before we launch into action can help us to live and work with a much greater sense of balance and well-being. The more we are mindful of our intentions each moment along the way, the more likely we are to arrive at a destination that we feel good about.

Remembering that even minute changes in the equations of a system can make a dramatic difference in its character, we can understand how making even subtle shifts in our intentions can create extraordinary changes in the quality of our lives.

Reaching Out to the Mystery

We live in a responsive universe. If you drop a stone in a pond, it both sends out and draws in ripples. Through heartfelt prayer, the energy of our intent reaches out, creating a reverberation in our deep psyche that reaches out to the Mystery and draws back the inspiration and blessing energy that may help us or others to deepen or accelerate a shift in the patterns of our life. Especially in times of great chaos, prayer can offer a sense of stability, meaning, direction, inspiration, balance, harmony, healing, and faith that can at times feel miraculous.

Life is continually challenging us to find the balance between who and how we are, who or how we can be, and who or how our environment is asking us to become. This dynamic and mysterious interplay of inner reality, potentiality, and outer reality is the true weaver of the fabric of our lives.

This weaving doesn't happen by isolating ourselves or by cutting ourselves off from the larger whole in which we live. The way living systems return to balance is by continually expanding to encompass more of the whole. While fear may cause us to constrict, separate, or withdraw, this is not the path to healing and balance. It is courage and love that guide us to step out and meet and befriend what we fear, to take it inside of ourselves, and learn from it in order to transform and heal ourselves. *That* is the true balancing act of our lives.

"Wholeness invokes balance."

—**Mary Jane Ryan**

"Each element of the cosmos is positively woven from all the others... The universe holds together, and only one way of considering it is really possible, that is, to take it as a whole, in one piece."

—**Pierre Teilhard de Chardin**

THREE

Life as a Learning Expedition:
A Model for Balance

The essence of health is an inner kind of balance.

—DR. ANDREW WEIL, M.D.

Earlier in his life, Joel was a research scientist, exploring as best he could the inner workings of the human brain. In those days, he used to dream about what the "ultimate experiment" might be to answer to the "ultimate questions." As he has grown older, wiser, and explored many disciplines, he has come to believe that he is living that ultimate experiment. Joel calls it "the learning expedition of my life. As I awaken, in the morning, and throughout the day, I often reflect to myself, 'I wonder what the learnings will be today?' Stepping out into the world my heart's prayer is a simple one: 'Teach me.' And I do my best to respond in an inquisitive way with whatever arises."

As you continue to tune in more mindfully to the learning expedition of your life, you will find that paradox is a great teacher. For example, you will learn the most about living in balance during times when you are out of balance. In the process, you will discover a greater balance that grows through holding both the experience of being in balance and that of being stretched out of balance. Once this new balance is defined, it invites a further expansion of learning in a never-ending cascade of dimensions of learning. Seeing that balance is really a verb—something you must constantly do—you open yourself to this balancing process as a continuous learning adventure. Morihei Ueshiba O'Sensei, regarded by many to be the greatest martial artist in modern times, deeply understood the larger flow of balancing. O'Sensei, the founder of the martial art of aikido, was once asked by his students, "How do you keep your balance all the time?" The master laughed and said: "The art is not in trying to keep your balance, but in losing it and seeing how fast you can regain it. The reason you don't see me out of balance is because I regain it so quickly!"

Embracing life as a learning expedition is the first step toward realizing balance. To understand this, it is helpful to understand the difference between living in your *comfort zone* and in your *learning zone*. Your comfort zone is what you are familiar with, what you already know so well the knowledge is almost automatic. Your learning zone is anything that stretches you beyond that, challenging you to learn new skills, new ways of relating. Ultimately, when we take to heart the lessons in our learning zone, we create for ourselves an expanded comfort zone, one far larger than we began with. In a

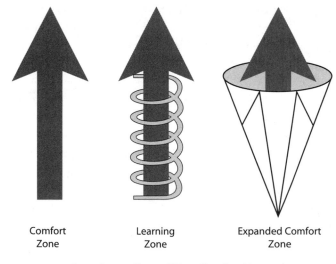

| Comfort Zone | Learning Zone | Expanded Comfort Zone |

Learning to Expand Your Comfort Zone

sense, all of our lives are a pattern of rest in the comfort zone and then stretching and learning in the learning zone. Then we rest again in the new, expanded comfort zone.

The journey toward balance begins by becoming mindful of the invisible walls, boundaries, conditions, and mindsets that define your current personal comfort zone, and then exploring the new frontiers of learning that are your learning zone. As one of our clients observed, "I have never learned anything in my comfort zone!" So, with awareness, step out and meet reality, and let it teach you. Once you step through all the invisible membranes of your fears, excuses, and self-limiting beliefs, and begin to befriend a larger world, you will have performed the miracle of expanding your comfort zone to previously unimaginable proportions. A mind once stretched to new dimensions will never return to its original size. And the learnings of a lifetime, and beyond, will never end.

The model on the following page has been very useful for individuals, teams, families, and communities to assess the quality of balance in their lives and to identify the needs and opportunities for learning. On your journey, it is helpful to be mindful of your passage through five zones of experience.

From top to bottom these are:

- The Burnout Zone

- The Upper Learning Zone

- "The Zone" of Optimal Performance (which is embedded within the heart of the Learning Zone)

- The Lower Learning Zone

- The Rustout Zone

Practicing the art of balance in an ever-changing world requires continuous learning. However, as you are probably aware, the glory of yesterday's hard won learning quickly pales as we encounter the next wave of new realities and challenges of our customers, kids, or environment. As the pace of change and challenge increases, anxiety grows and we are increasingly more motivated to discover and

"More than any time in history, mankind faces a crossroads. One path leads to despair and utter hopelessness, the other to total extinction. Let us pray that we have the wisdom to choose correctly."

—Woody Allen

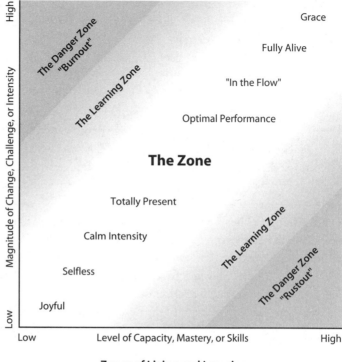

High

Magnitude of Change, Challenge, or Intensity

The Danger Zone "Burnout"

The Learning Zone

Grace

Fully Alive

"In the Flow"

Optimal Performance

The Zone

Totally Present

Calm Intensity

The Learning Zone

Selfless

The Danger Zone "Rustout"

Joyful

Low

Low   Level of Capacity, Mastery, or Skills   High

Zones of Living and Learning

rapidly learn new skills. After these new capabilities are mastered and integrated, however, the danger of relapsing into boredom or complacency often occurs. Suspended between these "killing fields"— the danger zones of extreme intensity and challenge, and the realms of immobilizing boredom and depression, the circumstances of life compel us to search for balance. This crucial balance is found by avoiding the painful extremes of burnout and rustout, and living with vitality in our Learning Zone. The stakes are high, and only the best learners will survive! In the journey of your lifetime, you have traversed each of these zones countless times. Let's visit each of them briefly and see what they have to teach us about balance.

As we discussed earlier, life in the universe survives within certain limits. When conditions go too far above or below those limits, or stay that way for too long, life is endangered. Thus, there is much wisdom in learning to manage your own life within "learningful limits." The Upper and Lower Learning Zones extend beyond "The Zone" into realms of both increasing and decreasing challenge. Here we stretch ourselves, and integrate our learnings in the never-ending cycles of learning that we call our lives. Beyond these reasonably tolerable Learning Zones, lie the forbidding and dangerous extremes of Burnout and Rustout, both of which may be visited for a time, and can contribute much to learning, but neither of which may be lived in, in a balanced way, for long.

At the heart of the Learning Zone (which includes the Upper Learning Zone, "The Zone," and the Lower Learning Zone), between the extremes of overwhelming distress and the inertia of boredom, lies a realm of extraordinary or peak performance. This quality of being is characterized by a state of individual and team performance that delivers the most energy efficient, exhilarating, and fulfilling experiences of human learning and potential. In the vernacular of sports, moments such as these are often described as being in "The Zone," a state of grace marked by effortless ease, power, precision, flow, ecstasy, certainty, or invincibility. Individuals or teams working in the The Zone are confident, highly efficient, and equipped with skills adequate to meet the demands of their situation. When we are in The Zone, we feel in balance, in harmony with ourselves and the world around us. Challenges are neither too strenuous as to create anxiety nor too routine as to create boredom. Though for the novice The Zone is elusive and difficult to enter, true masters in any field have learned to live and work in or near The Zone for much of their lives. These rare and esteemed leaders remind us that if we are willing to accept the learning challenge to live in balance with ourselves, we and others will benefit.

In psychology, this dynamic balance is often regarded as being "in the flow," a self-fulfilling state of optimal performance, extreme fulfillment and well-being, and remarkable brain performance. In the great spiritual traditions, such precious moments of grace are moments when we feel the Presence, Intelligence, or the Love of

"There are moments of glory that go beyond the human expectation, beyond the physical and emotional ability of the individual.
Something unexplainable takes over and breathes life into the known life.
One stands on the threshold of miracles that one cannot create voluntarily. The power of the moment adds up to a certain amount of religion in the performance. Call it a state of grace, or an act of faith… or an act of God. It is there, and the impossible becomes possible… The athlete goes beyond herself: she transcends the natural. She touches a piece of heaven and becomes the recipient of power from an unknown source."

—Patsy Neal, basketball player

Divine and Universal proportions manifesting in a deeply moving personal way in our lives. They offer us a glimpse of our true nature and of our potentials, which may spiritually nourish and deeply inspire our whole lives. In many domains of our life, these special times of balance are regarded as times of peak performance, extreme efficiency, or total quality moments when everything just clicks into place with no wasted energy or effort. Regardless of which frame of reference, or reverence, you choose, it is in these indelibly memorable moments that you catch a glimpse of the extra-ordinary balance that it is possible to realize and to weave more deeply into the fabric of your life.

Reflect for a moment on the times in your life when you were in "The Zone." During the moments of being "in the flow," times of grace, peak performance, or experience,

- How did it feel to you?

- What was happening within or around you?

- What circumstances supported you or triggered your experience?

- What strategies did you, or could you, use to enter "The Zone"?

Taking the time to look deeply into those special moments of flow and grace in your life, and asking yourself specific questions like these, can provide you with important clues into avenues of balance for you. Become a connoisseur of your own peak moments of balance, and learn what makes you "click"!

Anxiety and Beyond: The Upper Learning Zone

Beyond The Zone is a realm of less grace and more taxing learning. As the challenges in your life increase, you will find yourself moving from The Zone into the Upper Learning Zone, where heightened difficulties and distress stimulate your learning. If the challenges increase further still, you are in danger of passing into the upper danger zone called The Burnout Zone.

Pause for a moment to remember what it was like and how you felt at times when you began a new job, changed your first diaper, were asked to take on new responsibilities at work. Each of these situations gave you important feedback regarding the level of your skills and provided the opportunity to develop yourself. If you were able to rise to the occasion and learn what you were being asked to learn, the distress matured into the euphoric stress of mastery and accomplishment.

Joel remembers an example of this from his own experience. "As a teenager I was out skiing at Steven's Pass with some of my buddies. Most of them had been skiing for quite a bit longer than me. As we reached the top of one of the lifts, a friend said, 'Hey, have you ever skied Seventh Heaven?' 'No,' I said, 'What's it like?' 'Come on,' he said, 'I'll show you.' Not knowing what I was getting into, I followed him down a small slope and, to my surprise, onto a second chair lift. Before I knew it, I was heading nearly straight up a sheer face where I could look down at the chair below me between my legs. My heart sank and my mind began to race, wondering what I was going to find when I reached the top. When I got off the chair at the top, the slope was equally steep going down the other side, only this time people were skiing down it! How did I feel? Distressed—to put it mildly! More like panic, fear, in danger, dread, embarrassed, fearful, out of my league. Well, suffice it to say that I managed to skid my way down without hurting more than my ego. It was clear that there was some major learning yet to be achieved. And learn I did. Returning to the scene a few years later, my distress had transformed into joyful exhilaration and a sense of accomplishment. An experience that with lesser skills had put me way out of my Zone into anxiety and danger, was now one of sheer joy and delight. What had changed? I had learned skills that lifted my level of confidence. In the process, the bar went up on the intensity of challenge that I could meet and be in my Zone." Now ask yourself, what words best describe how you felt at those times when you were in the upper end

"Healing is embracing what is most feared; healing is opening what has been closed, softening what has hardened into obstruction, healing is learning to trust life."

—Jeanne Achterberg

of The Learning Zone? The following words are often used to describe how people have felt when they were in this zone: anxious, stressed, fearful, out of control, embarrassed, inadequate, suffering from low self-esteem.

The anxiety of being in The Upper Learning Zone is only natural, and it is still a place to learn when approached with awareness, wisdom, and respect. Learning here compels us to search for the resources and skills we need to develop greater self-mastery. As we grow through learning, we again experience the grace of returning to The Zone—only this time, having increased our knowledge, strength, and capacity, we enter at a higher level.

Skills for The Learning Zone

What does it take to do well in The Learning Zone? Many people are asking themselves these questions today, especially as the stakes for "learning how to learn" are becoming higher than ever and their sense of imbalance is consequently increasing.

A few years ago, our friend Peter Parks conducted a study on brain function and creativity at the Menninger Foundation in Kansas. First, he ran a battery of psychological tests to determine the "baseline" creativity level of each participant. Next, he trained the group to learn how to recognize and increase specific frequencies of brainwaves in the theta frequency band (between six and nine cycles per second) that are associated with enhanced creativity and intuition. After the training, he once again administered the creativity tests to see if there was a correlation between how successful people were in increasing their prevalence of theta brainwaves, and increasing the factors associated with creativity. One finding in particular stood out. There was a clear and strong correspondence between people's tolerance for ambiguity as measured by the psychological tests and the level of their theta brainwave activity. Interestingly, as people learned through feedback to increase their theta frequency brainwaves, they also showed an increase in their scores for tolerance for ambiguity associated with enhanced creativity.

Peter's ingenious study provides us with valuable insights that are helpful in our search for balance—particularly how to get the most out of The Learning Zone. Unless we can tolerate ambiguity and the unknown, we will have great trouble in The Learning Zone. As the great Nobel Prize winning chemist Ilya Prigogine once said, "The more rigid a system is, the more likely it is to collapse under pressure." In nature, rigid objects break or wear away, while more flexible and adaptable things learn, grow, and evolve. In contrast to those who cling to certainties, people with a high tolerance of ambiguity are more flexible and expansive in their thinking. Similarly, tense people quickly exhaust themselves, and people with "psychosclerosis" (rigid mindsets) who suffer from a "hardening of the attitudes," often isolate themselves or cut themselves off from meaningful relationships and learning.

To the degree that we are intolerant of ambiguity, we are prone to perceive situations as threatening rather than promising. When we lack information or encounter uncertainty, we are likely to feel uncomfortable and out of control. Yet as our lives grow more complex, three sources of ambiguity become more common: novelty, complexity, and insolvability.

Learning to develop our tolerance for ambiguity, rather than trying to avoid it, is an essential skill for living a balanced life in modern times because it creates flexibility. The more flexible we are, the better equipped we are to adapt to The Learning Zone, deal with stress, and learn from the surprises in our lives. These principles are, so to speak, "the rules of the game," and people who understand this are less likely to exhaust themselves struggling with life and more likely to live in harmony and balance.

"Security is mostly a superstition, it does not exist in nature, nor do the children of men as a whole experience it. Avoiding danger is no safer in the long run than outright exposure. Life is either a daring adventure or nothing at all!"

—**Helen Keller**

The Zone of Boredom and Frustration

At times in our lives it is only natural that we want to drop out of the flow and effortless grace of The Zone into The Lower Learning Zone. Quieter times such as these afford us a welcome opportunity to rest, recuperate, and integrate our learnings from more intense times.

Yet after a while, we begin to feel a bit bored and underutilized; we might want to stir things up, seek more adventure or challenge.

Pause for a moment to reflect on times in your life or work when you dropped into the lower reaches of The Learning Zone. Here, you were likely well equipped, possibly over-equipped, with the knowledge, skills, and confidence necessary for the levels of challenge in your life at that time. The unemployed, people in boring, repetitive jobs, and elderly housebound, are all likely dwellers in this domain. From our time as clinicians working with people with stress-related illnesses, we're convinced that as many were suffering from Rustout as from Burnout.

Thinking back to times in your life and work when you were in this domain, what words describe how you felt? Bored, frustrated, unproductive, unmotivated, wasting time, and suffering from low self-esteem?

These indicators tell us that it may be time to seek out the challenges and opportunities that we need to stretch ourselves. As we step out of The Comfort Zone and reach toward greater heights, once again we find ourselves in the sweet flow of The Zone. Are you starting to get a sense for the rhythm of this dance of learning?

Danger Zones: The Extremes of Burnout and Rustout

While optimal learning takes place in our Learning Zone, times of crisis, tragedy, and breakdown are also part of the learning journey. We humans cannot survive for long in the frigid polar regions or the scorching deserts, in the deep ocean, or highest mountain peaks, but a brief visit there with the right survival gear may be a powerfully transformative ordeal in our lives—that is, if we survive.

To optimize our learning as well as a sense of balance, we need to increase our vigilance and mindfulness as we move farther and farther out of The Zone into the nether regions of increasing or diminishing intensity or challenge. Generally speaking, only the most crazy, dull, and stupid among us will willingly put themselves in

"I will not die an
unlived life.
I will not live in fear of
falling or catching fire.
I choose to inhabit my
days, to allow my
living to open me,
to make me less afraid,
more accessible, to
loosen my heart
until it becomes a
wing, a torch, a
promise.
I choose to risk my
significance;
to live
so that which came to
me as seed
goes to the next as
blossom
and that which came
to me as blossom,
goes on as fruit."

—Dawna Markova

danger and stay there. Remember the story of the boiled frog who didn't notice that the water was slowly heating up? How easy it is to forget, especially when we are surrounded by other "frogs" with their heads down, working hard, hell-bent for... are they even sure what?

The truth is, we humans are simply not bioengineered to live in The Burnout Zone for sustained periods of time. Your body is equipped with the resources it needs to mobilize itself for brief "sprints" in that zone, but thinking you'll live there is as short-sighted as building your house on the slope of an active volcano. Your body is wiser than that. It will shut down by itself, either temporarily or permanently, depending on how extreme your situation gets.

If you study the physiology of balance in terms of biochemistry, you'll find that adrenaline and norepinephrine are the self-generated drugs of choice for brief periods of "fight or flight." But when you stay in a distressed or overwhelmed state for prolonged periods of time, your adrenal glands exhaust themselves, and the elevated stress levels of hormones actually begin to eat away the insides of your blood vessels, making them weaker and more liable to explode. Look how many people are taken out each year from the inside out with a stroke or a heart attack; nearly one-quarter of deaths! They are potent reminders of the dangers of imbalance.

Such conditions do not occur overnight, but are symptomatic of lives lived out of balance. Many of these people have lived too long in The Burnout Zone and did not know—or did not care to learn—how to shift out back into learningful limits. As pressure mounts, miles of tiny capillaries, constricted due to the stress of battling against an overstretched heart, pump harder and harder with increasing pressure to get enough blood, oxygen, and nutrients to your exhausted body. Add to this the habit and poor judgment of a mind, mindless and exhausted, clouded by distraction and confusion, which habitually elevates the stress hormone levels in the blood. Add to this the exacerbating influences of caffeine, sugar, and nicotine, plus arteries clogged from a high-fat diet, and you have the all-too-common makings of disaster. Is it any wonder that heart disease and strokes are the most common killers?

"It was the best of times, it was the worst of times,
it was the age of wisdom, it was the age of foolishness,
it was the epoch of belief, it was the epoch of incredulity,
it was the season of Light, it was the season of Darkness,
it was the spring of hope, it was the winter of despair,
we had everything before us, we had nothing before us..."

—Charles Dickens,
A Tale of Two Cities

Life as a Learning Expedition: A Model for Balance   37

Fortunately, there are plenty of alternatives. All of them involve taking the initiative and developing the skills necessary to take more control in our lives and to live in a more sanely balanced way. As part of a self-regulating system, your energy output needs to be matched with your ability to renew and refresh yourself. When you cross the line and the quality of healthy, homeostatic balance begins to slip, you quickly lose strength and vitality and slip into a potentially dangerous state. In this state of disintegration, the harder you struggle, the more exhausted and out of balance you become. After prolonged periods of unceasing distress, your resources are depleted, you are exhausted, your bloodstream is toxic rather than life-refreshing, and you are in danger.

Those chronically caught in The Rustout Zone are as much at risk as those chronically caught in The Burnout Zone. Suffering from extreme frustration, exhaustion, and low self-esteem, they often lapse into life-threatening despair or lash out in angry violent ways. Some feel despair about living in such a state, and in a disintegrating spiral of increasing self-depreciation, they may decide to take their own lives—over the course of many years or impulsively in a moment—affecting all who share their lives.

Understanding the gravity of such extremes states of imbalance, and the equally tragic missed opportunities to discover, develop, and express the incredible potentials of our lives, we often urge people who learn this model to not only apply it to their own lives, but to share it with the people they live and work most closely with. Just imagine how many lives might be saved or improved if each person reading this book were to be a little more mindful of the people in their lives who may not have even considered the possibility of living more in balance.

Life in The Learning Zone encourages a healthy balance between times in our lives when we are challenged to learn in order to meet a goal, and times when we are in a mode of rest, renewal, and integration. Living a healthy, balanced life means that we become aware where we stand on The Zone map, and to recognize when we are approaching the danger zones. Remember: Life is about balance. It's

"I'd rather be a failure at something I enjoy than a success at something I hate!"

—George Burns

"Be brave enough to live creatively. The creative place is where no one else has ever been. You have to leave the city of your comfort and go into the wilderness of intuition. You can't get there by bus, only hard work, risking, and by not quite knowing what you're doing. What you'll discover will be wonderful: yourself!"

—Alan Alda

about breathing in and breathing out, action and rest, intense learning and reflective integration; even waking and sleeping are allowed!

Lifelong Learning

The learning adventure of our lives continually reminds us that balanced living is achieved by seeking challenges when we are bored, and cultivating skills when we are challenged. It's an ongoing dance.

Imagine that you have exactly the skills and capabilities that you need to meet life's challenges. Things couldn't be better and you are in The Zone. And then, inevitably, things change. The pressures and demands upon you increase. What's the strategy to re-enter The Zone? You learn and develop new skills to meet the challenge. Take a class, get some coaching from a mentor, ask a peer to train you on that computer program you haven't learned but need for the project. As you learn, you find yourself moving back into The Zone. The challenges may remain the same for a time, but as your skills continue to grow you're likely to slip into boredom. This is no fun, and the work or way of life here is not very fulfilling. What's the strategy to move back toward "The Zone"? Easy, seek out more challenge. Take on some new responsibilities, challenge yourself to learn how to do something you've always wanted to learn, take that martial arts class that you've always wanted to take.

Balance, properly understood, is a cyclic dance of learning, meeting challenges, more learning, more accomplishments. At each step, you are able to bring a higher order of understanding to handle a greater degree of complexity in the challenge. Now, how long do you think these cycles of development and accomplishment go on? *Forever!* Lifelong learning is a way of life, not just a nice idea. As long as we keep on learning and seeking out new experiences, our brain keeps growing rich in making more and more complex connections. But if we stop learning and get stuck in the familiar, the integrity of our nervous system diminishes, like a once-strong muscle that weakens after a period of disuse.

If you look at the development of human culture over the past

"I am not bound to win but I am bound to be true. I am not bound to succeed but I am bound to live up to what light I have."

—Abraham Lincoln

tens of thousands of years, you will find an ever increasing intensity of challenge, complexity, and learning. Despite the comforts of our modern lives, the complexity and choices that we must face in a single week may exceed those that your great-great-grandparents faced in their entire lifetimes. And what about your children, and the world they will inherit?

In such a world, we need to cultivate awareness, to help us choose which zone we move toward. So, at different times throughout the day, pause to ask yourself:

- What zone am I in?
- What zone would I like to move toward?
- What do I need to do or not do to move in the desired direction?

Even at times when you feel totally overwhelmed or out of control, you can move toward your Zone simply by having the presence of mind to pause and reflect on these questions. The important question is not "Am I in The Zone?"; rather, it is "Do I know what zone I'm in and am I heading in the direction that I want to go?" The choice, as always, is your own.

Finding a fulfilling balance in your life may require that if you are really stressed at work, you look for opportunities to enrich yourself outside of work. Likewise, if you are bored at work, the challenge that gets you back in The Zone might be found by doing something in your community or with your kids. When in doubt, take one small step to improve your current situation. This may mean that you stop investing so much time and energy in activities or relationships that are unfulfilling, and begin to reprioritize your attention toward ones that are more rewarding to yourself and to others. Whatever you do to improve your situation can serve to generate the energy in your life necessary to create more overall balance. This doesn't mean that you don't explore possibilities to create more balance at work or at home, or wherever you need more challenge or development. It *does* mean you understand that the shift needed at

"A man of knowledge chooses a path with a heart and follows it and then he looks and rejoices and laughs and then he sees and knows. He knows that his life will be over altogether too soon. He knows that he as well as everybody else is not going anywhere. He knows because he sees... a man of knowledge endeavors and sweats and puffs and if one looks at him he is just like any ordinary man, except that the folly of his life is under control."

—Don Juan

any given time may be one on the inside, a change of heart or atti-tude, rather than a change in your job or relationship. Be sensitive to your needs, and ever-welcoming of deeper insights.

Living in the Zone: A Self-Test

The following practice will invite you to look deeply into the presence or absence of balance in the various arenas of your life. It is an exercise worth giving some quality time to, and may unfold as a sequence of contemplations over some days, or as an hour of more focused reflection.

First make a list of all the roles and identities that comprise your sense of yourself. You may want to list them on a piece of paper, or even write them down on Post-its, one statement per Post-it. To some you are a parent, to others a child. To some a follower, to oth-ers a leader. To some you are a friend, and to others a lover or a mate. You are a worker, a professional, an athlete, a musician, a writer. You are a physical being, a spiritual being, a deeply feeling and passion-ate being, an intellectual being. A member of a church or temple, of your neighborhood, professional societies, clubs, community, or the Rotary, a coach for the soccer team, a member of the golf league. You are a global citizen and a universal being. You are a great Mystery. Make as complete a list as you can of all the different elements of your identity that comprise the whole constellation of your Self.

On a separate piece of paper, draw The Zone diagram, with the Burnout and Rustout zones, the upper and lower realms of the Learning Zone, and The Zone of Optimal Performance running diag-onally up the middle. If you used Post-its you might want to map out The Zone diagram on a big piece of paper, or even use a window or a door. Pause to consider all the roles or identities that you just wrote down, and write or map those words onto The Zone diagram in the region that best describes where you stand on that particular quality of your life at this time.

Then step back and scan this "big picture" of your life. What does this say to you? Does it look like you are a burned-out boss? A

> "Each man has only one genuine vocation—to find the way to himself... His task is to discover his own destiny—not an arbitrary one—and live it out wholly and resolutely within himself. Everything else is only a would-be existence, an attempt at evasion, a flight back to the ideals of the masses, conformity, and fear of one's own inwardness."
>
> —Hermann Hesse

rusting-out lover? A peak performer in the mom or musician category? Does it seem that there is too much or too little going on to live a truly balanced life? Notice what areas of your life are way out of balance and calling for your attention to make some changes. Notice in what areas learning is really going on. Then continue by reflecting on the following questions:

- What areas in your life are most out of balance and calling for your immediate attention to make some changes?
- In which areas of your life are you most "overextended"?
- In which areas of your life are you most "underdeveloped"?
- In what areas in your life is the most learning going on?
- In which do you feel most challenged?
- In which do you feel like you need to raise the bar and challenge yourself more?
- In which areas of your life are you in your Zone?
- What activities, roles, or qualities of your Self are the sources of your greatest joy, satisfaction, or sense of accomplishment?
- Which aspects of your life are you most grateful for?
- Which do you have the most grief about?
- Which areas have you been ignoring that call for your attention?
- What elements of your wholeness have you left out and forgotten to even write down here?
- What strategies would help you to move toward The Zone in the areas of your life that you feel most out of balance?
- What are your top five priorities to give time and attention to in order to live your life in a more balanced way?
- What are the first steps you can take toward living in greater balance?

"The outward work can never be small if the inward one is great, and the outward work can never be great if the inward is small or of little worth... All works are surely dead if anything from the outside compels you to work. Even if it were God himself compelling you to work from the outside, your works would be dead. If your works are to live, then God must move you from the inside, from the innermost region of the soul—then they will really live. There is your life and there alone you live and your works live."

—Meister Eckhart

It's All About Learning!

Many of our friends from other cultures have commented that people in the modern West tend to be incredibly self-critical and unforgiving toward themselves. An exercise like the one we just completed invites you to look deeply enough to really catch a glimpse of a deeper insight into who you are, how you live, and what is truly possible. It may reveal ways in which you are living that you are truly grateful for and proud of. It may also remind you of choices that you have made, or paths you have chosen that you now regret or have some grief about. Welcome to the learning expedition of a lifetime!

It is helpful to keep in mind that this is really *all about learning!* When you are aware of the forces that shape your life, you have a choice and things can improve. When you live in a mindless way, the habits you have internalized rule your life. With this in mind, observe how the patterns of your life experience are shaped by your actions; your actions are guided by your intentions; your intentions reflect your values; your values are shaped by your beliefs; and your beliefs are shaped by your experiences and by the quality of insight or confusion with which you interpret them.

Making the changes necessary to improve the quality of your life requires a fierce commitment to continuous learning. And learning, whether about yourself, about others, about the ways of the world, or about the immensity of the mysterious universe, requires considerable courage.

Courage, Patience, and Forgiveness

In the early '80s it was reported that more than twice as many men and women died of suicide after returning from the war in Southeast Asia than died in combat. The only way these veterans knew to turn off the war inside was to take their lives. People in the Pentagon were stunned and many felt considerable grief at having contributed to such a deep wound in the world.

One day, shortly after the report was released, we received a call

"Inspiration follows aspiration."

—Rabindranath Tagore

"Life behaves in messy ways… continuously exploring systems bent on discovering what works are far more practical and successful than our attempts at efficiency. Such systems are not trying to reduce inputs in order to maximize outputs. They slosh around in the mess, involve many individuals, encourage discoveries, and move quickly past mistakes. They are learning all the time, engaging everyone in finding what works."

—Margaret Wheatley and Myron Kellner-Rogers

requesting us to help design and deliver an "Ultimate Warrior Training Program" for the U. S. Army Green Berets. Our hearts raced, and we definitely felt stretched way out of our Zone. This was a level of challenge that dramatically exceeded our perceptions of our capabilities. It also challenged many of our most deeply held values. Yet, after considerable soul-searching, we realized that we'd feel safer knowing that the next wave of troops had learned some of the kinds of lessons we are offering to you here in this book. We accepted the assignment, with promises of support from many of our mentors, whose guidance would be necessary to take on such an immense project.

Over the next three years, the government paid us to travel far and wide, and to talk soulfully with many incredible people from diverse traditions and professions about what they thought should be included in such a monumental program. Talking one day with Zong Rinpoche, the profoundly wise elder abbot of one of the largest monastic universities in Tibet, we explained that the men we were planning to train might well find themselves in a position to avert or trigger the next world war. The stakes were huge, and our hopes were that the team we'd put together would be able to impart some skills that would help these warriors to make wiser choices.

We asked the respected elder, "What do you think is the most important thing to teach these men?" He thought deeply for a moment, and then through his interpreter he replied, "Most of all it is important to teach them courage." "Us teach courage to the Green Berets?" we asked, taken aback. "How are we supposed to do that?" "Just teach them courage and everything will turn out for the best" was all he had to say. We lived with this conundrum for a number of years. Then one day we mentioned Rinpoche's advice to a friend who was a translator for the Dalai Lama. He laughed with delight and said, "Oh, that's so perfect. Did you know that in the Tibetan language, the word that we usually translate as *courage,* could also be translated as *patience* or *forgiveness*?" Upon hearing this, something deep inside of us burst open: *Teach them courage ... teach them patience ... teach them forgiveness.*

The moral of this story is that to make changes in our own lives, we all need to develop our courage, patience, and forgiveness for ourselves, and for the many other out-of-balance people whose mindless actions can cause so much grief. And this we can only learn when we have the courage and balance of mind to contemplate these two questions:

- What is really working in our lives?
- What is really not working?

We often say to clients, "You have to reward yourselves for making mistakes. If you don't take risks, if you are too self-protective and fearful about failure, then you will never step out of your Comfort Zone and into your Learning Zone. You will never realize what is possible. Not only will the quality of your life, work, and relationships suffer, but you honestly may not survive. A mistake is only a mistake if you fail to learn from it, or if you don't make those learnings visible to others who may benefit from your own learnings." This advice applies equally to individuals, to relationships, and to organizations searching for survival, sustainability, and for a more balanced way of life. Remember, learning is fed by feedback and led by questions:

- What feedback delights you?
- What feedback disturbs you?
- What feedback do you ignore?
- What questions are unconsciously driving your life?
- What questions would help you to focus your efforts to learn how to live a more balanced life?

You do not need to know the answers to these questions yet. By carefully observing the workings of your own mind and body, you will discover many clues for how to live in greater balance. We begin by stepping through the gateway of mindfulness.

> *"Wealth, position, and power become tiresome if the spiritual nature is not satisfied in its quest for meaning. As life progresses, the value of meditation and the cultivation of qualities of joy, equanimity, compassion, and love which give life its nobility and value will become more important. Amidst gain and loss, fame and defame, praise and blame, happiness/pleasure and sorrow/pain, the Awakened One urged us to keep a balanced mind. Only in this state can deep understanding arise, and the heart attain peace."*
>
> —Rina Sircar

FOUR

Mindfulness:
The Gateway to Balance

With an eye made quiet by the power of harmony and the deep power
of joy, we see into the heart of things.

—WILLIAM WORDSWORTH

Look out through your eyes right now, noticing the words on this page, and recognize that you are "seeing." Feel the contact of the book in your hands, noticing its texture, weight, and form, and know you are "touching." Watching the thoughts floating in your mind, wondering what will come next, know that you are "thinking." This lucid presence of mind that simply, effortlessly, notices what is true for you in the moment is called *mindfulness*. This dynamic state of attention is a deep, direct awareness of the present moment. It is your natural capacity and most crucial tool for discovering and sustaining balance.

Mindfulness is a presence of mind that we bring alive one moment at a time, right here and now. It brings clarity to our lives because the moment you realize that you have been mindlessly lost in your thoughts, you are awake again and back at the center of your life. Mindfulness allows you to recognize when you are out of balance and then to come back into balance, because it is the part of your mind that can notice what's happening. You've stopped falling off the tightrope—or at least you are aware of falling and can figure out how to get back on.

Because of the spaciousness that mindfulness creates around any experience—you aren't just noticing something, but you are aware that you are noticing it—it creates balance in the mind without grasping things too tightly, pushing them away, or confusing them with what they aren't. When we are mindful, we meet the moment completely, without being driven by our unconscious prejudices, assumptions, and conditioning. In this way, every moment of mindfulness becomes a moment of freedom that liberates us from mindless habit. That's why it is the cornerstone for creating balance in our lives.

Where Does Your Time Go?

Being mindfully focused is actually a more energy efficient state of living and working. The little bit of energy that you invest in staying mindful is far less than all the energy you burn up in the tension and distraction of ordinary mindless living. Just consider this: If you're an average American adult, over a lifetime you'd spend approximately:

- five years waiting in line,
- four years doing household chores,
- three years in meetings,
- six years waiting at red lights,
- one year watching T. V. commercials.

Although many of us feel that all we do is work, if you are like the average person, your attention is specifically focused on work-related tasks for only about thirty hours a week, and you spend approximately ten or more hours a week doing things irrelevant to your job while you're at work, such as daydreaming or talking with your coworkers about non-job-related things. You spend nearly as much time—approximately twenty hours each week—with your attention turned toward leisure activities, with about seven hours in front of the television, three hours reading, two hours in activities like working out or playing music, and about seven hours in social activities with family and friends, or going to parties or to entertainment. The remaining waking hours of your week are invested in basic maintenence activities such as commuting, eating, cooking, washing, shopping, puttering around, or in unstructured free time activities like just listening to music.

If you learn to bring greater mindfulness to even a fraction of these activities, you will add years of quality experience to your life and probably discover all sorts of time to do more of what you would like to in your life. Remember the old maxim: Choice follows awareness.

Once we begin to cultivate mindfulness, we can reclaim our life from the sinkholes of regret about doing things we really didn't want to be doing but were too unaware to realize it at the time: missed opportunities, escalating problems, and dangerous accidents. By reclaiming the time and energy lost in these ways, mindful living is like having an extended "quality of life" policy!

The Miracles of Mindfulness

The value of mindfulness is a universal theme common to all Eastern and Western wisdom traditions. Now scientists are discovering what contemplatives have been experiencing for a long time, as the health benefits of bringing this kind of dynamic awareness to our daily lives are being widely studied at Harvard Medical School, University of Massachusetts Medical Center, Stanford Research Center, the Menninger Clinic, and many other prestigious research centers. Although the benefits of effective stress reduction can be tasted almost immediately when one begins to live more mindfully, mindfulness taken deeply enough creates a profound state of inner balance that does more than reduce the harmful effects of stress in the body and mind. At its deepest levels, mindfulness ripens into the qualities of appreciation, love, and compassion. When this happens, we not only feel centered and good, but these positive states of psychospiritual caring and connectedness have immediate, measurable effects on enhancing

"The moment one gives close attention to anything, even a blade of grass, it becomes a mysterious, awesome, indescribably magnificent world in itself."
—Henry Miller

"There's an interesting transition that occurs naturally and spontaneously. We begin to find that, to the degree that there is bravery in ourselves—the willingness to look, to point directly at our own hearts—and to the degree that there is kindness toward ourselves, there is confidence that we can actually forget ourselves and open to the world."
—Ane Pema Chodron

immunological resilience, brain function, and the workings of the heart.

At its core, mindfulness is not different than love, and love is the greatest healing force there is. By nurturing our entire nervous system with the healing power of mindfulness in this way, we can maintain balance in our emotional lives and keep our bodies and minds functioning with optimal integrity. Thus, mindfulness provides a psychophysical basis of stability, which, in turn, provides the foundation for building stable and nurturing relationships.

Mindfulness is a perfect practice for people who live and work intensely. This rigorous and subtle practice cultivates such mental and emotional faculties as vivid mental clarity, deep listening, calm intensity, and authentic presence. The faculties that can be developed in this way are very important in balancing the complexity, intensity, stress, and change of our busy lives. Some other significant benefits of mindfulness include:

- improved focus, concentration, and precision
- enhanced quality of communication and relationships
- heightened clarity of your thinking and intentions
- improved efficiency and safety
- greater peace of mind and sense of flow
- mastery of stress
- insight and enhanced intuitive wisdom
- more authenticity, heart, soul, and caring in your life-work
- change resilience
- greater confidence, faith, and inner strength

Most importantly, mindfulness gives you a still point to return to in chaos, and it helps you notice where your energy is being expended. By noticing what you are paying attention to, you have more freedom to choose. In every domain of human

"These eyes through which I hoped to see God, are the eyes through which God sees me."

—Meister Eckhart

"A key to self-management is the capacity for self-observation. It is important to realize that self-observation is not the same as over criticism, judgmentalism, paralysis of analysis. It is rather a consistent monitoring of one's performance."

—Charles Garfield

experience, our ability to make wise choices, influence situations, and move toward greater balance depends upon the awareness we bring to the moment. The more mindless we are, the less we are in control of our lives, and the more out of balance we feel. Increasing mindfulness, therefore, is an essential tool for living, learning, and working in balance.

Because it seems so simple, it can be hard to believe that mindfulness can be of any importance in finding balance in our lives. But if you practice mindfulness, you will be surprised at your ability to change, radically and dramatically. This is like the trim-tab effect, where a massive ship can be more easily turned by putting a small rudder on the larger rudder, which helps it to move more easily. The place of the greatest leverage in your life is to practice mindfulness. It will give rise to a qualitative shift in your attention that will then allow you to easily make positive changes in the quality of your life.

Remember, in the mathematics of chaos science even the tiniest change in an equation will, over time, create a dramatically different structure and form of appearance. Each insight that you come to through mindfulness, if taken to heart, has the potential to substantially transform and reshape the course of your life.

"Learning how to be kind to ourselves, learning how to respect ourselves, is important. The reason it's important is that, fundamentally, when we look into our own hearts and begin to discover what is confused and what is brilliant, what is bitter and what is sweet, it isn't just ourselves that we're discovering. We're discovering the universe."

—Ane Pema Chodron

Being Awake

Have you ever stopped to consider how much of the time in your day you're fully present? For example, how much of the time are you really present when you're eating, and how much of the time is your mind wandering to memories of the past or fantasies of the future? How much are you really tasting the flavors and savoring the aromas of your meal, and how much of your attention is absorbed in watching TV, reading the paper, daydreaming, or talking with people as you put food in your body? When you're sleeping, how much of your energy goes into working out and wrestling with unresolved issues from the day, and how much of your energy is devoted to simply resting deeply and peacefully, restoring balance, and recharging your system? When you're talking with someone, what percentage of your attention is really present and listening, and what percentage is invested in thinking about other things or planning what you're going to do later?

There's an old Zen teaching story that speaks to this. The master is asked by his student, "How do you put enlightenment into action? How do you practice it in everyday life?" "I put enlightenment into action," replied the master, "by eating and sleeping." "But everyone sleeps and everyone eats," replied the student. "Quite so," says the master, "But it is a very rare person who really eats when they eat and sleeps when they sleep."

We are so often out of balance because we are not awake or, as we like to say, "no one is home." When no one's home, we are in a mindless trance, an all-too-familiar state of (un)consciousness where we are unknowingly lost in a fog of inner dialogues and daydreams that can lead us to miss our exit on the freeway, or miss an important communication from someone we are totally oblivious to—though they may be standing directly in front of us!

A classic example of this came from a woman who was in one of our corporate team training sessions. On her way home from work after the first day we had introduced the concept of mindfulness to her team, JoAnn picked up her young daughter from the local school on campus. Little Ana was sitting next to her, happily chirping away about all the exciting things that had happened to her in school that day. JoAnn was driving, preoccupied with things mulling around in her own mind, and she periodically mumbled, "Mmmmm...that's nice, dear...Uh huh..." in response to her daughter's animated tale and excited commentaries. After continuing on like this for a while, JoAnn suddenly felt a little hand tugging at her sleeve as they slowed down for a stoplight. "Anybody home, Mama? Anybody home?" came the piping little voice beside her.

"Wow, did I get the message, loud and clear," she told us the next day. "I really wasn't there for her, or for myself either, for that matter. I was just going through the motions like Mom on autopilot lost in the clouds of my thoughts. What a timely wake-up call that was for me!"

Why aren't we awake all the time? Is it even possible to be fully awake all of the time? Throughout the ages people have asked these questions and have experimented with various ways to increase mindfulness. We offer a few here.

Motivation and Mindfulness: Liberating the Spirit in our Lives

In his novel *Island,* Aldous Huxley tells the story of an island utopia. Understanding the importance of mindfulness for building optimal human relations, the founder of the community had trained a flock of myna birds and then set them free. The myna birds would land on windowsills and fence posts and deliver their wake up call to anyone around. Their message was "Wake up! Wake up! Pay attention... Attention... Here and now, boys, here and now, girls! Wake up! Wake up!"

We've introduced the notion of the "myna birds of mindfulness"—simple reminders to wake up and be present in your life—in most of the organizations we've worked with. In some places, this has taken inspiring high-tech forms, such as in certain divisions of Hewlett-Packard where, after our training session, people created screensavers proclaiming in brilliant colors: "Wake up!" "Breathe... Smile...Relax..." "Present...Open...Connected." One employee had even found a sign saying "WHOA!" and placed it in the middle of a busy corridor to remind people to slow down, focus, and re-balance. Another woman had the ingenious idea of putting a can of beans on her desk. Whenever her eyes would fall on this anomalous item in the middle of her desk, it would remind her to take a mindful breath and return to the present moment. When she got used to having the can there, she would find something else anomolous to replace it with!

One simple myna bird strategy is to wear your watch on the other wrist. Every time you check the time, you are reminded to

"Do not pursue the past. Do not lose yourself in the future. The past no longer is, and the future has not yet come. Look deeply at life, just as it is arising in the very here and now. Recognize it— invincible, unshakable. Care for it with your heart and mind."

—**The Buddha**

breathe, smile, and return to the stillness at your center, even for just a moment. By interrupting a familiar and often unconscious way of doing something routine, like looking at your watch, you can create an opening to pause and check in on the level of your wakefulness at that moment.

Another strategy is to set your watch to beep at intervals throughout the day, and to anchor its beeping with a mindful breath and the thought, "Wake up." A variation on this method was suggested to us by one of our teachers from the Tibetan tradition, the venerable Gen Lamrimpa (Gen-la), when he first came to the West for a two-year research and training program on the mastery of attention that we helped to coordinate. Gen-la is a colleague of the Dalai Lama, and is revered as a national treasure for the Tibetan people in exile. He lived on a very modest stipend from the Tibetan government to be a professional meditator. In this way, he could keep the well-spring of their profound knowledge vital as a living stream of tradition, rather than allow it to decay into fantasies about the miraculous mental powers of the ancient Tibetan yogis.

Having lived alone in a tiny hermitage in the Himalayas for nearly seventeen years, he didn't have much in the way of material possessions, and soon after he arrived, he asked if we could get him a wrist watch. When Gen-la made his request, he was explicit that he wanted a watch that could be set to beep once an hour, explaining to us that this would be an important aid to his meditation practice. We looked at each other somewhat quizzically, not quite understanding what he meant by this. Sensing our puzzlement, Gen-la explained to us that whenever he heard the beep, it would remind him that another precious hour of his life had just passed, and that his death was now an hour closer. Laughing, he explained that if he really took this to heart, he would stay more balanced and focused, be more loving and kind, and use every moment of his precious life to really make progress in his mental development and service to others. (In

Tibetan, "mindfulness" means "not to forget the object of your meditation.")

In numerous organizations we have worked with, teams have adopted a bell or chime of mindfulness, rung at random times during the day as a reminder for people to take a moment to come back to themselves. Each day the bell is passed to another person in the office, and as the gently melodious sound of the bell echoes out through the floor, people are invited to take a deep breath, to focus their mind and let it shine.

This time-honored technique actually stems from Southeast Asia where, for centuries, the villagers have kept alive the tradition of the "bell of mindfulness." In many ways, our workplaces have become our modern villages because we spend so much of our time there and have so many community and social interactions organized around our jobs. So what better place to ring the bell!

There's a mindfulness poem that accompanies this practice that we learned from our teacher Thich Nhat Hanh. You can use it when you hear the bell or use any other "myna bird" to return to the present moment. It goes like this: "Listen, listen. This wonderful sound brings me back to my true Self."

When you hear the bell, stop talking and thinking and just focus on your breathing with awareness for about three breaths, and enjoy your breathing. It seems so simple; it is hard to see how three breaths can help you find balance in your life. But the first step in achieving balance is to begin to see where your mind goes. Until you have awareness of where your attention is focused, you have little power to redirect your attention.

> *"The more and more you listen, the more and more you will hear. The more you hear, the more and more deeply you will understand."*
>
> **—Jamyang Kyentse Rinpoche**

Mindfulness of Breathing

The greatest strategy we have to offer for whenever you're feeling particularly frazzled, scattered, and out of balance is simply to return to the awareness of your breathing. Like an anchor in the midst of a stormy sea, breath awareness is a balancing force for the mind, anchoring you in the present.

We are made to live in harmony and balance between our inner and outer worlds. The breath offers a vital key to understanding this dynamic relationship. In many of the world's spiritual traditions the words for *breath* and for *Spirit* are the same. In contemporary science, breathing is regarded not only as a vital balancing force in all mind-body functioning, but as the only function that can take place both unconsciously and also be very easily consciously controlled. If you take these ideas to heart, you will realize that the simple practice of mindful breathing actually teaches you to balance in the center of the gateway where your conscious and unconscious minds meet, where your inner and outer worlds join, and where your ordinary, limited sense of Self encounters your boundless Universal Self.

Each breath teaches us many lessons about balance, reminding us of our interconnectedness with the whole world. Each breath also affirms that our life depends upon finding a balance between taking in and putting out, and reminds us that "inside" and "outside" are dancing with each other, and that they can be harmoniously reconciled as long as we can create the space and time for both inner and outer.

With each inhalation the lungs fill and the heart rate increases a bit to counteract the pressure of the lungs upon it. With each exhalation we release, relax, and our heart rate slows down. Similarly, we too can find greater balance in our lives when we can harness the energy, and exhilaration of initiating some course of action, and then, having given it our complete attention, we relax and let go into a joyful flow of awareness, action, and discovery.

If you carefully observe the flow of your breathing, you will discover that in the midst of constant change there are *still points*. These are revealed at the very climax of the inhalation before the exhalation begins, and at the bottom of the exhalation before the next inhalation begins. Taking this principle to heart, you may find the wisdom in pausing after you finish something and before you start the next thing to collect yourself, to fully focus your attention, or to get clear on your intention. With practice, you can learn to be more fully present with change by building frequent pauses into your busy day.

These needn't be long in duration, but the more frequently we stop, scan, and tune ourselves toward a more balanced state, the more we will be able to bring greater flow, sensitivity, wisdom, and care into the moments that follow.

Building more still points into your life provides a welcome opportunity to harvest insights and to apply them. This is like pausing to push the clear button on your calculator after the computations have become so numerous that they are all getting confused. The blank slate allows you to begin again, fresh and clear.

The technique is very simple: As you inhale, know that you're breathing in . . . as you exhale, know that you're breathing out . . . as you watch your breath, mindfully experience the flow of sensations that come with breathing.

The more effortlessly and naturally you ride the waves of your breath, the more effective this technique will be. This is not an exercise to control or change your breath in any way. It isn't about breathing deeper or slower, or trying to manipulate the breath as in some yoga or deep breathing exercises. In fact, strictly speaking, this isn't even an exercise, but simply a focusing of awareness into what is already going on by itself. In essence, it's a letting go of trying to control, and allowing the power of awareness to do the balancing work by itself. Simply relax into the breath, feeling it just as it is.

Mindful breathing accomplishes one of the greatest miracles of life: It brings your mind and body into synch with each other and into focus, so that your mind-body-spirit can work together with balanced presence. Because your mental functioning and quality of consciousness is so closely linked to the way you breathe, mindful breathing can have a focusing, calming, and vitalizing effect for your whole mind and body.

As a technique for balancing energy, focusing on the rising and falling movement of your abdomen is especially effective. Follow your breath and simply notice the natural rising and falling sensations of the movement itself. Practiced in this way, mindfulness of breathing can become like a centering heartbeat, a focused and flowing pulse creating a wave of awareness that you can use to steady

"Concentrate, and listen not with your ears—
But with the heart.
Then, not listening with the heart, do so
With the breath.
The ear is limited to ordinary listening;
The heart (mind) to the rational.
Listening with the breath, one experiences
All things in purity."
—Chuang Tzu

yourself as you ride through every activity of your life. With mindfulness of breathing as your home base, you can focus your attention and direct it to observe anything, or to perform any action, with greater presence and equanimity.

Some of our friends use this with their children. Whenever one of the kids is upset, overly excited, or about to have a tantrum, s/he is gently reminded to "go to your breath." How different an approach from being told merely to "go to your room!" Once the children have had a short while to calm and balance themselves with their breathing, they can then speak more clearly about what happened, how they feel, and what they need. Imagine how different your life would have been if this had been a family practice when you were growing up!

Beth, a client of ours, used mindfulness of breathing to handle a breakdown in communications with one of her customers. She was part of a team that provided technical support to other departments in a large insurance company. Keeping their information systems online and running efficiently was a high priority, because if one of their systems went down it could cost millions of dollars a day. One day a major breakdown occurred, and a very upset customer called, speaking abusively. Beth had enough presence of mind to say, "Look, we're both pretty upset about this situation. It would be easy for us both to get out of balance here and waste a lot of time. How about if we try getting focused first? Can you come over to my office and let's talk about this in person?" Her client agreed and came right over.

As they began to talk, Beth said, "I know that you're really upset, and I'd really like to see us figure this design issue out. Let's take a minute to cool our jets and get focused first, that way we can let our minds clear so we can think straight, OK?" The client had to admit that that was a good idea. "Look, it's real simple," Beth said. "Let's just be quiet for a couple of minutes and breathe together. Let your mind get focused with the breath, breathing in with full awareness and breathing out with full awareness. . . . that's it." After a couple of minutes, Beth said, "Wow, that really helped. My mind's a lot clearer now and I think I may have a solution to your problem." Her customer agreed that he was more focused and able to concentrate as well. Within a very short time they arrived at a very efficient solution to a complex problem, and got to work bringing the system back online.

Later that afternoon, the customer called Beth and thanked her for taking the time to get focused and centered. "By the way," the customer said, "Thanks for that breathing technique. It's really simple, but it sure works." The next day Beth learned that this customer had also left a voice message for her manager, and talked to the senior vice president of her department telling them what good service he'd received from her.

In a profound and simple way, cultivating a mindful awareness of the flow of the breath provides you with a continual reading on the overall status of balance and flow in your life.

If you learn to anchor your mindful awareness in the flow of your breath as a backdrop for all the experiences of your life, then refreshing your mindfulness is never more than a breath away.

So . . . whenever you're feeling frazzled and out of balance, come back to your breath.

Mindfulness of Your Body

The second base of mindfulness is to be mindful of your body. Right now as you sit here, become aware of your posture. Notice what the sensations of your hands are, and feel the sensations of your bottom touching the seat. Smile to yourself as you come out of the clouds of your thoughts and land with full awareness in your body.

Throughout the day, one of the simplest ways of getting focused and mastering stress is to become mindful of the position that your body is in. When you pay attention to your body frequently throughout the day, you recognize the accumulation of tensions and you're better able to let them go more easily and swiftly. As a result, you are less likely to accumulate a lot of tension and, therefore, less likely to develop stress-related illnesses. In this way,

"The best antidote to stress—besides altering your life so it's less stressful—is learning to manage it through mind-body methods such as meditation, mindfulness, guided imagery, and deep breathing. Recent Harvard studies have found that these techniques can successfully treat a host of... health problems."

—Dr. Alice Domar, Chief of Women's Health Programs at Harvard Medical School's Division of Behavioral Medicine and Mind/Body Medical Institute

"Most men pursue pleasure with such breathless haste they hurry past it."

—Soren Kierkegaard

mindfulness is the basic foundation of preventive medicine.

There's a very simple, powerful method for weaving body awareness into your daily life. As you breathe, feel the rising and falling of your chest or abdomen. Feel the stream of sensations as the breath flows into and out of your nostrils. At the top of the inhalation, in the pause, tune in to a *touch point:* notice your bottom touching the chair, or the sensations of your hands or your lips touching. Then, ride the wave of sensations of the outflowing breath, and at the bottom of the exhalation, tune again into a moment of mindfulness of your body.

Awareness Sweep

Another way to strengthen body mindfulness is by sweeping your awareness throughout your body, part by part. Begin at the top of your head, and as you breathe, allow your inhalations to focus your attention in this region. Simply be aware of any sensations or vibrations that you experience here. Then allow your mindful attention to travel down, noticing any sensations or vibrations at the back of your head, on either side of your head, or around your face. Whatever you notice, you're simply aware of, with no judgments.

Now, allow your mindfulness to gently sweep down into your neck and throat... as you breathe, your mindfulness travels across into your shoulders. Then allow your mindfulness to move through your right arm, traveling down from the shoulder to the finger tips, and then down through your left arm to your fingertips. Become mindful of your chest and rib cage, and then your abdomen and back... and then gradually sweeping this wave of mindfulness down into and through your hips, buttocks, and genitals. And then sweeping it down through your legs one at a time or both together... being mindful of your thighs... and then of your knees... Don't forget your ankles and feet, and finally your toes.

When you reach your toes, smile, breathe, and focus your attention once again at the top of your head. Again let your awareness

"We have concluded from our work with hundreds of patients that anything you can accomplish with an acupuncture needle you can do with your mind."

—Elmer Green at the Menninger Foundation

"Awareness in itself is healing."

—Fritz Perls

move and scan through your body, lighting up each part of your body with awareness.

As you sweep your awareness through your body, welcome whatever comes to your attention. If what you encounter is pleasurable or painful, let those feelings flow into and through your awareness of the present, ever-changing moment. Let your mindfulness pass through your body like a warm wave passing through an icefield, allowing any places of holding or tightness to release. Let your mindfulness sweep through your body like a magnet passing over a pile of jumbled iron filings. With each pass through your body, feel your energies beginning to align and to flow more smoothly and harmoniously. As you learn to listen to your body, it will reveal a treasury of insights to you.

Noticing Your Thoughts

Having built a foundation of mindfulness with your breath and body, the next base of mindfulness to develop is that of thinking. According to some researchers, 90 percent of the thoughts we think are reruns of thoughts we've already had before!

You can learn to simply and heartfully watch the changing images and listen to the endless flow of inner voices, without needing to get involved in them. However, this is not as easy as it sounds. If you're like most people, you've spent your whole life identifying with these voices, and struggling with them without really considering that these thoughts are only thoughts, and they really have little power over you unless you give it to them. Your real source of balance lies in remembering that you are more than the chatter that you hear in your head. You are also the presence of mind that knows these thoughts, as well as the space of awareness in which all these many thoughts coalesce and dissolve. When we hold our thoughts lightly, like wispy cloud formations dancing in a deep clear sky of mind, we are able to see through them to the creative intelligence that underlies and sustains them.

"Mindfulness is the practice of aiming your attention, moment to moment, in the direction of your purpose. It is called mindfulness because you have to keep your purpose in mind as you watch your attention. Then, whenever you notice that your aim has drifted off, you calmly realign it."

—**Frank Andrews**

You can choose which thoughts or voices to follow and which ones to merely let pass by with mindfulness and a compassionate, patient smile. This smile will protect you from taking any of these voices too seriously, trying too hard, or being too judgmental, as you learn to sit quietly by the stream of your mind. Here are a series of exercises to increase your mindfulness of thoughts.

Past, Present, and Future

Begin by sitting quietly, focusing your attention with a few moments of mindful breathing. Build the strength and continuity of your attention by breathing your mindful awareness into this moment, and letting it continue as an unbroken stream of awareness into this next moment. Stay fully focused and mindfully present with each moment and each breath.

Now, rest your hands on your knees, right hand on the right knee, and left on left. As you breathe, draw your attention to the stream of your thoughts. Staying mindful of each moment, whenever you notice a thought that's a memory of the past, tap gently with your left hand, indicating to yourself that you're aware of a special kind of thought called a memory. If you like, you can anchor it by saying mentally to yourself, *past.* And whenever you notice that you're having a thought that's a fantasy of the future, then tap on your right knee and if you like, mentally note *future.* Whenever your attention is totally focused here and now in the present moment, just smile to yourself and enjoy the ride.

As thoughts arise, just view them as clouds floating through the sky of your mind, or as different taxi cabs racing here and there in the mind. Remember not to hitch a ride on any of them! Avoid the tendency to mindlessly climb aboard and get lost in those thoughts. Simply let the thoughts come and go. Stay mindfully focused, and keep tapping your left knee for thoughts of the past and your right knee for thoughts of the future.

After a few minutes, reflect to yourself. Has your attention been drawn more to memories of the past, to fantasies or plans for the

"Yesterday is but a dream,
tomorrow is but a vision.
But today well lived makes every yesterday a dream of happiness, and every tomorrow a vision of hope.
Look well, therefore, to this day."

—Sanskrit proverb

future, or balanced more in the present? Objectively, learningfully, and without criticism, simply notice which ways your attention is most drawn.

As your powers of mindfulness grow, you'll gain more and more insight into how your mind works. Understanding more and more about your patterns of attention, you'll come to a clearer recognition of the patterns of mind that you'd like to strengthen as well as the patterns of mind that you'd like to reduce.

Pleasant, Unpleasant, and Neutral

Once again now, as you watch the flow of thoughts passing through your mind, be mindful of three kinds of thoughts. When you notice judging thoughts or disliking thoughts that feel unpleasant, mark them by tapping your left knee. And when you notice experiences that trigger appreciative, pleasant thoughts or acceptance, tap your right knee. When you're neither judging nor accepting, but are merely "neutral" and present, then just sit quietly and mindfully ride the waves of the breath.

Once again, avoid the tendency to dive in and get carried away or caught up with the content of your thoughts. Simply notice and be mindful that those tendencies are activated in your thinking process. Ultimately, you'll learn to be mindful of whatever you're thinking, and by being more mindful of what you're thinking you'll be able to direct your thinking as you wish.

"Understanding is the fruit of looking deeply... This present moment contains the past and the future. The secret of transformation... lies in our handling of this very moment."

—Thich Nhat Hanh

Mindfulness Brings Understanding and Understanding Cultivates Balance

When you practice mindfulness, you begin to see clearly what is really going on inside you. As you see more clearly, you find that you can just naturally come into balance. And as you do, you come to three very important realizations about how your mind works.

The contents, qualities, and states of your mind are constantly moving and ceaselessly changing. You can no more stop this flow than you can stop a powerful river or stop the wind. And if you could stop it, it would cease to be the river, the wind, or the mind.

Within or beneath this flowing movement of mind is a deep, quiet inner stillness that is completely undisturbed by all the movement. It is a quality of presence, like the open sky, completely undisturbed by the fierce winds of thoughts, images, and feelings that blow through the mind. This sky-like presence of mind can contain any experience; it is completely unstained by any of the contents of the mind. It is always clean, clear, and open to whatever flows through it.

The movement and the stillness are both present in your mind at every moment. You can't have movement without stillness or stillness without movement. You can't have silence without sound or sound without silence.

A very wise young friend of ours named Caton explained this difficult point quite simply to his mom on the way to daycare one morning when he was about five years old. Laurie, his mother, asked him if he knew where his thoughts came from. "The thoughts come out of the quiet in my mind, Mom," Caton said quite knowingly. Mom smiled, taking his wisdom to heart, and then asked him, "Well, then where do you think the thoughts go when you are done thinking them?" With a giggle Caton replied, "They melt back into the quiet of my mind, Mom."

The Wheel of Mindfulness

The essence of mindfulness is to be aware of what you are sensing, feeling, thinking, wanting, and intending to do at any given moment. Like any other life skill, mindfulness grows with practice. As you learn to understand how your perceptions, feelings, thoughts, desires, and intentions influence your body, your communications, and your behavior, you will feel more confident and better equipped to guide the course of your life and find balance moment to moment, day to day. The wheel of mindfulness illustrated on page

"In the Native way we are encouraged to recognize that every moment is a sacred moment, and every action, when imbued with dedication and commitment to benefit all beings, is a sacred act."

—Dhyani Ywahoo

66 offers a simple yet powerful compass for charting the course of your life.

This navigation tool helps you to discover and to describe to yourself what is true for you in each moment in each dimension of your being. By knowing what is true for yourself in terms of what you are perceiving, thinking, feeling, wanting, and intending, you will be more likely to recognize options, make wiser decisions, and to honestly and accurately communicate your experience to others. For greater clarity in any situation, focus the beam of your mindfulness to illuminate each of the following five domains:

I notice... **Mindfulness of Perception and Action.** In this moment of experience what do you notice going on? What is the raw sensory data available to you directly through the doorways of your sense perceptions—what do you see, hear, smell, touch, or taste? What you are looking to discover here is the kind of objective information that a video camera or tape recorder would pick up if they were turned on to record this experience, with no overlay of judgment or interpretation.

I feel... **Mindfulness of Emotions and Feelings.** How does this experience make you feel? Do you feel anxious or at ease, happy or sad, mad or glad, depressed or excited? What words best describe the emotional tone of your experience in this moment? Be watchful of the tendency to respond by saying "I feel that..." Adding the word *that* after *I feel* probably indicates that you're moving into thinking and judging rather than staying with your actual emotional response.

I think... **Mindfulness of Thinking, Thoughts, and Imagination.** What are your thoughts or "internal conversations" about your experience? Are you creatively thinking about a situation, or are you merely replaying old thoughts? What is the story you're telling yourself about a situation—your thoughts, fantasies, and assumptions? Recognizing the old stories helps you to live in a more grounded way

"One instant of total awareness, is one instant of perfect freedom and enlightenment."

—**Manjushri**

*"The thought manifests as the word;
The word manifests as the deed;
The deed develops into habit;
And habit hardens into character:
So watch the thought and its ways with care,
And let it spring from love
Born out of concern for all beings."*

—**The Buddha**

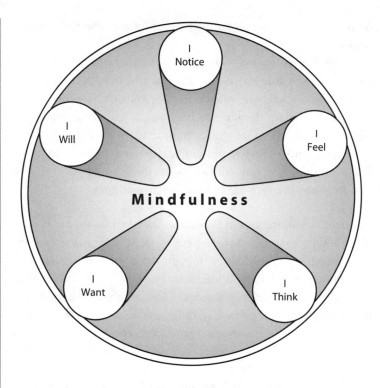

The Wheel of Mindfulness

and liberates you from mistaking your thoughts and assumptions for reality!

I want . . . **Mindfulness of Values, Intentions, and Desires.** What are your values, intentions, and motivations? What do you really want or need? Having clarity on your values, desires, intentions, and motivations is essential for effective communication and action.

I will . . . **Moving Mindfulness into Action.** What action are you willing to take in this situation? What are you unwilling to do? What are you willing to stop doing? Bringing mindfulness across the threshold of awareness into the domain of conscious action is the key to transformation. When you consider and then communicate to others what you are and are not willing to do, you become a conscious co-creator of your experience, rather than being unconsciously enslaved to it. And remember, your actions and inactions speak more loudly than your words. Be mindful of the impact that all your communications have on others.

A Mindfulness Week in Review

Here's another useful technique you can use to help you stay mindfully in balance every day. First, pick one day a week to set aside some time for mindful reflection on the larger picture of your life. Even a few minutes with the following questions can make a big difference in restoring your sense of balance:

- What have I been paying the most attention to in my life this week?
- What elements of my experience are calling for greater attention?
- What specific activities do I want to bring greater awareness to?
- How will becoming more aware improve the quality of my life, my relationships, and my work?
- What indicators have reminded me that I had drifted off into mindlessness?

By giving yourself the gift of a few minutes each week to evaluate the level of awareness that you're bringing to the things that matter most to you, you'll be able to fine-tune and reset your attention patterns before you get too far off course. Then once a month, enjoy a special "day of mindfulness" celebration. On the day of the month that corresponds to your birthday, invite yourself to mindfully explore something new and different. Even for a little while that day do something, in some way, that you've never done before. The freshness of mind that you bring to experiencing something for the first time is a good way to refresh your taste of mindfulness!

"We cannot do great things in life; we can only do small things with great love."

—**Mother Teresa**

"In the beginner's mind there are few possibilities. In the master's mind there are many."

—**Shunryu Suzuki Roshi**

Bringing the Mind Home

The cultivation of mindfulness is a lifelong process. Here are some useful distinctions to remember as you begin to integrate this vital tool for balance:

- Self-awareness is not the same as self-centeredness. When I am truly aware of myself, I am more in touch with everything around me, more available and sensitive. In fact, I can be more spacious and relaxed, and less self-protective.

- I can be aware of others only to the degree that I am willing to be aware of myself.

- Mindfulness requires being fully present, here and now. Because it is easy to drift into memories of the past or fantasies of the future, the pursuit of awareness in the here and now calls for practice and dedication. As we often say to our clients: "You can only manage the moment!" *Every moment is an opportunity to increase your awareness.*

"How do we know if our practice is a real practice?
Only by one thing: more and more, we just see the wonder. What is the wonder? I don't know. We can't know such things through thinking. But we always know it when it's there."

—Charlotte Joko Beck

A good place to begin is exactly where you are. So right now ... begin by bringing your mind home from wherever it may be straying. When the mind comes home, it becomes present and peaceful. With mindfulness, right now, you are aware that you are seeing these words, and may even smile to yourself with delight as you know that you know. You are aware of the texture and weight of the book in your hands, or of the thoughts and associations triggered by reading these words.

Outwardly, be aware of your surroundings. Notice what you see and hear in the world around you. Then, drawing your attention inward, first tune into what's most real and true for you as a physical being right now. Mindfully sense your position and posture. Quietly observe the natural movement and flow of your breathing.

One helpful technique here, suggested by Vietnamese monk

Thich Nhat Hanh, is to mentally add the words *arriving* as you breathe in, and *home* as you breathe out, silently letting these words guide you into a steady focus on the present moment balancing of your own rhythmic breathing. *Arriving...Home...* Your mental energy will gradually begin to settle and stabilize in this way, with the calming, balancing effect of mindful breathing. Then direct your mindful attention to the flow of sensations and vibrations moving within and through your body.

Next, open the focus of your attention to mindfully observe the flow of your thoughts, your internal conversations, and the emotional feelings that color this moment of your life. Simply, effortlessly, easily bring your mind home to focus and rest within yourself. Dwell in the calm, clarity, and peace of mind that's always here, mindfully observing the flow of experiences.

Having brought your attention back to yourself as home base, now you can open and expand your attention to reach back out into your world again. As you do this, maintain your awareness of your thoughts, feelings, breath, and body...mindfully present and balanced, focused and flowing from moment to moment.

Mindfulness is not some strange abstract or imaginary exercise. It's a proactive way to bring your life alive and in balance, and to discover what is real and true for you. As we have been saying, because you can change only what you're aware of, mindfulness lays the foundation for living in greater balance and harmony. With a clearer, more objective, and appreciative view of your current reality, you'll be better able to recognize and evaluate your options for moving forward. By helping you stay focused on what you are doing and thinking, and helping you recognize when you may be getting off track, the power of mindfulness helps continuously to counteract the tendency to get out of balance.

"It is good to have an end to journey toward; but it is the journey that matters in the end."

—Ursula K. LeGuin

Mind-Body-Spirit Harmony: Fine-Tuning Our Primary Instrument

"Integrity implies an integration of soul, heart, mind and body....
It is humanity becoming all that we are... A luminous thread in
a seamless garment... Integrity implies a new way of being—with
others and in the universe. It implies caring; a quality of attention
which involves a total commitment to looking, listening, feeling,
sensing, intuiting, being..."

—ANNE HILLMAN

OUR JOURNEY TO BALANCE IS TRULY
one that incorporates more and more dimensions of our reality into a unified whole. Though we may think of body, mind, emotions, energy, and
spirit as distinct dimensions, they are inseparably interrelated. Loss of balance in our outer lives reflects a cascade of inner imbalances: Imbalance in
our behavior is often reflective of our emotional imbalance; emotional
imbalance reflects imbalance in our biochemical and energy systems; these

reflect the turbulence within our mind; and our mental imbalance is rooted in the conscious or unconscious confusion that arises when we relate to our world from a point of view of separation instead of connectedness, communication, and wholeness. The closer we come to knowing and living in a way that honors and reflects wholeness, at every dimension of our being, the greater will be the quality of harmony and balance that we experience in our lives.

In a sense, no aspect of ourselves can be separated from all the others. If we cut through confusion with a deep insight that beholds the wholeness of ourselves and our world more clearly, we will have greater peace. Inner peace puts us in touch with reality and brings a balance of mind that is less subject to conflicting emotions. As emotional turbulence subsides, and our emotions become more balanced, our biochemistry shifts to promote greater harmony throughout the body. As our body, emotions, and mind are in greater harmony and balance, we are more likely to see clearly, care deeply, and act wisely in bringing more balance alive in our own lives and in the lives of those we meet.

By learning to observe the changes of mind and body, we are able to consciously influence them. A well-known axiom in psychophysiological training comes from our friends and mentors, Drs. Elmer and Alyce Green, the grandparents of biofeedback. The Greens explained that "every change in the physiological state is accompanied by a corresponding change in the mental-emotional state, conscious or unconscious; and conversely, every change in the mental-emotional state, conscious or unconscious, is accompanied by a corresponding change in the physiological state." Simply put, this means that every change in the body is reflected in a change in the mind and vice versa.

If you carefully observe yourself, you will discover that these dimensions are actually inseparable. There are no hard and fast boundaries along what we call "body," "emotions," "thoughts," "energy," and "soul" or "spirit." Words, thoughts, and concepts are helpful for limited tasks, yet they exist purely in our minds; the living reality of our seamless wholeness is indivisible.

For the purpose of learning, it is important that we separate these concepts here in order to discuss each. But it is equally vital for a true sense of balance that we also learn to weave our body-mind-spirit into a unified whole. A simple way to do that is with the breath. For example, as you inhale, sense and feel your physicality and form, thinking or softly saying to yourself, "body." Resting in the silent pause at the fullness of your inhalation, feel and affirm your radiant luminosity, thinking, "mind." Exhaling, open your heart and mind to its unobstructed, essential wholeness, thinking, "spirit."

> *Inhaling... Stillness... Exhaling...*
> *Body... Mind... Spirit...*
> *Form... Radiance... Essence...*

Understanding how this method works, you can change your contemplations to integrate and balance any trinity of concepts that you choose. If you anchor this balancing technique during quiet moments of undistracted contemplation, you will soon discover that you are able to awaken this same sense of balancing wholeness in the midst of your more active life. In this way, each breath—21,600 times each day—becomes an opportunity to arrive home and to affirm your balance in wholeness.

Now, keeping the reality of wholeness in mind, we will take a look at the strands that make up the fabric of our selves.

☺

FIVE

Physical Balance: Lessons from and for the Body

Body is that portion of Soul that can be perceived by the five senses.

—WILLIAM BLAKE

Delphine's soft, small fist wrapped firmly around Michelle's thumb. Standing, wobbling, toddling forward, she took a step, and then another step. A smile of glee and delight burst forth and a giggle radiated from her joyful being as if to say, "Yahoo! I did it! I really did it! I took my first steps."

Delphine's experiment in walking continued throughout the day with more and more steps added. Her little body learned fast. The next day brought new triumphs. Climbing from the floor, up her mother's leg, she pulled herself up to a standing position. Balancing carefully, one hand on her mom's knee, she stepped out. The room hushed. Two dozen adult eyes watched. A small step perhaps for humankind, but a huge first untethered step for Delphine. Step...wobble...pause...wobble...center...breathe...then another step...then a moment to crouch...don't touch the earth...then standing and continuing. A wave of shared and sympathetic joy burst forth from big and little hearts around the room.

Our bodies, big and little, offer many insights into the nature of balance. As human beings we come fully equipped with myriad sensory systems. While we pay primary attention to the five senses that speak the loudest, there are other sensory voices that we rely upon so instinctively, such as balance, that are seldom brought to our full conscious awareness—that is, until they fail us.

In this chapter, we invite you to explore with us ways of bringing your life more into balance through nourishing yourself, exercising, and resting in wiser ways. We begin with some lessons that your physical body has to offer about balance.

Mirror Images

Sit or stand naked in front of a mirror, to observe and discover the laws of form and balance revealed by your body. In-formed we are balanced, more or less. The symmetry of left and right mirror images is apparent in your face, arms, torso, breasts, genitals, internal organs, legs, feet, and toes. Front side and back side, top and bottom, left and right, inside and outside... all weave together into the wholeness and perfect balance that we call our body. Even the dual lobes that form the left and right hemispheres of your brain show an amazing symmetry in both their form and function.

Those of us who are women have likely heard from our health care providers that our breasts should be nearly completely symmetrical with each other, "like the wings of a butterfly," as Michelle's doctor once told her, and that any lumps or bumps in one breast should be mirrored by similar ones in the location on the other breast. If they are not, they should be checked out more closely.

Observing the functions of the body, balance is further revealed in the rhythms and cycles of activity over time. Breathing in, pause...breathing out, pause...breathing in...and out...Activity...rest...agitation...sleeping...waking up! Hunger...eating...defecating...Thirst...drinking...satisfaction...urinating...Ovulating...menstruating...menopause...

Youth...strength...elderhood....Wellness...illness....Births...
deaths...births...deaths....

The body reveals balance and symmetry at every turn—seldom
absolutely perfect, but always dynamic. Both structurally and func-
tionally, balance reveals itself through the body in form and space, in
movement and stillness, measurable and mysterious.

Rhythm and Balance

There is an intimate relationship between rhythm and balance.
In Mickey Hart's *Drumming at the Edge of Magic,* the Nigerian drum-
mer Babatunde Olatunji describes the capacity of drumming to create realignment within the human system: "Where I come from we
say that rhythm is the soul of life, because the whole universe revolves
around rhythms, and when we get out of rhythm, that's when we get
into trouble. For this reason, the drum, next to the human voice, is
the most important instrument. It's very special."

Our need for and delight in rhythmic, bilateral movement has
its genesis in the rhythms we experienced in the womb. From the
first instant of our life, we are woven into form through the rhythms
and pulsations of our mother's heartbeat and breathing, the rhythms
of her walking and talking, her activity and rest, and the changing
balance of biochemicals that flowed through our united veins. As
our own heart began to beat, our form emerged as a dance between
the harmonic wave forms and pulsations of our own internal
rhythms and those of our mother, and of the environment in which
she lived. From the moment of our birth, the dance that is our life
has continued to be woven on a loom of many rhythms. Consciously
or unconsciously, the balance or imbalance of our inner rhythms and
outer rhythms work in harmony or disharmony to weave the fabric
of our lives. Is it any wonder that such miraculously simple things as
walking, sleeping, dancing, playing or listening to music, watching
the sun rise or set, or making love bring us such joy and delight?
They ground us in rhythms that carry us back to touch the wisdom
and strength of our very source.

*"When you lose the
rhythm of the
drumbeat of God ,
you are lost from the
peace and rhythm
of life."*

—Cheyenne saying

*"Mr. Duffy lives a
short distance away
from his body."*

—James Joyce

Dancing and many forms of exercise can help you find a rhythmic doorway into the experience of dynamic balance, as can many of the following exercises. Notice how the theme of rhythm is woven into the deep fabric of so many exercises and principles in this book, and into the wisdom you naturally bring to living life in balance.

Rocking into Balance

Find a place to sit down where you have room to rock from side to side and from front to back. Now begin by rocking gently from side to side. Left and right . . . left and right. If you like, you can synchronize your movements with your breathing. Gradually allow the movements to become more and more subtle, rocking closer to center with each rock. As the rocking becomes subtler, sense that you are coming into a finer alignment with a sense of balance. When you finally feel like you have arrived at the center of perfect balance, then quietly remain there with full awareness for a few moments.

When you are ready, rock gently forward and back. In the same way as before, allow the movements to become more subtle. As the movements become less and less, let your mindfulness also grow more subtle. Once again, feel yourself coming to a sense of balance. When you arrive at the center of this crossroads, savor the deep, sweet sense of balance that you find here.

For many people this simple exercise is a powerful tool for finding balance of both mind and body. Once you get a feeling for it, you can use this to find your center of balance whenever and wherever you like.

Cross Crawl

As human beings, many of our movements are bilateral, involving a coordination between both sides of our body. Walking, crawling, and swimming are good examples. Movements to the left are balanced by movements to the right, and vice versa. Notice how

"I believe that just being conscious of our ability to shift our rhythms within the fabric of a frenetic society will make our hours less anxious, our days less stressful, and our lives more complete. It will, simply enough, make us happier. Happiness has a rhythm, too. Happy people seem to live less frenetically. They have more time in their lives. They are more in the moment. This happiness is available to all of us."

—Stephan Rechtschaffen

78   Living in Balance

your arms swing in rhythm and balance with your footsteps.

In our workshops, we often invite people to stand up and do simple stretching exercises that are designed to promote balance in the body and brain. For example, begin with your hands touching right in front of you. As you inhale, let your right hand rise up and your left hand come down. As you exhale, let your hands come smoothly back to the center. Then as you inhale, let your left hand rise up and your right hand come down. Coordinate these alternating movements with your breathing, and allow them to be smooth and fluid in motion. For further effect, you can experiment with shifting your gaze from side to side in coordination with your moving and breathing. Once you have established a fluid pattern and rhythm of movement, then experiment to see if you can reverse it or do its mirror image. As you begin, a movement may be awkward and jerky, but with practice it will become more even and natural. Keep it simple at first, and experiment to discover what works for you.

As your familiarity with these kinds of exercises grows, you can begin to further enhance and expand the "cross-crawl" effects with your imagination. As your hands move upward, imagine them coming down. As you push forward, imagine pulling back. As you push upward, imagine drawing downward. As you step forward, imagine stepping backward. As you do these exercises, the contrast of these actual and mental movements acts to "depolarize" many habitual patterns of moving, perceiving, and thinking, and opens both your mind and body to new possibilities and a balanced freedom of movement.

"I have no doubt whatever that most people live whether physically, intellectually, or morally, in a very restricted circle of their potential being. They make use of a very small portion of their possible consciousness... Much like a man who, out of his whole bodily organism should get into a habit of using and moving only his little finger... We all have reservoirs of life to draw upon, of which we do not dream!"

—**William James**

Side Switching

Another strategy that you can use to explore balance is an exercise in "switching sides." Each of us has a preferred side, a tendency to perform actions with one hand—for example, when brushing your hair, or answering the phone, or even wearing your watch. Ball players, skiers, skaters, and martial artists generally have a favored side for pitching, batting, turning, or rolling. Insight into balance can be enhanced by switching sides, such as switch-hitting in baseball, shooting baskets with the other hand, or brushing your teeth with your nondominant hand. Even switching your watch to your other wrist for a day will offer many interesting insights into balance in the interplay of your muscles, eyes, and thinking. The novelty of side switching will intensify your attention to the subtle, usually unnoticed cues about balance from your body. The key insight of this exercise is in the intensified attention that comes when you introduce novelty by changing the "balance settings" in your life. If you look, listen, and feel for it, lessons on balance are available—all the time.

Contrasting Balance and Imbalance

Experiment with standing, sitting, and walking. First, simply be mindful of when you are balanced, and when you are not. When you are mindful of an imbalance, zoom in with your mindfulness and investigate how that feels. Perhaps even exaggerate the position a bit so you can really get a feeling for how that is in your body. In the same way, when you notice that you really do feel balanced, zoom in with your mindful awareness and explore what and how that is for you. If possible, fine-tune your position and your awareness and refine this sense of balance. See if you can make it even more perfect, and then notice how that feels. Continue to live in this experiment and continue to let the balance inherent in your body teach you.

Balance Through Nutrition

Not only can we learn about balance from the body, but we also need to provide the conditions of balance *for* the body—proper food, exercise, and sleep—so it can work in an optimally balanced way. Let's begin by taking a look at our food choices.

Some people live to eat. Others eat to live. We invest so much time, energy, money, and attention into feeding ourselves, yet health statistics indicate that nearly 90 percent of all disease is linked to unwise choices in feeding ourselves. Food choices are deeply linked to many of the mindless habits in our lives.

From one point of view, eating is essentially a form of self-medication. We nourish ourselves but we also alter our biochemistry and thus our state of mind or consciousness each time we eat. If you doubt this, go without eating too long, and see what happens to your mental-emotional-physical state. We all know how eating some food leaves us feeling heavy, dull, lethargic, or sleepy, while eating other foods leaves us feeling more calm, balanced, or energized. At least three times a day, the food choices you make bring you more, or less, into balance. Being mindful of your food choices and how you feel after you eat different foods is an essential key to balance. Until recently, there has been little interest in our culture for learning about healthy food habits. Most doctors currently practicing have had less than an hour of formal instruction on nutrition, though they spent nearly a decade in medical school. But with growing concern over increasing health care costs, and the startling findings that so many of our diseases are linked to our eating habits and to the unwise practices used in growing food, many people are taking a greater interest in healthier nutrition and ways of growing food that are less harmful to our bodies and to the environment.

Simply put, your body is a walking, talking biochemical factory. What you eat directly and immediately affects your biochemical balance, the chemistry of your blood, and the ability of the countless sensitive biochemical processes in your body to function. The body is made to maintain health, to be effective at cleansing itself of elements that may cause disease. But if the immunological defenses of the body are overburdened trying to get rid of large amounts of imbalancing substances in the body, then our ability to maintain our health, restore our vitality, or to ward off disease is severely compromised.

We live in times that tax our bodies. Some say that the nutrition in our food is less than 10 percent of what it was a hundred years ago because the nutrients in the soil in which our food grows has been severely depleted by erosion, modern farming methods, and abuse of the soil with chemicals. Our food is so saturated with pesticides that the breast milk of every mother tested in the United States had

Choice follows awareness.
With balance in mind, consider:
Pounds of edible product produced on an acre of prime land:
Apples 20,000
Potatoes 40,000
Celery 60,000
Beef 250

How often a child dies of malnutrition and starvation: Every 2.3 seconds
Number of children who die each day due to malnutrition and starvation: 3800
Number of people who will starve to death this year: 20,000,000
Number of people who could be fed if Americans reduced their intake of meat by only 10%: 100,000,000

higher levels of contaminants than would be allowable to sell in store-bought milk. Walking into a grocery store, we often have to balance two competing voices in our minds: one that says how tasty and attractive those foods are, the other that wonders how laden with pesticide and fertilizer residue they are, and what our risks are in eating them or feeding them to children who are in their formative years.

For better or for worse, the food you eat has very powerful biochemical consequences in your body. The good news is, with the right understanding and mindfulness, you can learn to control these consequences by the amount and types of food you choose.

Understanding that nutrition is a vast and complex field, we'd like to simply offer some information and a few guidelines here to help you make wise decisions regarding your food choices, which, in turn, will help you to create more balance in your life. If you are interested in learning more about nutrition, seek out a professional or read books to help you sort out a balanced nutritional strategy. There are many recent pioneering books advocating food choices based on new research, considering factors such as metabolic balancing, individual blood and body types, genetic ancestry, and mind-body interrelationships. For a list of suggested readings on this subject please refer to the Resource Guide at the end of this book.

Nutrition, Stress, and Balance

The ability of your body to maintain adequate reserves of energy against the impact of stress depends to a large extent on a well-balanced and nutritionally sound diet. The food you eat, and the way you eat it, play a significant role in your total feeling of physical and mental well-being. A poorly designed and digested diet may counteract many of the benefits you could obtain from other strategies for balancing your life. Individual dietary needs vary a great deal. Read through the suggestions that follow and experiment to find your own optimal approach.

Most common cause of death in the US: Heart disease
Risk of heart attack for an average American man: 50%
Risk of death from heart attack by average American man who consumes no meat, dairy products, or egg: 4%
Amount of all cancers in US that are diet related: 40%
Increased risk of breast cancer for women who eat meat daily compared to less than once a week: 3.8 time higher.

Amount of federal poultry inspectors who said they would not eat chicken: 75%

Your food choices can change the world.
—**Source: EarthSave**

Relax at meals. The amount of nutrients you absorb from your food is partially determined by your eating habits. If you are tense and eat quickly, your food will not be properly chewed and mixed with saliva. This prevents your body from being able to extract all the necessary nutrients from your food, and adds additional stress on your gastrointestinal tract. Your appetite takes twenty minutes to register that you're full, so if you eat too quickly you may also eat too much. Slow your meal down by enjoying your surroundings and the conversation. Learn to enjoy the sensations of chewing your food. Begin to think of eating as a process that includes the preparation, tastes, aromas, textures, and environment as, well as the meal itself.

Set a meal schedule. A regular schedule for meal time is generally best for the digestive system. Snacking between meals and eating late at night is hard on your body. If you need to snack, try fruits, sliced fresh vegetables, nuts, or whole grain crackers. Plan your snacks ahead to avoid junk.

Listen to your appetite. Learn to listen to your body's needs. Are you truly hungry? Many people eat because of boredom, anxiety, or the need for oral gratification. Pay attention to what you're feeling as you reach for food. Because the same part of our brain that regulates our appetite is also linked to the control of our emotions and our sexuality, disordered eating often reflects unbalanced states of emotional distress, such as loneliness or unhappiness. If you feel you are eating more for emotional reasons than for physical nourishment, counseling may be helpful.

Eat simply. Read labels, know your ingredients, and avoid additives. When food contains excessive fats, chemical preservatives, or by-products from processing, the internal organs—stomach, liver, gallbladder, intestines, and kidneys—have to work harder at their specific tasks. Try to eat fresh, unprocessed whole foods as much as possible.

"This food is the gift of the whole universe— the earth, the sky, and much hard work. May we live in a way that is worthy of this food. May we transform our unskillful states of mind and learn to eat with moderation. May we eat foods that only nourish us and prevent illness. We accept this food so that we may realize the way of understanding and love."

—Zen Meal Blessing

Avoid caffeine. Caffeine is a stimulant that triggers a stress response in your body, stimulating the nervous system, the heart, and the respiratory system. Headaches, nervousness, irritability, elevation of blood pressure, and stomach problems can occur even with doses as low as 200–500 mg/day. (Eight ounces of drip coffee contain 220 mg of caffeine; eight ounces of percolated coffee contain 175 mg. Cans of soda pop contain 35–50 mg.) Wake up in the morning with gentle exercise, stretching, or a cool shower and a glass of juice rather than coffee. Instead of a coffee break, try grain beverages and herb teas, or have a big glass of water. Take a short brisk walk and breathe deeply. Keep decaffeinated coffee to a minimum. It is not 100 percent caffeine free and the most common decaffeinating process uses toxic chemicals to remove the caffeine.

Reduce sugar. Sugar is a stress-producing food in two ways. When you eat sugar, your body interprets the increased blood sugar level as a sign that you are in a "fight or flight" situation. Your whole body is stimulated and readied for action. This "sugar rush" throws your entire system out of balance, and may produce dramatic swings in energy and fatigue, often known as the "sugar blues." Reduce your intake of simple sugars as much as possible. If you can't eliminate sugar completely, try to avoid eating sugary foods by themselves, and have your sweets at the end of a meal rich in protein and complex carbohydrates. To counterbalance the harmful effects of sugar and to build your energy reserves, increase your intake of fresh whole vegetables, fruits, and grains.

Increase your fiber intake. Some people experience constipation when under stress. In addition to discomfort, this condition can cause fatigue and toxic buildup in the body. Exercise regularly, drink plenty of fluids, and eat a diet high in roughage. Supplement with bran, psyllium, or flax when necessary.

Drink plenty of fluids. Current research underscores the vital importance of drinking plenty of water each day. Your body is com-

> *"What is the use of planning to be able to eat next week, unless I can really enjoy the meals when they come. If I am so busy planning how to eat next week that I cannot fully enjoy what I am eating now, I will be in the same predicament when next week's meals become now."*
> —Alan Watts

posed of more than two-thirds water, just like the planet, and every organ needs a sufficient amount of liquid to function properly. Sodium retention can be a stress response for some people, particularly when fluid intake is low. This puts an extra burden on your heart, lungs, kidneys, muscles, skin, and brain! To keep these vital organs in balance and working at optimal levels, researchers recommend drinking six to eight glasses of water each day.

Reduce salt. High blood pressure, or hypertension, is a disease that is often related to stress. Although some individuals may need medication to control this condition, others may find substantial improvement with lifestyle changes such as relaxation training and dietary changes. Lowering salt consumption helps hypertension in some people. If recommended by your doctor, and as a general preventive measure, reduce your salt intake to below five grams per day. Read labels of prepared foods to determine exactly what is in the food you are eating. Try herbs and spices for flavor instead. Once you have cut down on salt, you may find your sensitivity to other tastes increases.

Maintain a healthy weight. The majority of longevity studies indicate that ideal weights for a long life range from 10 pounds underweight up to five to ten pounds overweight. Although many researchers believe obesity to be a health and stress hazard, weighing a few extra pounds is actually much healthier than continuously losing and gaining weight through fad diets. Once again, the best guideline here is to avoid extremes, and cultivate the balanced middle way.

Get enough vitamins and minerals. Under conditions of high stress, the body uses increased amounts of some nutrients, particularly water-soluble vitamins and certain minerals. Unless these nutrients are replaced, the body's supply can be rapidly depleted. Extra supplements of vitamin C, B-complex, calcium, potassium, zinc, and magnesium are often recommended for prevention and treatment of stress. Include in your diet on a regular basis those

"May this water as it flows through me become medicine, and strengthen the earth and purify and bring food for people, and renew the people."
—**Thundercloud's Water Medicine Prayer**

foods known to be naturally high in these nutrients, such as leafy green vegetables, sea vegetables, whole grains, wheat germ, nutritional or brewer's yeast, nuts, seeds, and fruits.

Be aware of allergies. Food allergies may be a hidden nutritional stress for some people. Even foods that are nutritionally sound for a majority of people may produce allergic reactions for specific individuals. Symptoms of food allergies might include bloating, nausea, headaches, skin irritation, or irritability. These symptoms may be mild or severe. Onset may occur immediately after eating the food, or may take up to several hours. In some mild allergic reactions, no symptoms will be experienced if the allergic food has not been eaten for three or four days, but will occur if the individual eats the food several days in a row. If you think food allergies may be a problem for you, observe your reactions to different foods and different combinations of foods and consult a physician who understands food allergies for further testing.

Get enough variety in your diet. To prepare your body and mind to effectively handle the accelerating stresses of daily life, a moderate, balanced diet with plenty of variety is the key. Any diet that emphasizes excessive amounts of any one food or type of food necessarily excludes a broad range of nutrients. Learn to listen to your body's needs, and plan your meals so there is plenty of variety. Include both cooked and raw foods; all colors of vegetables (be sure to include leafy greens); a variety of protein sources; nuts and seeds; and a variety of whole grains, such as brown rice, millet, bulgur, quinoa, oats, buckwheat, and whole wheat.

Balance Through Exercise

You were made to move! For millions of years your ancestors roamed the savannahs, swam in shallow inland seas, climbed trees, ran, walked, rolled, and frolicked in the fields. They lived an active

"We develop this sense of interconnectedness by acknowledging all that is eaten in its original form; envisioning the wheat that comprises the bread, the milk of the cow, the pod of the pea. The ocean of the fish. And the sun which feeds them all. We take in the sacred, the germ of life, like the Eucharist, in gratitude and respect."

—Stephen Levine

and embodied existence. Is it any wonder that it feels so good when you exercise and why you can feel so funky when you don't? Your body is not made to sit still in front of a computer monitor or TV for long periods of time, no matter what your boss, or those little people in the TV say. To maintain a healthy sense of balance in life, it is necessary to get up and stretch or move at frequent intervals throughout the day.

Every tradition of exercise and physical development is, in essence, a discipline of balance: the balance of activity and rest, of contracting and relaxing, of integrating and balancing left side and right side, front and back, and of hundreds of subtle complementary moves and functions that are necessary for physical balance and health. Just go to a gym and watch the cycle of exercises or weight machines that a person follows in a well-programmed workout and you will see balance at work. Similarly, go to any well conceived stretching or yoga, tai chi, or martial arts class, and you will see balance in action. Each move is followed by its mirror opposite, or by a movement or stretch that works the opposing muscle groups. Stretching backward is followed by stretching forward, reaching out to the left is balanced by a stretch to the right. As our understanding of optimal fitness expands, it is becoming more common to complement the high arousal achieved in an intense aerobics workout with at least five or ten minutes of deep relaxation at the end of a workout. Your body is made to move and to optimize its function through the dynamic balance of myriad exquisite components and functions. The more deeply and completely you understand your body, the more in balance you will live.

The topic of exercise is a deep, vast, and exciting one with much to teach us about finding balance in our lives. Rather than attempt to go into great detail in this book, we'd like to simply offer a few basic guidelines and some ideas on finding balance through exercise that you may not get from other sources. From here we encourage you to check with your health care specialists, or to check into the resources we've listed at the end of this book.

"A smile can change the situation of the world."

—**Thich Nhat Hanh**

The Basics

Exercise thirty minutes per day at least five days per week. This is the USDA's most recent recommendation. This could involve walking, jogging, riding a bicycle, or working in the garden, and need not necessarily include more complex rituals that involve club memberships, costly equipment, or access to a locker room. Numerous studies show that just this much moderate exercise can produce dramatically enhanced immunological function, resistance to disease, and prolonged life, so take this advice to heart!

Find an activity (or a variety of activities) that you enjoy. It is unlikely that you will sustain a exercise routine if you don't enjoy what you are doing. Experiment and find activities that work for you: walking, bike riding, working out at a gym, yoga, tai chi, the list is almost endless.

Take your pick: solo or social? Depending on your inclination, working out can be either a solo or a social ritual. For many of us, working out is not much fun unless we are connecting with and being supported by others. For others who are busy with people all day long, solo exercise time provides a welcome opportunity to integrate the experiences of the day, and for creative reflection and deep listening, which are so necessary for our lives.

Make some of your exercise aerobic. Aerobic exercise increases the efficiency of your heart. While ordinary people have a resting heart beat of, on average, seventy beats per minute, trained athletes may have resting heart rates of less than forty beats per minute. For an average person, seventy milliliters of blood are pumped with each beat, while for an athlete it may go up to one hundred fifty milliliters. At rest your heart pumps five liters of blood per minute. During intense exercise it may pump up to thirty liters per minute—a bathtubful every two minutes! Over the course of a lifetime your heart beats over 2,500,000,000 times. Reducing your resting heart rate with exercise by ten beats a minute would mean saving nearly

"When you walk, walk. When you run, run. By all means don't wobble."

—Zen poem

twenty days of work for your heart over the course of each year.

Conditioning your cardiovascular system requires learning how to maintain your heart rate in your target zone for at least twenty minutes in a state that is not overly relaxed or overstrained. Your target zone lies between 60 and 80 percent of your maximal heart rate. For effective aerobic training, you must find and sustain a balance in this range; below 60 percent of your capacity you will achieve little fitness benefit, and above 80 percent there is little added benefit.

Most fitness experts recommend that the lower and upper limits for your target zone can be determined with the following formula:

Lower limit: 170 minus your age = _____ beats per minute

Upper limit: 220 minus your age = _____ beats per minute

To determine if you are in your target zone you must check your pulse immediately upon stopping exercise; once exercise is stopped or slowed down, your pulse changes very quickly. Ideally, find the beat within one second, and then count for ten seconds, and multiply by six to get your beats per minute. If you check your pulse and find it is below your target zone, then increase the intensity of your workout to get in your target zone. If the pulse is too high, balance that out by stepping down the intensity of your workout.

We call the ideal five-phase aerobic workout a WACSR:

1. Warm Up: Start out slow and gradually build the intensity of your workout.

2. Aerobic Phase: Maintain a balanced intensity in your workout that keeps you in your target zone for at least twenty minutes. Check your pulse as often as you need to, and adjust the intensity of your workout to stay in your target zone.

3. Cool Down: Gradually reduce the intensity of your workout, allowing your heart rate to slow down. Slow your pace and begin to feel the vitality and strength within your body.

"A pump when I picture the muscle I want is worth ten with my mind drifting."

—Arnold Schwarzenegger

"Beware of a man who laughs and his belly does not jiggle; that is a dangerous person."

—Confucius

4. Stretch: Take some time for balanced stretching. Breathe deeply and begin to savor the revitalization of your body.

5. Relaxation: To optimize the balance you gain through exercise, follow the natural wisdom of your body and take a rest. As you know from times of working and playing hard, or from making love and then snuggling up to enjoy the afterglow that follows, after a time of increased arousal, your body will naturally rebound into deep natural relaxation. When you work out, hit the shower, and then jet off to work without adding the relaxation phase, you miss the integration and deep balancing phase of your workout, and this is the best part.

To take advantage of this naturally balancing cycle, add on an extra ten to fifteen minutes of deep relaxation onto the final phase of your workout. Because your body may cool down as you relax, it can be helpful to have a blanket or a sweat suit handy. Lie down on a soft mat, kick back in the hammock, or sit comfortably and let the effortless and natural rhythms of your breath and the balancing wisdom of your body carry you into a state of deep relaxation. When it is time to return to activity, notice how intensely peaceful, calm, and alert you are. People often notice that they get as much deep rest and revitalization during fifteen minutes of this kind of relaxation as they get during hours of good sleep. Carry this calm intensity into whatever activity may follow.

Be strong, inside and out. To develop strength, weight or resistance training is suggested. Here balance is achieved through balancing the development of opposing muscle groups. Work biceps, then triceps. Push, then pull. Build the body in balance.

Develop flexibility. To find balance and move through the world with grace and power, we need flexibility. Follow stretches to the right by stretches to the left, and back bends by forward bends. Stretch deeply and comfortably in order to find an expanded range of motion.

Pick a theme for your workout. This may be a quality or strength that you would like to build in yourself through your training. It may be a question or theme that you would like to ponder. Make an agreement with yourself to let this theme be the primary focus for this time and agree with yourself to also remain watchful of traffic or aspects of your environment that you must attend to for safety.

Do a Dardick. Serving as a physician at the center for Olympic athletes, Dr. Irving Dardick developed an unusual system of exercise that builds upon many of the insights into balance that you have been learning. From his extensive research with peak performers and with people suffering from chronic illness, Dr. Dardick discovered that people who built into their days frequent short periods of high-arousal activity followed by a period of deep relaxation were often able to dramatically improve their physical resilience. This ususally resulted in a major upswing in their physical, mental, and emotional health, and an overall increase in the quality of balance in their lives.

From the perspective of balance, folks who are depressed tend to benefit most through exercise, while folks who are suffering from anxiety need to learn to slow down and meditate more. Alternating waves of arousal and waves of recovery through successive rhythms of both exercise and meditation or deep relaxation can provide immediate benefits from a preventive as well as a restorative point of view. "Doing a Dardick" can be very quick and simple:

"I never hit a shot, not even in practice, without having a very sharp, in-focus picture of it in my head."

—Jack Nicklaus

1. Boost your activity level

First, check your pre-activity heart rate. Then, launch into vigorous activity for one to five minutes: go run around the block, do some push-ups, climb a few flights of stairs, or increase your activity in a way that works for wherever you are at the time.

2. Deeply relax

Sit or lie down comfortably and mindfully ride the naturally slowing waves of your breathing and the slowing rhythm of your heart into a pool of deep revitalizing relaxation. Ideally relax until your heart rate has dropped to a rate slower than it was at when you first began. As you relax, you might notice that you yawn or deeply sigh. These are often indicators that you are releasing accumulated tensions, so welcome them if they happen naturally.

3. Carryover

Carry the calm vitality and sense of deep mind-body balance resulting from this brief time back into whatever activity will follow.

You can repeat this Dardick cycle as often as every fifteen minutes, or at least a few times during the day. Especially on days when you are doing sedentary work, making time to move or stretch can be like stirring the soup so it doesn't stick to the sides of the pot and burn.

Go for a mindful bike ride, a run, or a walk. Make a mental commitment to be fully present from point A to point B in your workout. When you arrive, make a mental note of how fully present you were, and then pick the next "milepost" or marker. For example, give yourself the challenge to be fully present as you walk from your house to the corner. Notice how you did and then challenge yourself to stay mindful while you walk to the next intersection. Continue setting goals for yourself as you go.

Drift with mindfulness. Run or work out freely and simply witness where your mind wanders to. What do you notice in the world around you? What aspects of inner physical or mental experience call for your attention? What are the values, aspirations, or yearnings that work to organize and focus your attention? Just let your awareness drift where it wants to go without imposing any specific focus upon it. Simply follow the movements of your mind with mindfulness and see where it takes you.

Exercise in nature. Whenever possible, get outside in nature and move. Though this takes some discipline to overcome your inertia, once you do finally get out into the fresh air, you will most certainly

"If the heart wanders or is distracted, bring it back to the point quite gently. . . and even if you did nothing during the whole of your hour. . . but bring your heart back, though it went away every time you bring it back, your hour would be very well employed."

—**St. Francis de Sales**

experience the benefits. We often suggest to people that one important strategy for living a balanced life is to spend an hour every day in nature. If you combine this with exercise, you will learn about balance from two great teachers, your body and the natural world. Let them teach you, and listen deeply.

Sleep: The Great Balancer

As we work with thousands of people a year, we find that a large proportion of them have difficulty really sleeping well. Because information on nutrition and exercise are more commonly found than information on quality sleep, and because you will spend from one quarter to one-third of your life sleeping, we'd like to take some time here to help you better understand the importance of quality sleep for living in balance. If you don't sleep well, you might find some lifesavers here, and if you do have good sleep habits, this section will affirm and clarify much of what you have intuitively learned.

National estimates are that 25 percent of the population has difficulty sleeping, and that as many as 80 percent of the population are sleep deprived. Being sleep deprived also means that we're deficient in REM or dream-time cycles, an important source of inner balancing and guidance. Twenty percent of doctor visits are related to exhaustion, and more than half of the burnout cases that find their way to a doctor's office are people suffering from sleep deprivation. And the vast majority of people who suffer from sleep deprivation are not even aware of it!

Pause for a moment to let this soak in. If sleep is so fundamental to our health that we spend nearly one-third of our life doing it, is it any wonder that if so many people are not getting enough sleep, that so many things in our world are so out of balance?

Sleep deprivation is due in part to the unrealistic expectations of our lifestyles that often drastically underestimate how much sleep we need—ideally seven and a half to nine hours per night. It is also due to the fact that many people simply have trouble sleeping even if

"Study the patient rather than the disease...
Observe... if he sleeps or is suffering from lack of sleep; the content and origin of his dreams... one has to study all these signs and to analyze what they portend."
—Hippocrates' advice to physicians more than 20 centuries ago

they have the time. In many cases, sleeping problems are stress related. People get so wound up, accumulate so much stress and tension, and drink so much caffeine during the day that they have difficulty unwinding and shifting out of a stress-arousal mode in order to fall asleep, and stay asleep. And often people's systems are so out of balance that they have developed physiological problems that contribute to the difficulty of getting enough sleep.

Natural Rhythms of Rest

As you begin to rebuild healthier patterns of sleep, it is important, first of all, to understand that our natural waking and sleeping patterns are very different from the culturally imposed norms. The sensitive biological being that you are is made to awaken peacefully with the singing of the birds or the first gentle rays of the dawn—not with a screaming alarm. Second, as you may have noticed, your energy and alertness levels naturally wax and wane throughout the day with some periods of clarity and alertness, and other times when you are so drowsy and dull you can barely keep your eyes open. These rhythms and cycles of activity and rest are clues to your natural balanced state.

Looking at the working and resting cycles of other living creatures, we gain some interesting insights into how out of balance we humans are. For instance, think of the intensity with which a hummingbird works, flapping its tiny wings with lightning speed and its little heart beating at hundreds of beats a minute. Yet the hummingbird spends 82 percent of its time resting, not flying around. A lion spends only 6 percent of its time on the prowl, and 75 percent of its time resting, while a walrus rests for 67 percent of the day. Observing our closer mammalian cousins, the spider monkey rests for 63 percent of its time, and the gorilla rests a full 51 percent of the day. In the case of each of these creatures unfettered by our societal expectations, periods of activity and rest weave naturally together into the balancing rhythms of each day.

"Do few things but do them well, simple joys are holy."
—**St. Francis of Assisi**

"Do as much as you can and take it easy."
—**Tara Tulku**

The Importance of Sleep

Quality sleep is essential for a balanced life. During sleep, the body rests, cleanses, and purifies itself. It repairs, rebuilds, grows, and heals itself. During sleep, the stresses, strains, and tensions accumulated throughout the day are ideally released, and, in our dreams, to some degree resolved. In dreams, the mind is open to creative levels of the psyche, and we are able to tap the wellspring of deep inspiration, insights, and even premonitions that may profoundly inspire and guide our lives. And in deep sleep, our brain slows way down, and all the "mental programs" that we run cease to operate, allowing us to rest in a state of pure being. When our circuits are jammed with stress, and we tumble into bed exhausted and wake ourselves up with alarms, we are less likely to realize the full benefits sleep has to offer.

"Our truest life is when we are in our dreams awake!"
—**Henry David Thoreau**

Improving the Quality of Your Sleep

A powerful key to learning how to rest effectively comes through understanding the stages of sleep and anticipating your own sleep cycles. The stages of sleep, each lasting about ninety minutes have much to teach us about balance. When you first fall asleep, you pass through a brief period of intense semiconscious mental imagery and then spend a short while in dreams. Next you dive into a deeper, more peaceful and dreamless state. During this time, your brainwaves slow down into the delta frequencies of one to three cycles per second, and you rest in a state of deep, dreamless sleep. It is in this state, called "Stage IV sleep," where you get your deepest, most healing and harmonizing rest. In this dreamless stage, we are in a profound state of inner balance where our body rests at ease like a drop floating in harmony with the ocean of the universe.

"For those who are awake, the cosmos is One."
—**Herakleitos**

After some time, your biological clock leads to a shift in your biochemistry and an increase in brain rhythms as they accelerate to a theta frequency of four to eight cycles per second. Once again you enter REM, or rapid eye movement sleep, where you are likely to experience dreams. Though many people say that they do not dream, this is not because they aren't dreaming, but simply because they are unable to maintain enough mindful vigilance while they are in these more subtle states of mind-brain function to notice or remember them. As mindfulness grows in our waking life, we are more likely to be aware of our thinking and fantasies throughout the day. This lays a foundation of awareness necessary to begin to recognize and remember our nightime dreams. As our waking mindfulness deepens, we may even learn how to "lucidly dream"—which is like becoming a virtual reality composer working with the limitless creative potentials of our own internal dreamscape. When mindfulness is perfected, this lucid, peaceful presence of mind can be maintained even during the most deep and quiet periods of dreamless sleep.

At about ninety minutes after falling asleep, we reach the most superficial stage of sleep. Here we are more likely to awaken or to be aroused by sounds or movements around us, or worries or pains within us. And then as the earth turns, the whole cycle begins again. Once again, we go deeply asleep, though likely not quite as deep as during the first sleep cycle. Then again we dream, and then move into a more superficial sleep where we are more likely to be awakened by sounds or movements around us. In this way, the sleep cycles continue throughout the night carrying us rhythmically through balancing cycles of deep sleep, dreaming, and shallow sleep. With each ninety-minute cycle our sleep is more shallow. At the end of each cycle we rise toward the waking state, until finally at the end of one and a half, three, four and a half, six, seven and a half, or nine hours we naturally pop through into ordinary reality and wake up.

Understanding these natural cycles of sleep, you can come to some very useful insights:

- First, your deepest sleep happens during your first sleep cycles and the amount of rest you gain is progressively less with later cycles. If you have only a limited amount of time to sleep, then plan to sleep for one and a half, three, four and a half, or six hours.

"What occurs around you and within you reflects your own mind and shows you the dream you are weaving."

—Dhyani Ywahoo

- Second, if you need to set an alarm, ideally set it to go off at the end of a ninety minute cycle. If you wake up in the middle of a sleep cycle you are more likely to feel groggy and disoriented.

- For most of us mammals, our deepest, quietest metabolic time of the day is in the wee hours of the morning, an hour or two before dawn. If at all possible, this is a very wise time to stay asleep.

- You need to dream. Quality dream time is essential to living a healthy and well-balanced life. In studies where people are prevented from dreaming, they quickly become agitated, disoriented, and dangerously imbalanced. Next to breathing and drinking water, it seems that dreaming is the most essential vital function of our life.

The healing, harmonizing, and balancing power of dreams can also be understood by realizing that the body is actually a biological oscillator embedded within the larger resonant fields of the earth. In dreaming sleep and in deep meditation, the predominant brain wave frequency matches the rhythms of the pulse of the planetary electromagnetic field called the Schumann resonance field. Thus when we sleep and dream, our little biophysical oscillator comes to rest and balance in sympathetic resonance with the rhythms of the larger planetary field. This, combined with the profound and miraculous biochemical changes accompanying sleep, results in our awakening feeling refreshed, renewed, and realigned.

"To my right (in the South) the angel Michael, 'Who is like God'—lovingkindness; To my left (in the North) Gabriel, Divine strength—courage; In front of me (in the East) Uriel, Divine light:—vision; Behind me (in the West) Raphael, Divine healing; Above me (in the Center) Shekinah, Divine Feminine—She Who Dwells Within."

—A bedtime meditation, adapted by Michelle Levey from a Rabbinic Midrash

How I Lay Me Down to Sleep

People who know how to release stress throughout the day are often able to sleep more deeply and efficiently. In general it is always a good idea to take some time to deeply relax when you first get into bed. Here are two simple methods you can use:

- Tense your whole body, hold it for a moment, and then completely relax. Then, tense again, half as much as the time before, hold, then relax deeply again. Then for a third time, tense half as much as the time before, hold it, and then deeply, completely relax.

- Imagine that your body is like an ice field, and that your mind and breath are like warm sunlight. Using your breath to help your awareness to focus and flow throughout your body, gently allow your awareness to travel through your body like a warm breeze flowing through the ice, warming and dissolving any places of tightness or tension. Continue to sweep the warmth of your awareness through your whole body until you are deeply relaxed or fall asleep. If your body quivers or twitches, or if you notice any deep sighs, ahhhh, recognize these as signs of tension being released.

Each of us is different and must learn to understand our own natural cycles and needs for sleep. Some people need nine hours of sleep to function optimally—even if they think they should get only five. One classic example is a woman who was a client of ours. She had a German husband who insisted that they needed no more than six hours of sleep each night. When she came to see us for treatment, she was a nervous wreck. She hadn't slept more than six hours for many years and was suffering from many stress-related symptoms. As we worked together, we came to recognize that she was deeply exhausted. We offered her some suggestions for resetting her internal clock. As she got more sleep, her symptoms went away, and she felt much more energized, hospitable, and alive.

Keep in mind that your biological clock is calibrated by your exposure to light. If possible, avoid the common practice of blasting yourself with bright lights—like when you turn on the bathroom lights to brush your teeth—for at least an hour before you plan to go to sleep. If possible, put dimmers on the lights in the rooms you spend time in prior to sleep, or simply use a soft night light rather than the regular lights.

- If possible, sleep in a quiet, dark room, with some fresh air at about sixty degrees.

- Use quilts or blankets and avoid electric blankets that create considerable imbalance in your body's own bioelectric field. In a pinch, use an electric blanket to heat up a cold bed and then unplug it during your sleeping time.

- Establish a regular sleeping schedule, but don't go to bed until you are sleepy. If you can't fall asleep within twenty minutes, get up and return when you are sleepy.

- A nightcap before sleep does not improve sleep. Though it may help you to relax and fall asleep, your sleep will be less deep and restful, and more easily interrupted.

- Avoid drinking caffeinated beverages for at least four hours before bedtime. And keep in mind that nicotine is also a stimulant that will interfere with restful sleep.

- If at all possible, avoid sleeping pills and learn skills to sleep more naturally. Sleeping pills can be addictive and should be used for very short periods of time only—never more than three nights in a row. They also lead to imbalanced sleep cycles and daytime fatigue that then is often worsened by using caffeine. Never combine sleeping pills with alcohol!

- Because the mind entering into sleep is highly suggestible to the images you feed it, avoid watching TV just before bed, or falling asleep with the TV or the radio on. Instead, we suggest that you either fall asleep quietly, or if you prefer, with soothing and uplifting music. You might also experiment with reading something that is inspiring or that nourishes your soul before you go to sleep. We often read to each other before bed, or give each other a foot rub or back rub to relax, and when we do this is a very special time. You will be amazed at the balance this can offer to the frenetic pace of life, and at the difference this can make in how well you sleep.

"A person is not a thing or a process, but an opening through which the absolute manifests."
—**Martin Heidegger**

"Our normal waking consciousness, rational consciousness as we call it, is but one special type of consciousness, whilst all about it parted by the flimsiest of screens, there lie potential forms of consciousness entirely different. We may go through life without suspecting their existence; but apply the requisite stimuli and at a touch they are there in all their completeness, definite types of mentality which probably somewhere have their field of application."

(continued on page 101)

- Sleeping with your head to the north optimizes the quality of your rest. Your body is actually charged like a big bioelectric magnet. Your head has an electrical polarity similar to the north pole, while your feet have a polarity like the south pole. If you could imagine your body floating in a pool of water like the needle of a compass, your body would naturally come to rest in alignment and in synch with the geomagnetic environment when your head is toward the north and your feet to the south. Thus, sleeping with your head to the north aligns your body in a naturally balanced way with your larger environment. This alignment is more deeply restful than if you were to sleep oriented in another direction. If it is difficult to orient yourself to sleep with your head to the north, east is your second best choice.

- If you suffer from chronic or severe insomnia, talk to your doctor or make an appointment for an evaluation at a sleep disorder clinic.

- If you are so inclined, taking some time for prayer or meditation before sleep can greatly improve the quality and depth of your sleep.

- Upon awakening, remember that a study showed that people who woke up with an alarm, leaped out of bed, and charged off to work were actually less productive during the day than people who got off to a slower and more mindful start. So take time to meditate, stretch, or do yoga or tai chi, spend quality time with the people you love, go for a walk, and so on. In the long run, such "time-wasters" will actually enhance the quality of balance, effectiveness, and productivity you bring to a busy day at work.

Balancing Cycles of Clarity and Drowsiness Throughout the Day

We all know how at times we can be so drowsy that we can hardly keep our eyes open or hold a pen in our hand. Then, twenty or thirty minutes later, we are again more clear-minded and focused. This is because these ninety-minute circadian cycles during sleep actually continue throughout the day. Understanding this, a number of insights are helpful in order to balance and optimize your energy levels throughout the day.

At times when your energy is naturally slumping, it's generally unwise to make a habit of reviving yourself with caffeine. Though it will artificially elevate your energy and alertness level for a short while, it also puts more strain on your body by overriding your body's natural balancing mechanisms. Caffeine simply makes your already tired body work even harder in order to make the shift in your biochemistry and energy level to get the rest it needs.

Fit your task to your energy and alertness level. If you are feeling drowsy and find it difficult to concentrate, this is not the time to balance the books or prepare a detailed spreadsheet. Instead, rouse yourself to do something more active like run some errand, walk materials across the office, or take a walk around the block. At least shift the focus of your work to tackle a project that you can be in a more imaginative or creative state with, such as brainstorming some design ideas or drawing a sketch. After a while, when your mind is more clear, you'll be better prepared to turn your attention to more focused work.

"No account of the universe in its totality can be final, which leaves other forms of consciousness quite disregarded. How to regard them is the question—for they are so discontinuous with ordinary consciousness. Yet they may determine attitudes though they cannot furnish formulas, and open a region though they fail to give a map. At any rate they forbid a premature closing of our accounts of reality."

—William James

Power Napping and Theta Twitching

If your energy and ability to focus is on the wane, consider taking a brief nap. If you don't have time for a whole sleep cycle, you can practice a wonderful, quick method that we call "theta twitching."

Theta is the name of the brainwave states that are most predominant during dreams, deep relaxation, or in deep lucid states of meditation. You likely know the feeling you have sometimes just when you're falling asleep, and the body jerks and sometimes wakes you or your partner up? This twitch is a signal that you have just released a big load of accumulated stress and tension as you crossed the waking threshold into theta.

So, to theta twitch on purpose, sit down at your desk after a good lunch, or later in the afternoon when you are feeling kind of drowsy. Rest your elbow on your desk or on the arm of your chair, close your eyes, breathe, relax, let sounds and thoughts float by, and drift deeply into sleep. As you doze off, you will lose muscle tension, and your arm will drop, most likely waking you up. When you do wake up, stay relaxed and mellow, and propping your arm up again, go for another round. See how easily and quickly you are able to drop again across the threshold of waking and into sleep After one or two twitches, check your energy and alertness level. Most people will notice that even after these few brief moments they feel refreshed and renewed.

Learning to Optimize Your Energy Level

Understand that the quality of your life and work are determined in large part by how wisely you manage your energy. If you work a twelve-hour day at 20 percent efficiency, you may have worked hard but not really done much quality work. On the other hand, if you manage your energy more effectively and work at 60 or 80 percent efficiency, you may accomplish more working only six or eight hours. For people who are "knowledge workers," we know that in a half hour of inspired work, weeks or even months of more labored efforts can be achieved.

One of our teachers, Brother David Steindl-Rast, reminds us that lessons in balance are available in each moment if we only pause to listen to the wisdom of our heart. "The heart is a leisurely muscle," he says. "It differs from all other muscles. How many pushups can you make before the muscles in your arms and stomach get so tired that you have to stop? But your heart muscle goes on working for as long as you live. It does not get tired, because there is a phase of rest built into every single heartbeat. Our physical heart works leisurely. And when we speak of the heart in a wider sense, the idea is implied that life-giving leisure lies at the very center.... Seen in this light, leisure is not the privilege of a few who can afford to take time, but the virtue of all who are willing to give time to what takes time—to give as much time as a task rightly takes."

Understanding this, develop your personal skills and support those you work with in learning how to manage their energy levels throughout the day. Wise managers who understand the wisdom in this will support their people in taking breaks to eat, exercise, or even nap during the work day. They recognize that people should be rewarded not on the basis of the time they work, but on the quality of results they are able to produce. Because our rhythms and cycles vary, develop working relationships where you and your coworkers can cover for each other as you take care of your needs throughout the day, and help each other to be mutually successful.

"Here is the very heart and soul of the matter: If you look to lead, invest at least 40% of your time managing yourself—your ethics, character, principle, purpose, motivation, and conduct. Invest at least 30% managing those with authority over you, and 15% managing your peers. Use the remainder to induce those you 'work for' to understand and practice the theory... if you don't understand that you should be working for your mislabeled 'subordinates' you haven't understood anything. Lead yourself, lead your superiors, lead your peers, and free your people to do the same. All else is trivial!"

—Dee Hock, Founder of VISA Card

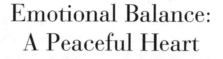

SIX

Emotional Balance:
A Peaceful Heart

In this century, human knowledge is extremely expanded and developed.
But this is mainly knowledge of the external world.... You spend a large
amount of the best human brain power looking outside—too much—
and it seems you do not spend adequate effort to look within, to think
inwardly.... Perhaps now that the Western sciences have reached down
into the atom and out into the cosmos finally to realize the extreme vulnerability of all life and value, it is becoming credible, even obvious, that
the field of what we call "inner science"—dealing with the inner
things—is of supreme importance. Certainly physics designed the
bombs, biology the germ warfare, chemistry the nerve gas, and so on,
but it will be the unhealthy emotions of individuals that will trigger
these horrors. These emotions can only be controlled, reshaped, and
rechanneled, by technologies developed from successful inner science.

—THE DALAI LAMA

Having explored the physical
dimensions of balance in our
bodies, we now move to examine
the closely related sphere of our emotional lives. The heart forms a good
bridge linking these two worlds. While still a physical organ, the heart also
represents for many of us the vital center of emotional tones and textures.

Day after day, year after year, your heart keeps beating, teaching you
about balance with each pulse. With every beat, millions of sensitive cells

work together in a complex rhythm that keeps things flowing through every moment of your life. Thirty-six thousand heartbeats a day, over 1,000,000 beats per month, add up to well over 2,500,000,000 heartbeats in a lifetime. The heart muscle represents the most intelligent and well managed workforce in the world.

For your heart, as well as for your life, the secret to success is in finding a dynamic flowing balance between phases of working and resting, pulsing and resting, activity and receptivity, to be nourished so that it can pulse again. It's doing... and then pausing to just be. The heart is able to keep going strong and steady, without a break, for a lifetime because it knows how to focus and then flow, and it has the flexibility to adapt to each micromoment along the way.

There is a wisdom in our heart worth listening to for a lifetime. Though our thinking is useful for many things, we often confuse our thoughts about reality for the actual direct encounter with it. Learning to recognize when you are "in your head" or "heart-centered" is an essential skill for finding balance. The need for balancing heart and mind has been apparent to seekers of inner peace for a long time. From his meditative hermitage, over a hundred years ago, the Christian contemplative Theophane the Recluse, shared his intimate insights into this subject. With careful observation he noted his awareness, advising us in the language of his day:

"For so long as the mind remains in the head, where thoughts jostle one another, it has no time to concentrate on one thing. But when attention descends into the heart, it attracts all the powers of the soul and body into one point there."

Decades of inspired global service work led our friend and teacher Ram Dass to witness and relieve considerable suffering in the world. Yet still so much remains. As he reminds us, "There are many levels of the heart. And the human heart will break because it empathizes. The deeper heart... looks at the universe, just as it is, in a non reactive way and says, 'Ah so,' 'Yes'. And it includes your human heart which is breaking, but your identity isn't only with your human heart. Your identity is with a deeper, intuitive heart wisdom which is different. You don't deny the pain, but you don't get reactive to it."

"Our scientific power has outrun our spiritual power. We have guided missiles and misguided men. Our hope for creative living lies in our ability to reestablish the spiritual needs of our lives in personal character and social justice. Without this spiritual and moral reawakening we shall destroy ourselves in the misuse of our own instruments."

—Rev. Martin Luther King Jr.

"The hardest state to be in," he reminds us, "is one in which you keep your heart open to the suffering that exists around you, and simultaneously keep your discriminative wisdom.... Once you understand that true compassion is the blending of the open heart and quiet mind, it is still difficult to find the balance. Most often we start out doing these things sequentially. We open our hearts and get lost in the melodramas, then we meditate and regain our quiet center by pulling back in from so much openness. Then we once again open and get sucked back into the dance. So it goes cycle after cycle. It takes a good while to get the balance...You have to stay right on the edge of that balance. It seems impossible, but you can do it. At first, when you achieve this balance, it is self-consciously maintained. Ultimately, however, you merely become the statement of the amalgam of the open heart and the quiet mind. Then there is no more struggle; it's just the way you are."

"Our first teacher is our own heart."

—**Cheyenne saying**

Life Signs

The heart is a powerhouse, a bioelectric miracle generating a bio-electric field that is 40 to 60 times stronger than the field generated by your brain. By biological standards, this is very strong. The bio-electric field generated by the heart ripples through your whole body and far beyond. If you could set up the right kind of sensitive scanning device across town from someone and zero in on him or her, you'd find that the information wave generated each time our hearts beat could be picked up for miles around you. Each time you enter a room, the beating of your heart announces your presence and informs other biological entities in the room as to how at peace or in conflict you are underneath your surface appearance.

"Words that come from the heart enter the heart."

—**Moses Ibn Ezra**

The workings of the heart are influenced by the two branches of your autonomic nervous system: the sympathetic system that is associated with the stress-arousal response and the parasympathetic system that is associated with the relaxation response. These two work together to speed up and slow down your heart rate sort of like the accelerator and brake of a car.

When we are anxious or stressed, the heart "drives" jerkily, like the car of a beginner driver who is unsure of himself and keeps stepping on the brake while he has his foot on the accelerator. Signals of stress, followed by signals of tentative comfort, then another surge of anxiety or doubt, and a moment of gentling reassurance—the interplay of these conflicting emotional reactions can wreak havoc on our poor heart, not to mention all the other physiological systems that go along for the ride. All the while, our internal turbulence broadcasts loud and clear to all those around us, affecting them negatively as well.

On the other hand, when we are in a more peaceful, balanced, loving, or appreciative mode, our heart purrs along like a car under the hand of a skilled driver on an open road. The heart rate is coherent rather than incoherent, steady instead of jerky, more musical in its waveforms than the noisy signals during stress. It is clear by the good vibes we are putting out that we are in harmony and balance, and likely we are safe to approach or depend upon.

You probably know from experience what it is like to walk into a room when there has been an argument; you can feel the tension in the air. Similarly, you may know what a "contact high" you can get to be with someone who is truly peaceful, loving, kind, or joyful. Even if you are consciously out of touch with what's going on for you, your mind-body is belting out the broadcast for all to hear. To the degree that other people are stressed, imbalanced, or distracted, their ability to tune in, to be sensitive to you, or to empathize with you will be eclipsed. To the degree that they are present, balanced, and at peace with themselves, they'll be more likely to be sensitive to what is really going on for you. The following three-part sequence of heart-opening and stretching exercises will help you to live from your heart.

Heart to Heart

Imagine someone in front of you toward whom you feel much tenderness, friendship, love, or compassionate concern. This could

"Love has to spring spontaneously from within and it is in no way amenable to any form of inner or outer force. Love and coercion can never go together; but though love cannot be forced on anyone, it can be awakened in him through love itself. Love is essentially self communicative; those who do not have it catch it from those who have it. True love is unconquerable and irresistible, and it goes on gathering power and spreading itself, until eventually it transforms everyone whom it touches."

—**Meher Baba**

be a loved one, a close friend, or even a pet. As vividly as possible, with your eyes closed, sense or imagine the presence of this being before you now. Allow yourself to get in touch with the genuine sense of love and care that you feel for this special one.

Now begin to focus on this person's heart, not the physical organ that pumps blood, but rather that center of love that lies at the "heart" of each person. Reach out now—actually raising your arms and reaching out with your physical hands—and imagine cradling in your hands this person's place of deepest feeling, really touching his or her heart. Imagine that as you breathe in, a feeling of love and care wells up within you and fills your own heart. As you exhale, this wellspring of love within you—visualized as streams of light or energy—flows from your heart out through your arms and hands, and pours gently into this person's heart. In a deep and silent way, offer this love and care, and imagine that it is being received in the way the person most needs at this time.

Now, imagine that this person reaches back to touch your heart. Imagine your eyes meeting in recognition, appreciation, and understanding. Imagine seeing each other with total love and forgiveness. Let any memories that block your hearts be dissolved and healed in the joy of this heart-to-heart meeting. Imagine looking deeply into one another's eyes with heartfelt love and mutual respect. Feel the satisfaction and the intimacy of this flow between you.

Focus your attention again on the image of your loved one or friend. Visualize the image of this person condensing into a small bright sphere of light that you tenderly hold in your hands. As you breathe, gently place this luminous sphere in the center of your own heart. Imagine it shining brightly, like a gently glowing sun that shines with a light of love and peacefulness, dispelling any darkness within or around you.

"Lord, make me an instrument of thy peace.
Where there is hatred, let me sow love;
Where there is injury, pardon;
Where there is doubt, faith;
Where there is despair, hope;
Where there is darkness, light;
Where there is sadness, joy."
—Saint Francis Prayer

Touching Your Heart

With both of your hands now, reach up and touch your own heart. As you breathe, imagine filling your heart with feelings of love directed toward yourself. Imagine what it is like to be here fully for yourself with the same love and care that you might offer to others.

Understanding that it is difficult to receive the care of others if you are unable to give love to yourself, breathe in the love now. Feel the sense of genuine self-love well up within your entire being. Use the natural cycles of your breath to circulate this feeling of love, moving from your heart out through your arms and hands, and back into your heart again.

As you establish this flow between your hands and heart, begin to extend and circulate this feeling through your whole body now. With each breath, send ripples of love and care from your heart out to every cell and fiber of your body, to every nook and cranny of your mind. Fill yourself with love. Fill yourself with light. Let it move and flow and circulate through every dimension of your being. Send this loving light to those regions that are in pain or that cry out for attention. Let this love flow as light to dissolve any seeds of disease that may lie hidden in your mind or body. Imagine this light vitalizing and strengthening your undeveloped potentials for love, wisdom, power, and understanding.

Radiating Love and Light

Breathing gently now, imagine yourself filled with light and love. Begin to feel the power and the presence of this love and light within you. Begin to shine it out into the world.

Resting in this vitalized state, imagine beaming your feelings of well-being and love out to dispel any darkness or fear in the world. From your heart, send ripples of this loving light to your loved ones and friends, to all who live in suffering or fear, to all those leaders with the power to help or harm. Imagine this light as a beacon of love, a broadcast of caring that will be received by others in the way that they most need to be touched at this time.

Now simply rest in the flow of the breath. Effortlessly be filled, effortlessly extend who you are and what you have to offer, to yourself...to others...to everyone...in whatever way they need it. Radiate your own love and light out into the world. Imagine it bringing light into darkness. Imagine it fanning the powerful flames of wisdom, love, and understanding in the hearts and minds of others.

Take a moment to appreciate how the inner changes you're making within yourself are touching the world in wonderful ways. Appreciate how these quiet moments of inner work have generated an atmosphere of greater harmony, balance, and well-being in the world.

Emotions That Kill, Emotions That Heal

For human beings, one of the most powerful forces in shaping our world is the strength of our emotions. Our emotions lead to healing and to killing, to giving life or taking it. And only when we are aware of, understand, and know how to balance our emotions, along with our bodies, minds, and spirits, are we able to truly live in balance.

Most of us reading this book likely come from cultures that have little understanding of what Eastern wisdom traditions call the "inner sciences." As a result, most of us have inherited fairly primitive tools for working with the incredible power of our emotions, and thus we are emotionally way out of balance. Some people even pride themselves on not being very emotionally sensitive, joking that, "Oh, I had an emotion once and it went away!" When it comes to living, this is not something you want to brag about.

How intense does your emotional state have to be before you are aware of it and can put a name to it? How sensitive are you to noticing how your body is affected by your emotional states? How easy is it for you to put into words what you are feeling emotionally? How do you tell the difference between frustration and anger, happiness and sadness, fear or trust? Your answers to all of these questions are clues to whether you have alexythymia or not.

Do You Suffer from Alexythymia?

The term *alexythymia* was first used by Harvard psychiatrist Dr. Peter Sifneos in an attempt to describe a problem shared by a large

"...My joy is like spring, so warm it makes flowers bloom in all walks of life. My pain is like a river of tears, so full it fills up the four oceans. Please call me by my true names, so I can hear all my cries and my laughs at once, so I can see that my joy and pain are one. Please call me by my true names, so I can wake up, and so the door of my heart can be left open, the door of compassion."

—from Thich Nhat Hanh's poem "Please Call Me By My True Names" proportion of patients suffering from various stress-linked medical disorders. Looking at the Greek roots for the word we discover that *alexy* means "no words," and *thymia* means "for feelings."

It's a dangerous state. If we have no words for our feelings, we are not in touch with our internal state until the subtle whispers have turned to painful screams within or around us. The more alexythymic we are, the further out of balance we get before we even have a conscious clue that something is not quite right. For this reason, alexythymia is regarded as a dangerous precursor to nearly every stress-related illness. Additionally, when we are out of touch with ourselves, we are far more likely to get stressed about being stressed, or to get anxious about being anxious, and to have small imbalances escalate out of control into major crises. Losing our balance, we are more likely to set off a whole cascade of problems in the lives of others, and the impacts may echo for generations to come.

For many people the first encounter with the notion of alexythymia is a fierce wake-up call. They immediately recognize people in their own lives who fit the description, and they often silently wonder to themselves, "How well does this describe me?"

Alexythymia is essentially a social disease that is most often transmitted to children from parents who are out of touch with their own feelings. It develops over childhood as we go to our dad, for example, saying that we are feeling hungry, and he negates our experience saying, "You can't be hungry! You just ate a sandwich!" or when we go to our mom feeling cold, and she responds by telling us, "You can't be cold, honey. It's eighty degrees in here and you have your sweater on." When our authority figures make a habit of ignoring or negating our own deeply felt experience, when they lack the patience, skills, or caring to help us figure out what was really going on, they put us in danger of developing alexythymia.

When this happens early in our lives, we begin to ignore our feelings, confuse our needs, distrust our interpretations of our own deep personal experience, and thwart our development of self-balancing skills necessary for knowing what we feel and describing what is true for us. Though we may come of age physically and assume

"Do not seek with cold eyes to find blemishes, Or the roses will turn to thorns as you gaze."

—Sabistari

"Human capacity is equal to human cruelty, and it's up to each of us to tip the balance."

—Alice Walker

our position as a "mature" adult in society, unless we heal this deficiency with ourselves, we are prone to be out of touch with what is going on within us and with other people, to unknowingly pass this condition on to our own children, and to be doomed to live our lives in a precarious, unbalanced way.

Though in many settings people scoff with disdain at approaches that they describe as "touchy-feely," there is considerable hard evidence to suggest that people who are out of touch with their feelings are especially vulnerable and at risk in the face of stressful change. And no matter how out of touch we may be, our warm, feeling bodies continue to be deeply affected by the experiences of our life, continue to pump out the biochemicals that heal or harm us, and keep broadcasting loud and clear the intensity of our feelings and needs, even if we choose to ignore them.

"You can't get there from 'not here'."

—**Richard Moon**

Reversing Alexythymia

Before you get too depressed, keep in mind that alexythymia can be cured. It takes some discipline, mindfulness, patience, and time. Here are some helpful guidelines. Keep in mind that emotional states are best described in a single word or an image. Remember, if you hear yourself saying, "I feel that...," then you are probably describing your thoughts and judgments about a situation, rather than an actual feeling (which is often experienced as a bodily sensation). With this in mind, and with a patient smile of mindfulness:

- Keep a log book next to your phone and make a note of how you feel each time you hang up the phone. How did that call affect you emotionally? Are you feeling anxious or relieved? Happy, angry, or afraid? Hopeful, doubtful, or confused?

- Make a similar written or mental note after each, or most, of the encounters you have during the day. How do you feel when you see your kids when you come home from work?

After seeing your neighbor in the elevator? When walking out of that meeting?

- When listening to the radio or watching TV, after each segment, notice the emotional impact of that segment. Are you delighted or depressed when you hear someone talk about the election? Do you feel peaceful and loving, or agitated and disturbed after that last episode? Just as certain foods can balance or unbalance your body, your selection of media also has a direct impact on your biochemistry and your health. As you tune in and understand how the sensitive being that you are is being soothed, irritated, inspired, or drained by ingesting certain media, you may choose to change your "media diet" in order to optimize your chances of living a more balanced life.

Understanding that your emotional responses are tied to your mindset, look behind your emotional responses in these situations to gain insight into the beliefs, values, expectations, or assumptions that lead you to interpret the objective raw data of your experience with the particular emotional charge that it has for you. Because the same situation may make one person happy, another person sad, and a third person angry, search for the factors that make your feelings uniquely your own, and remember that you *can* change your mind.

Cleaning Up Toxic Emotions

As we talk with people about times when they lost their balance in life, few people tell us about losing their physical balance, as in falling when skiing or riding a bike. Rather, they usually talk about getting emotionally upset. That is not surprising. Strong, roller-coaster emotions, be they positive or negative, do have a dramatic impact on our sense of balance, and strong emotions tend to drive us into behaviors that often create more imbalance in our own lives and in the lives of others.

Pause to reflect for a few moments on the times in your life when

"Suffering is not enough. Life is both dreadful and wonderful. To practice meditation is to be in touch with both aspects. Smiling means that we are ourselves, that we have sovereignty over ourselves, that we are not drowned in forgetfulness. How can I smile when I am filled with so much sorrow? It is natural—you need to smile to your sorrow because you are more than your sorrow."

—**Thich Nhat Hanh**

you have felt, and acted, most in or out of balance. How would you describe the predominant emotions during those times: Blind rage? Joy? Grief stricken? Head over heels in love? Wonderstruck?

There are numerous studies that draw a correlation between people's emotions and their physical health. One study conducted by Howard Friedman, professor at the University of California Riverside, analyzed a hundred different such studies. His analysis showed clearly that certain emotional states are absolutely toxic. The imbalance created by being chronically depressed, anxious, pessimistic, irritated, or critical actually doubles one's chances of developing a major disease! It's no wonder that in Buddhist traditions these negative mindstates are described as "afflictive emotions" or "mental poisons" believed to be at the root of a host of problematic human conditions.

To modern science it is clear that there are powerful links among the centers of the brain that regulate our responses to emotions and to immunological function and the cardiovascular system. These connections work powerfully to promote health and balance by boosting our defenses against disease when we are generating positive mental states such as love, appreciation, compassion, and empathy. Yet under the influence of stress hormones and other neurochemicals that are released when we are feeling negative emotions, these same connections hamper the ability of the immune system to protect us from diseases. Toxic emotions and unbalanced states of mind create conditions in the body that make us vulnerable to developing serious illnesses such as cancer, heart disease, and diabetes. Toxic emotions also raise our blood pressure and cholesterol levels, and change our blood chemistry to leave more deposits that clog our arteries.

On the other hand, people who are genuinely optimistic, appreciative, kind, loving, and compassionate are far less susceptible to disease. Their hearts and brains exhibit far more balanced, coherent, and energy-efficient functioning. The biochemistry of a loving, positive mindstate promotes measurable balance, revitalization, and immunological strength throughout the systems of the body.

"Emphasizing only happiness or only suffering to the exclusion of the other is limiting the experience. When you blend the good and the bad you learn to dance and flow with both expressions. Learning from both sides of the experience you become more whole and integrated. No event is all black or all white... Personally, I prefer not to dwell too much on the happiness without reaching into the misery."

—David Chethlahe Paladin

Speaking on the new field of psychoneurocardiology, at a large conference that we chaired for the Menninger Foundation and Life Sciences Institute, Dr. Miroslav Borysenko observed that "the brain is everywhere in the body!" There are special proteins, called neuropeptides, that are produced specifically for each emotion. Until recently it was thought that neuropeptides were manufactured solely in the brain, but scientists now have seen that neuropeptides are also made in our skin, liver, and other organs as well. As Dr. Borysenko says, "there's anger in your blood; there's compassion in your blood."

In short, loving mindstates feed us; while negative mindstates bleed us of our strength and vitality. The key to this, however, lies not in the words that people say or the affirmations they tell to themselves, but in the genuineness and authenticity of their attitudes and feelings.

It's Up to You

If we felt total equanimity toward the experiences of our lives, we would be unlikely to ever feel out of balance. We would relate to everything that happened to us with a Buddha-like acceptance. But as long as we are human and experience preferences, we will be prone to tumble into emotional reactions of liking or disliking, attraction or aversion. We want something; we are afraid of losing what we have. The many subtle shades, intensities, and durations of our emotional reactions play upon the exquisitely sensitive instrument of our body.

As sensitive creatures, we are vulnerable to be wounded by the words and deeds of unkind, suffering people. Yet people often poison their own mindstreams and bloodstreams for decades, replaying simulations and frustrations over a minor insult of a person long dead. We have to ask ourselves, "Who is causing this suffering?" The only person who can turn your bloodstream into a toxic swamp or into a healing elixir of long life, is you. No one can make you feel angry or happy. Moment to moment, your mental-emotional-bio-chemical-physiological state changes. And regardless of how kind or

"If I told patients to raise their blood levels of immune globulins or killer T-cells, no one would know how. But if I can teach them to love themselves and others fully, the same change happens automatically. The truth is: Love heals."

—Bernie Siegel

"Knowing others is intelligence. Knowing yourself is true wisdom. Mastering others is strength. Mastering yourself is true power."

—Tao Te Ching

nasty anyone "out there" is to you, no matter how much you may blame others for how you feel, you alone determine the quality, intensity, duration, and direction of your response. Through mindfulness we can learn to be on the lookout for toxic emotions like aversion, hatred, and bitterness. Instead of making things worse by taking a negative situation personally and trying to push the pain away, we can develop a growing emotional equanimity that allows us to stay open to pain, understand it, and even generate a wholesome healing response such as compassion.

Emotional Intelligence: What Is Your EQ?

Walking down the aisles of the information systems area at Hewlett-Packard, we noticed a color copy posted on a cubicle. The words leaped out at us, "In the corporate world, it is IQ that gets you hired, and EQ, emotional intelligence, that gets you promoted." It was an excerpt from *Emotional Intelligence,* the bestselling book written by our friend Daniel Goleman, science editor for the *New York Times.*

Understanding the five dimensions of emotional intelligence is very helpful in cultivating a more balanced emotional state. These are:

- Mindfulness or Self-Awareness: Just what we've been saying—only when you know what you feel can you make decisions that will bring you happiness and satisfaction.

- Managing Your Feelings: In the absence of awareness, emotional reactivity and habits control your life. Learning to recognize and control emotional impulsiveness, to soothe anxiety and upset, to restore balance following stressful encounters, and to have anxiety or anger that is appropriate but not overblown requires a high level of mindfulness and skill.

- Motivation: Your attitudes and intentions will color your emotional response to difficult situations. Cultivating an

"In the deeps are the violence and terror of which psychology has warned us. But if you ride these monsters deeper down, if you drop with them farther over the world's rim, you find what our sciences cannot locate or name, the substrate, the ocean or matrix or ether which buoys the rest, which gives goodness its power for good, and evil its power for evil, the unified field; our complex and inexplicable caring for each other, and for our life together here. This is given. It is not learned."

—Annie Dillard

attitude of optimism, trust, confidence, and respect goes a long way in boosting your EQ.

- Empathy: Your sensitivity to the unspoken and spoken feelings of others is another vital key to good relationships, whether in love or work.

- Social Skills: Faced with the intense and often imbalanced emotional reactions of others, developing the ability to stay mindful, centered, and at ease will help you to establish and maintain quality relationships.

Expanding on the practice of mindfulness, EQ has created a very powerful and effective "one-two punch" for helping many of our clients get a handle on the work they need to do on themselves to deal with stress more effectively and find greater balance in their lives. Once people take to heart that they alone are in control of their emotional reactivity, a path of learning opens up that is both humbling and exciting. The key is not to rate yourself on never losing your equilibrium, but on how often you lose it, how intensely you lose it, and for how long. If you measure your success in this way, you will find that with sincere practice, your emotional balance will improve.

Guidance from an Equanimous Elder

In 1984, Michelle had the good fortune to study with a revered meditation master during a three-month retreat at the Insight Meditation Society in Barre, Massachusetts. The teacher was an old Bengali woman named Dipama, who lived in Calcutta, India, and taught in the Burmese tradition. A householder and mother herself, Dipama taught that even the simplest activities of everyday life, such as ironing or washing the dishes, could become the supports for developing mindfulness, equanimity, joy, compassion, and love. Many people came from all over the world to visit Dipama in her simple home in one of the poorest parts of the planet to learn the arts of mindful living from this humble master.

"The salvation of the world lies in the human heart."

—Vaclav Havel, President of Czechoslovakia addressing the US Congress

"God, Grant me the serenity to accept the things I cannot change, the courage to change the things I can. And the wisdom to know the difference."

—St. Francis of Assisi

Dipama, whose name means "Mother of Light," was one of those rare people who embodied an abiding sense of peaceful equanimity. During one of the small group interviews Michelle attended at the retreat, a question came up about working with emotions. The young woman who had asked the question was desperately struggling with roller coaster rides of intense emotions that were disturbing her meditative practice. After listening quietly yet intently, Dipama responded that a tendency to be emotional was not a hindrance to meditation practice. Emotions reveal the presence of a mind that is open and sensitive, or "soft," as Dipama put it ever so gently. "Just watch and don't identify with the emotions," she said. "Increase mindfulness of *noticing* and the concentration. Like everything else, emotions are impermanent. Watch them arise and pass away, like clouds in the sky."

The key to restoring inner emotional balance, Michelle learned, lay in not fighting with our emotions, but in simply accepting their being there as a natural expression of our minds, and not adding fuel to the fire of emotional turbulence raging within. By seeing our emotions simply for what they are, we allow them to settle back more easily and naturally into the clear inner openness from which they arise.

A Practice of Gratitude

One day, we met a wise man from Chicago. He gave us a simple challenge that we took to heart and that has changed our life ever since. This is it: How often do you look for beauty in your world?

Can you imagine how your life would shift if you took this challenge to heart? What if, as you walk or drive down the street, you were to actually seek out beauty and things to rejoice in? As you sit and talk with other people, what if you were to decide to focus on what is beautiful about these people rather than being critical and judgmental? As you sit around your home or watch TV, what if you focused your heart and mind to notice the many blessings in your life and dwell less on the irritations? Such a shift can bring

"The whole cosmos is being renewed moment by moment... To those among us who have entered into this mystery through faith it need not be explained; to others it cannot be explained. But to the extent to which we have given room in our hearts to gratitude, we all have a share in this reality, by whatever name we may call it. It is a reality which we shall never fully take hold of. All that matters is that we let it take hold of us... which leads us to integrity within ourselves, to concord with one another and to union with the very Source of Life."

—**Brother David Steindl-Rast**

emotional balance to your life in a beautiful way.

Both ancient teachings and modern medical research agree that one of the quickest, most direct routes to restoring balance in our lives is to dwell in gratitude and appreciation. The moment you shift from a mindstate of negativity or judgment to one of appreciation there are immediate effects at many levels of your being. Your brain function becomes more balanced, harmonized, and supple; your heart begins to pump in a much more coherent and harmoniously balanced rhythm; and biochemical changes trigger a host of healthful balancing reactions throughout your body.

In the medicine ways of indigenous people, the restorative power of gratitude was well understood. The heart filled with gratitude generates actions and prayers that complete the circle among the giver, the receiver, and the sacred source of the gift. To offer prayers of thanksgiving is a gesture of rejoicing in discovering the many gifts that life brings us. Here is a practice we often teach as a way to dwell in gratitude and thanksgiving:

Sitting quietly, shift toward dynamic balance with a few minutes of mindful breathing. Bring to mind someone whom you are deeply grateful for. As you breathe in, take this person to heart. Breathing out, let your heartfelt gratitude shine deeply and brightly to them and through them. Continue for as long as you like, letting each breath take to heart a loved one, a friend, someone who has been kind to you, someone who is teaching you patience or how to forgive. Let each breath shine from the depths of your being through the depths of their being in order to light up their life with your love. Taking your eyes, your ears, your hands, your intelligence to heart, bless them in a similar way with the heartfelt radiance of your appreciation. Whoever or whatever comes to mind, gather them into your heart, one at a time, or all together. Taking these many gifts to heart, complete and affirm the circle with gratitude, assuring that the stream of blessings in your life and in the universe will be unbroken.

"We live in illusion and the appearance of things.
There is a Reality.
You are that Reality.
Seeing this, you know that you are everything.
And being everything, you are nothing.
That is all."
—Kalu Rinpoche

Three Realities to Keep in Mind

In every situation that you encounter, there are three levels of reality to be mindful of. Understanding each of these is essential to working effectively with emotions:

What is *really* happening, that is, What is *"the truth?"* Don't be fooled into thinking you can know the whole truth of a situation. Regardless of what you think, the Great Mystery is undoubtedly at work behind the scenes in this situation in ways too complex, too vast, too subtle, too deep for you to fully comprehend. Be wise enough not to be fooled by your limited perspective, and humble enough to wonder, "What is really going on here that I cannot comprehend?"

What do your senses tell you about this situation, that is, what you see, hear, smell, and so on? In seeing, what you see is only an image or interpretation in your mind. Likewise for all your other perceptions: hearing, just sounds in the mind; touching, only tactile sensations registering in the mind; in tasting and smelling, only tastes and touches. Your perceptions are only your perceptions! They are only mental re-presentations of what is really going on. Before you get out of balance, pause to wonder, "What is really going on?"

What are your assumptions, interpretations, beliefs, and feelings about what is happening? Remember, your assumptions and interpretations are again merely mental constructs that help you to describe and explain your experience! They are stories you tell yourself to make sense of the world; they are not a direct experience of reality. Always pause to wonder what is really going on.

Emotional balance depends on how mindfully you are able to relate to each of these three realities—what is, what you perceive, and what you think—and to how they influence each other. When we confuse our thoughts or even our perceptions for what is really going on "out there," then we are in danger of losing perspective and tumbling into emotional reactivity. The balance of certainty and

> *"Understanding a process enables a person to gain control of that process or to gain freedom from being controlled by it. Thus, analytic understanding of the atomic components of blind rage—what triggers it, how it directs itself, how it mobilizes mental, verbal and physical energies and so on enables an habitually angry person to begin to control his or her temper, perhaps finally to become free of its control."*
>
> —The Dalai Lama

mystery is found in learning to regard each of these realities for what they are!

Managing Emotional Energy

"Sometimes I go about with pity for myself and all the while Great Winds are carrying me across the sky."

—Ojibway saying

Mindless emotional reactivity is one of the most powerful and destructive forces in the universe. So to live more in balance, learn to mindfully observe the interplay among your thoughts, emotions, and behavior. Experimenting with the following strategies will help you learn to better understand and deal with your emotions, particularly at times when you notice strong emotional states rising within you:

- Shift your attention from what is outwardly going on to focus on the internal pattern of physical sensations related to your emotional feelings.

- Ask yourself, what does this emotional state really feel like? Where and how do I feel this in my body? Befriend intense or negative emotional states by recognizing them; smiling to yourself; making a mental note: "Ah, this is anger (or fear, or jealousy) . . . . of course!"

"Despair is often the first step on the path of spiritual life and many people do not awaken to the Reality of God and the experience of transformation in their lives till they go through the experience of emptiness, disillusion, and despair."

—Father Bede Griffiths

- Identify what thoughts and mental habits or "tape loops" are associated with the feeling. What are you telling yourself about the feeling? It is one thing to have a financial setback and experience fear. But is the fear coming from a story of utter doom that has you on the street as a bag lady in a matter of days, while the reality is that you will probably be able to cope just fine? Oftentimes we unconsciously make matters worse for ourselves by fantasizing the worst.

- Empathize with the feelings of other people and the circumstances that may have led to their suffering. Remember, when others act cruelly or insensitively, that no one can act that way unless they are suffering themselves.

- Painful emotional states may be intensified by getting angry about being angry or feeling guilty about feeling guilty. Learning to recognize and accept old, conditioned emotional reactions is the first step toward learning new, healthier ways of feeling and expressing your emotional truth.

- Develop emotional flexibility. Practice intensifying and diminishing your emotional intensity in different situations. Experiment with changing your emotional state and recognizing how much choice you really can have in how you respond to different circumstances.

- Learn from your experience. Analyze intense situations after they are over and clarify for yourself how you might learn from this situation in order to commit to a more effective and compassionate response next time.

With a heart balanced by mindfulness, you can learn to:

- examine your current situation;
- examine your reaction patterns;
- examine your options;
- examine your ideal visions, goals, intentions, and desired outcomes; and
- make the wisest decision for moving forward.

When in doubt, choose a course of action that is either kind (will avoid causing harm to yourself or others), or helpful (bringing benefit to yourself and others in both the short and long term).

"We know finite disappointment, but we know infinite hope."
—Rev. Martin Luther King Jr.

"The only way out is through."
—Robert Frost

SEVEN

The Balanced Mindstate

Mind is the forerunner of all things.

—BUDDHA

Balance, as we know it, begins and ends in our minds. To find true balance of mind, you must learn to balance mental agitation with mental stability, and mental dullness with a vivid clarity of mind. As you learn to do this, you'll experience an exquisite quality of peace of mind, and the deep, steady concentration that allows you to understand life deeply.

Living a life of balance also means finding a healthy balance between the functions of our active mind, such as thinking, intention, and imagination, and the more direct and immediate experience of reality offered by our receptive, open, or quiet mind, such as mindful attention, a deeply felt sense of aliveness, and intuition. It's hard to have balance when you don't even know one half of the equation!

Finally, to realize a truly balanced mind, we must know ourselves in all our uniqueness and dimensionality. This means cultivating a spaciousness of mind that can hold the relativity of our ordinary identity, the limited and partial "stories" we construct and keep telling ourselves about our favorite character—our self—and our "true nature" or authentic Self which is infinitely more omnidimensional and Universal in nature.

Gaining insight into these different states of mind is essential as we gradually learn how balance is lost and can be regained in our lives, moment to moment. Like many themes in your search for balance and wholeness, it is likely that you will have a better understanding of some of these dimensions of mind than of others. Learning to discover, develop, and balance these many facets of the jewel of your mind is part of living your life in an ever-evolving and dynamically balanced way.

Illusion, Confusion, and Reality

We often remember the advice offered to us by Gen Lamrimpa as we were about to embark on a year-long, silent retreat. With tender compassion and a peaceful smile, the Tibetan yogi reminded us, "As you look more and more deeply into your experience you will discover many dimensions and realities of yourself of which you were previously unaware." How true these words rang for us and should ring for you.

Keep in mind that as you peer into the depths of your own mind you will behold the appearance of many subtle images, thoughts, and patterns. Some of these mental experiences will be quite compelling, some will seem more like fragments of frantic cartoons, while still others will appear as ephemeral dream images. None of these has a concrete reality—all of them are like cloud formations that you imbue with your own meaning.

Just as the water in a pond will be moved and shaped into complex waves and images by the passing of wind or light, so too your remarkably sensitive mind/brain is bombarded by countless stimuli giving rise to a complex display of mental reverberations. Some of these mental appearances will please you, while others may displease, disgust, or even frighten you. Familiar and unfamiliar images will arise, abide momentarily, and then dissolve like so many wispy clouds in the deep clear space of your mind. But just as we saw with our emotions, these intangible inner appearances have tremendous power to influence your life, change your physiology, and compel you into action.

Again, we in the West have had little mind training. On his first trip to the West, a visiting Tibetan lama was amazed to see how little

"We don't understand the operations of our minds and hence don't operate them very well."

—Charles Tart

"Let me see if this be real.
Let me see if this be real.
This Life I am Living
Ye who possesses the skies,
Let me see if this be real
This life I am Living."

—Tewa People

control most people in this culture seemed to have over their minds, and how strongly driven they were by the tyranny of their thoughts. After a full day of interviews, he turned to his translator in disbelief and exclaimed, "These people seem to be giving all their power away to their thoughts! When I want my mind to be focused on something, I put it there and it stays there as long as I want. If a thought comes to my mind that I do not wish to entertain, I simply do not dwell on it. These people have not yet learned how to do this . . . ."

Remember that the more you come to center yourself in a stance of open-minded, open-hearted, quietly smiling, self-observing mindfulness, the better equipped you will be to find true balance by recognizing this ceaseless flow of mental images to be merely a passing show of changing appearances in the mind and not imbue them with so much power. Though these thoughts, images, or feelings may be easily confused with actual reality, they are truly insubstantial. Like images in a dream, they exist only as ephemeral shadows and flickerings that represent the unimaginably deep reality of yourself, others, and the world in which you live. The dawning of this realization is quite liberating for some, while for others it may be frightening at first to discover how illusory the dream fabrications of our own thoughts truly are.

"Once one knows the secrets of the mind, one will uncover the nature of all realities. By knowing the one, one will know all. This is the nature of the mind."

—Traditional Tibetan Saying

Balance from the Inside Out

Our inner and outer worlds reflect each other. When our minds are dominated by fear, anxiety, or preoccupation with ourselves, the world may appear hostile or threatening. When our minds are at peace, the world and the people in it are beheld as a source of wonder and delight. You likely know from experience that when your mind is agitated and unbalanced, the world appears to you as separate from or even antagonistic to yourself. In fact, the more unbalanced and agitated we are, the more separate, anxious, or alone we are likely to feel.

As we learn to relax, focus, and move more toward a deeper sense of balance, our mind-brain-body becomes less tense, more peaceful, and we begin to feel more trusting of and connected to the world. As the internal flow of energy and activity within us becomes more balanced, we begin to experience greater wholeness and harmony in relationship to others.

The key to this shift is the quality and depth of our mindful and caring attention. With practice we learn to turn scattered distraction into momentary concentration, and then to sustain that concentration as a flow of mindful awareness into action. The more wholeheartedly present we are with whatever we are doing, the more our mind will function in balanced ways. This translates into moving into and through our world in a more peaceful, powerful, energy efficient, kinder, and wiser way.

"At the root of all war is fear."

—Thomas Merton

Learning How to Stop the War

The summer Joel graduated from the University of Washington, he met Zen writer and teacher Paul Reps, who touched him deeply.

"I was young, wide-eyed, and intent on exploring the further reaches of human potential. Having devoured nearly everything in print on the research in human consciousness and completed my first wave of research into the human mind-brain-spirit, I was filled with far more questions than answers, and had launched into the first of nearly four years of travel and study to seek the answers that my academic studies did not provide.

"When we are capable of stopping, we begin to see."

—Thich Nhat Hanh

"I was offered a job setting up an international conference on consciousness research that was to be held at a beautiful contemplative center nestled on Kootenay Lake in the Canadian Rockies. Arriving two weeks early to prepare for the conference, I discovered a wonderful and eccentric companion in residence at the retreat center who, at first glance, appeared like an elder elf with bright eyes, deep gaze, and the presence of one deep in Spirit. We took a mutual interest in each other and Reps invited me to join him for tea and conversation every day at four.

"During our conversations Reps, a marvelous storyteller, would invite me into his memories, traveling through the Orient in search of the great wisdom masters who were still alive in the middle of this century. Reps, I discovered, was one of the first Westerners to travel to the East to study and translate the wisdom teaching of the Zen traditions. One day, over tea, he told me a story about the power of the tranquil mind.

"In the early '50s, Reps, who was then in his forties, had traveled to Japan en route to visit a respected Zen master in Korea. He went to the passport office to apply for his visa and was politely informed that his request was denied due to the conflict that had just broken out in Korea. Frustrated, Reps walked away from the counter and sat down quietly in the waiting area. He had traveled thousands of miles to a foreign land with the plan to study with this master in Korea. He was deeply disappointed, perhaps even angry, at being told he could not complete his journey. He realized that at that moment there was not only a war starting in Korea, but also another raging inside of himself. Recognizing that his internal conflict had the potential to erupt and create conflict in the world around him, he wondered what to do. Pausing for a few moments of mindful breathing, he then reached into his bag, mindfully pulled out his thermos, and poured himself a cup of tea. With a calm and focused mind, he watched the steam rising, swirling, and dissolving into the air. He smelled the fragrance of the tea, tasted its bitter flavor, and enjoyed its warmth and wetness. Finishing his tea, he put his cup back on his thermos, put his thermos in his bag, and pulled out a pen and paper upon which he wrote a haiku poem.

"Mindfully, he walked back to the clerk behind the counter, bowed, and presented him with his poem and his passport. The clerk read the poem, and it brought tears to his eyes. Looking up deeply into the quiet strength in Reps' eyes, the clerk smiled, bowed with respect, picked up Reps' passport, and stamped it for passage to Korea. Reps' haiku read:

"Drinking a cup of tea, I stopped the war."

Reflect for a moment on how this story speaks to you, and to the interplay of balance and imbalance, war and peace in your mind-body, relationships, and environment. Imagine living in the balance

"Breathing in, I know that anger is in me. Breathing out, I know this feeling is unpleasant... Breathing in, I feel calm. Breathing out, I am strong enough to care for this anger."

—Thich Nhat Hanh

of mind that would allow you to recognize and befriend your own "inner enemies" and to make peace with the conflicts raging within your own mind. See yourself as a true and noble warrior, armed with the wisdom, inner strength, compassion, courage, and vigilance necessary to recognize and transform all of your inner enemies. Consider how you would like to be able to respond to the inner enemies who speak to you with the voices of irritation, frustration, disappointment. How would you like to respond to the stabs of doubt or self-judgment, or to the demons of resentment and fear, the plagues of pride or jealousy? Imagine or sense the inspiration you could draw from a deeper, more steady center of balance if you were to recognize and stop the wars when they are whispers, rather than waiting till they are screams, when they are tiny skirmishes, rather than raging atomic wars. Envision the peace and power you can find in your life when you learn to be more patient, tolerant, forgiving, and honest with what is going on within you so that your internal conflicts don't escalate and erupt into your outer relationships, causing grief and imbalance in the lives of others.

You *Can* Change Your Mind!

It is common for people just beginning to develop greater mindfulness to initially feel a bit overwhelmed at how wild and out of control their mind seems to be. But, if you have supportive friends, patient and insightful mentors, effective techniques, and the personal discipline necessary to put what you learn into practice, you can swiftly develop confidence in your ability to calm your mind.

Many of the people we've worked with are classic examples of people who are highly sensitive, stressed, or have been diagnosed with Attention Deficit Disorder (ADD). These people are usually high-intensity, high-energy sorts of people who are erratic, easily distracted, easily excited, or depressed. As a result, they often have a long history of frustration, poor self-esteem, and alienation from others who are impatient or uncompassionate toward them. What they learn when they calm their minds is that their personalities seem to change totally.

Lynn was an executive on the fast track in her telecommunications firm when she came to see Joel as a patient at the medical center. Her doctor had referred her for stress-related panic attacks, headaches, and stomach problems. Outwardly Lynn was attractive and highly controlled. Though she generally managed to keep a fairly cool and calm appearance, her internal turmoil was revealed as noticeable flushing of her face and neck, flared nostrils, perspiration beading at her brow, and a telltale racing pulse that was noticeable at her throat or temples. Inwardly she was prone to many swift and abrupt fluctuations in her thoughts and feelings.

As part of their work together, Joel and Lynn used a mirror and an instrument that monitored the changes in Lynn's skin temperature and skin conductance—two measures that are sensitive indicators of the level of physiological stress response. The mirror offered visual feedback on her furrowed brow, tense eyes, and flushing. The monitor showed decreases in skin temperature when she was stressed, and warming hands as she relaxed, as well as elevated skin conductance when her palms were sweaty under stress, and decreased readings when she relaxed. The mirror and monitor were visible to both of them, providing valuable feedback while they experimented with various techniques to help Lynn understand and master the intensity of her stress response. "On her first visit, it was clear by watching her physiological changes that her mental stress was strongly effecting her physiology," Joel comments. "The changes in her mental state were dramatically mirrored in swift, erratic changes in her body, as indicated by dramatic and abrupt increases and decreases in her skin temperature and skin conductance. At first these physiological changes seemed totally unconscious and out of her control. Yet as her mindful awareness developed, Lynn began to gain insight into how her mental stress tended to escalate. As she began to get more focused, and to bring more awareness into the interplay of her mental state, her pounding heart rate, her sweaty hands, and flushing neck, she recognized ways she could break the cycle and bring her stress response under control."

As Lynn learned and practiced new skills, she found that she

"The unhappiness and suffering that we experience arise through our inability to control our own minds, and the happiness that we wish to achieve will only be achieved by learning to control our minds... You can use Inner Science to educate each individual to understand himself or herself, to control his or her negative emotions and distorted notions, and to cultivate his or her highest potentials of love and wisdom."

—The Dalai Lama with Robert Thurman

could relate to her stress in a more spacious and playful manner. She learned to smile to herself as she tuned into her internal dialogue. She learned to make choices for how to respond to stressful situations that didn't intensify the distress. As the weeks passed, she learned to consciously control her stress responses. As she did, she maintained the same passionate intensity and breadth of responses, but was able to move between different states of mind and body in a much smoother, more balanced, and less erratic way. She began to feel more naturally calm, confident, and in control, and the frequency and intensity of her painful headaches and stomach problems diminished.

A year later, when Joel met Lynn at the market, she smiled and gave him a warm hug. "You know, that work we did together was the first stage of a long and wonderful journey." she said. "Since I last saw you I haven't had a single panic attack, and when I feel a headache coming on, I can usually relax it away. This has given me the confidence to finish my MBA and make some changes in my life and relationship that have been long overdue. I can't begin to thank you enough for holding up the mirror so I could see myself in a brighter light."

"What made the difference for you, Lynn?" Joel asked, knowing that something had made this work on herself a real priority. "You know, what really got me motivated to understand and change myself was seeing my five-year-old daughter begin to have worries, headaches, and stomachaches just like Mommy," she explained. "I realized that I probably picked up some of my strategies for dealing with stress from my mom, and I made a commitment to myself to learn and model for my daughter some wiser, healthier, more balanced ways of dealing with the stresses that come with living in our modern world."

Stories We Tell Ourselves

The major cause of stress for most people arises from self-generated anxiety and worries. Because the body responds equally to

> "I believe that any event from a person's past immediately becomes a myth (a personal story)."
>
> —David Chethlahe Paladin

> "Wisdom tells me I am nothing.
> Love tells me I am everything.
> And between the two my life flows."
>
> —Nisargadatta Maharaj

mental images as to sensory ones, learning to monitor and sort through our thoughts can be a major step to finding greater balance.

Here's a "mindfulness of thinking" technique that comes from a tribe in Africa. From an early age, children there were trained to be mindful of their thinking. If a person became aware of a foreboding thought like, "Oh no, what if there is a lion hiding behind that tree waiting to eat me?" they learned first to recognize and then release the thought by saying to themselves, "This is a story that doesn't need to happen!"

We use this technique often. For example, one of us may be chopping vegetables with a sharp knife and the thought pops up, "I'd better be careful or I'll cut myself." Or we're in a rush driving on the freeway and the image of getting pulled over by the state patrol jumps to mind. The key is to first notice your thoughts and then, if they are harmful or unproductive, to say to yourself, "This is a story that doesn't need to happen." This technique is not about getting rid of negative thoughts or about the power of positive thinking. If a stress inducing "doom and gloom" kind of thought comes to mind, you acknowledge it, you don't try to get rid of it, to hold on to it, or even analyze it. You simply honor it and let it go.

Balance is also found by recognizing that some of those stories that pop into our minds are ones we'd like to see happen. In response to a desirable thought like, "Maybe there is a watering hole over there," or "I hope the baby I am carrying will be healthy and a leader for the people," the members of the African tribe would add to themselves, "And this is a healing story!" In your life you might bless or energize thoughts such as, "I know I'll do a great job on that presentation," or "This meal is going to be delicious," or "This lump is probably benign," by thinking or saying, "Yes, this is a healing story."

In our work with leaders and teams, we often teach this technique as a way of strengthening mindfulness of our unconscious, and often self-sabotaging, inner dialogue. Many people have found it very simple and useful. For example, while out on his morning jog, the service manager for a medical instrument division we worked with in Australia, noticed a worrisome train of thoughts

"Out of this aboriginal sensible muchness, attention carves out objects, which conception then names and identifies forever—in the sky 'constellations', on the earth 'beach', 'sea', 'cliff', 'bushes', 'grass'. Out of time we cut out 'days' and 'nights', 'summers' and 'winters'. We say what each part of the sensible continuum is, and all these abstracted 'whats' are merely concepts. The intellectual life of man consists almost wholly in his substitution of a conceptual order for the perceptual order in which his experience originally comes."

—William James

racing through his mind, "Whoa!" he said to himself, "This is definitely a story that doesn't need to happen!" Immediately he felt his pulse rate slow down, his tension level drop, and his mind come into a more clear, focused, and balanced state. "It was amazing," he said to us over breakfast, "to see how immediate the effects of this applied self-awareness really are. I recognized that the mental scenario I was running was actually running me. The worries had a life of their own, and they were catapulting me in a direction that I would not choose to go. It's scary how much physical and mental stress I can create for myself through my own imagination. I would guess that most of the time I'm not aware of what I'm thinking, and that this is really the source of a lot of my stress and tension. In this case, instead of dwelling on the problem like I tend to do out of habit, my heightened self-awareness enabled me to think more creatively about the situation. When I got back from my walk, I made a few calls and then phoned the client who had a problem with our system. We worked out a solution that was really a "win-win" for their company and for ours. Over the long run, this will only increase their confidence in our ability to deliver and will increase our advantage over our competitors. Seeing how immediate of an advantage I could gain by recognizing and sorting out my thoughts is really a boost for my self-confidence and likely for my effectiveness on the job as well!"

Recognizing your flow of thoughts will help you smile to yourself and get playfully creative. For example, if you notice thoughts like, "I'll never get this done," "I'll mess this up," "They'll think I'm incompetent," or "My presentation will be a bomb," it may be helpful to smile to yourself and say, "This is a story that doesn't need to happen." And if you notice thoughts like, "My client will love this design," or "People are really going to love this idea!" anchor it by affirming, "And this is a healing story!"

Original Confusion and Mistaken Identity

Imbalance in our lives is rooted in a fundamental mental confusion regarding who we really are. This confusion leads us to

---

"Why are you unhappy? Because 99% of the things you do, think, and feel are about your self. And there isn't one!"

—Wei Wu Wei

"This pure Mind, which is the source of all things, shines forever with the radiance of its own perfection. But most people are not aware of it and think that the Mind is just the faculty that sees, hears, feels, and knows. Blinded by their own sight, hearing, feeling, and knowing they do not perceive the radiance of the source."

—Zen Master Huang-po

misperceive ourselves and our world, and leads to out-of-balance thinking and relating.

This original confusion is largely a case of mistaken identity. We know only a tiny fragment of the totality of ourselves and have lived our lives ignorant of our true nature. This is mainly due to habit. Who and what we call ourselves is based on a story that we keep telling ourselves over and over again. Over time, we forget that this story is only a story, and we come to believe and live in the story, rather than in the deep, vast, intense mystery of our totality. Research in the cognitive sciences suggests that we think tens of thousands of thoughts each day. Yet as many as 90 percent of these thoughts are thoughts that we thought yesterday—mindless reruns, cycling through our minds again and again and again. Habit energies of the mind programming and reprogramming themselves into endless cycles of confusion, distortion, entropy, and dullness. If this is true for you, can you imagine how much creative potential and energy you could liberate if you were to live more wakefully?

Thoughts—good, bad, beautiful, ugly, new, or reruns—are merely thoughts. Stories. Descriptions. Abstractions. Reality is far more than a collection of your thoughts, far more than the volumes of descriptions and explanations that you generate. *Wake up.* Be mindful and amused by the passage of thoughts you take so personally and so seriously. Thoughts are thinking themselves. Look through them and discover reality.

If we take these ideas to heart, we realize that the limiting story we tell ourselves revolves around an imaginary and unquestioned identity that we come to know as our "favorite character"—our self. Over time, without even knowing it, we believe our personal myth, and forget that the story is only a story and not reality.

To find deep and lasting balance in our lives, we must learn to see our personal story as merely a story, and to expand our insight into the true depth and mystery of our Self. As we do this, we discover that who we are is far more profound and extraordinary than we may have ever dreamed! Like the dweller in Plato's cave who had the courage to leave the familiar shadow world of his cave to step out

"We are luminous beings. We are perceivers. We are an awareness. We are not objects.
We have no solidity. We are boundless. The world of objects and solidity is a way of making our passage on earth convenient. It is only a description that was created to help us. We or rather our reasons, forget that the description is only a description and thus we entrap the totality of ourselves in a vicious circle from which we rarely emerge in a lifetime. We are perceivers. The world that we perceive though is an illusion. It was created by a description that was told to us since the moment we were born."

—**Don Juan**

into the vast, brightly colored world, our journey toward balance requires courage and may at times be both exciting and terrifying. The key teaching points to remember here are:

- Stories are stories.
- Reality is reality.
- Mistaking our stories for reality is a sure path to losing both perspective and balance.

True Nature

Years ago we discovered a wonderful radio series entitled *Moon over Morocco,* which is produced by the ZBS Foundation. Early on in this magical, mystical *Raiders of the Lost Ark*–style spoof, the hero, Jack Flanders, finds himself walking down a crowded street in Morocco. He is approached by a mysterious man who asks for a light. "Do you come to Morocco to seek the Mazamuda?" he whispers to Jack mysteriously. "Who are you?" asks Jack. "Do you know who are you?" the mysterious man asks Jack in return. "No..." stammers Jack. "You don't," the mysterious man chuckles, finishing Jack's thought.

So, what about you? Yes you, the one holding this book and looking out through your eyes at the words upon this page. "Do you know who are you?" If you are like most of us, this is a difficult question to answer. It is easy to list a variety of titles, roles, and vital statistics, but how much does that really describe who you truly are? Scientists and mystics will tell us that anything, or anyone, examined deeply enough reveals a profound indescribable Mystery. As futurist Peter Russell reminds his callers on his answering machine, "Hello. This is not an answering machine; it is a questioning machine. The questions are: 'Who are you?' and 'What do you want?'. If you think these are trivial questions, consider that most people go through their entire lives without finding the answer to either one." Do you know who you are? If you think you know the answer, look again more deeply.

At the core of our Self is a reality that is the very authenticity of our true nature. It is universal in nature, and the foundation of our ordinary personal self. Its nature is openness, wholeness, clarity, oneness, and peace. It is the source of all true love, healing, power, and intelligence in our lives. In essence it is not separable from your ordinary mind or sense of self any more than the water of the ocean is separable from the waves.

When, through mindfulness, the turbulence of our ordinary minds comes to balance, we discover what mind truly is when it is not busy fabricating and projecting illusions of separateness. We discover this deep true nature of mind in moments of peace, love, presence, clarity, calm, compassion, empathy, unity, or wholeness. Because it is the foundation and source of reality, it transcends separation and perceives wholeness. This awakened mind functions beyond the limitations of ordinary perception, and beyond the limitations of time and space. The awakened, universal, oceanic mind is the basis of all healing, the source of our intuitive intelligence, inspiration, and revelation. This is the medium through which prayer and extraordinary human faculties function. It also is the source of peace that the balanced state manifests.

Though the universal mind is unmeasurable, invisible, and impossible to grasp, in every moment of mindfulness, patience, love, heartfelt appreciation, or compassion, the presence of this deep universal nature is present in our lives. The universal mind is grounded in reality, not in self-generated fantasies or stories. Its foundation is wholeness. As the ground from which all things spring, it is the essence of love that infuses all things.

Though our personal self is born and dies, the universal Self is birthless and deathless. Talking with respected leaders of many of the world's great spiritual traditions, there is a universal agreement that if we live our lives in such a way that we balance our personal self-importance with a deeper wisdom of our true Self, we will be less afraid of death because we have already discovered our deathless nature. Many of our teachers have commented, "If you die (to the limited illusion of your personal self) before you die, then

"Emptiness is two things at once: the absence of self and the presence of the Divine. Thus as self decreases, the Divine increases."
—**Bernadette Roberts**

when you die, you won't die." The wise Rebbe Yerachmiel ben Yisrael illuminated this point in a letter to his beloved spiritual son, Aaron Hershel:

When we look at the world from the perspective of manifestation we see birth and we see death. But when we look at the world from the perspective of wholeness, there is no birth and no death. Manifestation and wholeness, being and emptiness, are poles of God's Greater Unity. Only God is whole and complete: Yes, Reb Yerachmiel ben Yisrael is gone, but the One who wore his face these many years is ever present. And that One wears your face, dear friend, as well. What we truly are is God manifest in time (Yesh) and eternity (Ayin). Know this, live well, and die easy. You have been a blessing to me beyond what words can convey. Remember, love is stronger than death (Song of Songs 8:6). Shortly I will be no more. Let our love grow ever stronger.

Creative Intelligence: The Synergy of Active and Quiet Minds

The wisdom traditions remind us in countless tongues that just as balance is found in the presence of the all embracing wholeness of the Universal Mind and its reflection as myriad personal minds, the presence of balance is similarly echoed within our personal minds as the dynamism of the active-creative-imaginative mind, which is complemented and balanced by our quiet-receptive-intuitive mind. Understanding and developing the vital balance between these two aspects of our personal mind is essential to living a healthy, balanced life. Let's take a closer look at the dynamic synergy between these complementary mental forces.

Using the power tools of intention, thinking, and imagination, the active mind shapes thoughts and perceptions to give meaning to the fluid chaos of our experience of the world. These creative "doing" functions of your active mind are balanced by the quiet mind, whose faculties are the formless, receptive, and reflective qual-

"Our thinking capacity is associated with the biological brain, the reflective capacity is associated with consciousness, and the ability to know that we know—the capacity for direct awareness—is associated with the generative ground... the Life-force whose creative intelligence underlies, sustains, and transcends... the cosmos... awakens the intuition that a living presence permeates the universe."

—Duane Elgin

ities of mind—including mindful attention or presence, deeply felt direct experience, and open-mindedness. The quiet mind encounters reality deeply and directly, without bias or distortion. The quality of our intuitive intelligence is a direct reflection of the mastery we have in developing our quiet mind skills.

Like everything else in nature, there needs to be a balance between our active and quiet minds. This can be hard, because we have been trained only to pay attention to (and be overinvested in) the active mind. But with mindfulness, you can begin to experience both. As you talk, also deeply listen. Notice how the active foreground display of your abstract thoughts or imaginings emerge and shape themselves against the backdrop of quiet mindful awareness. Within this deep stillness of the mind, experience how images arise, develop, and dissolve back into the open clear field of awareness. Observe and sense how images and associations cascade through the space of the quiet receptive mind like clouds forming and disappearing when warm moist winds pass over a ridge in the high mountains. As you learn to balance creative activity with reflective receptivity of your mind, you will discover the key to unlocking mental balance.

From Fixation to Flow

Though the deep natural state of mind is one of radiance and unimpeded flow of experience, the ordinary mind's habits of perception and thought tend to fixate and freeze the dynamic flow. In psychology this tendency is called reification. This tendency toward fixation leads us to misperceive and misconceive the appearances of ourselves, other people, and the various things in the world within and around us as solid, rather than beholding them as the ever-changing, fluid, radiant, and dynamic fields of energy that they are. This is what we mean when we say that people create "stories" about their experience—solidifying the meaning and making assumptions about the way things will turn out. However, by learning to find a balance between the tendency of the ordinary mind toward fixation

"I wanted only to live in accord with the promptings which came from my true self. Why was it so difficult?"

—Hermann Hesse

"The Great Way is not difficult for those who have no preferences. Make the smallest distinction and heaven and earth are set infinitely apart. If you wish to see the truth then hold no opinions for or against anything. To set up what you like against what you dislike is the disease of the mind. When the deep meaning of things is not understood the mind's essential peace is disturbed to no avail."

—Sengstan

and freezing the flow, and the universal mind's radiance and flow, we discover a natural freedom of mind that beholds the relativity of things and their appearance of solidity, while sensing or feeling their fluid, radiant nature at a deeper level of intuition. When we learn to do this, we are more able to respond to reality as it presents itself, rather than our ideas about it.

Feeling Fluid

To understand this, begin by sitting quietly. Because long-held patterns of thought tend to fixate in our bodies, focus first on your body. Notice the furrows in your brow, your posture and gestures as you talk, the hot spots where you hold tension around your eyes, in your neck or shoulders, or in your gut. As you become aware of these regions, tune into any of the patterns of mind—the attitudes, images, or feelings—that lead you to hold your body in these particular molds.

Now begin to use the flow of your breathing to help you to develop a balance between the focusing and flowing of your attention. Use your inhalations to help you draw your attention into any region in your body where you notice a sense of tension, holding, or fixation. Then as you exhale, allow the tension in that region to release, relax, and dissolve into a sense of radiance or fluidity. With each breath allow your awareness first to focus and then to flow within any regions of your body where you feel any tension, constriction, or fixation. In some regions you may need to linger for a number of breaths to allow these "ice-fields" of tension to dissolve in the warmth of your penetrating awareness. In other regions you will find that one or two breaths will be sufficient to focus and dissolve fixation into flow.

As you continue to seek out and dissolve physical fixation points into flow, be mindful of any fixation points in your thoughts or feelings. These may be associated with regions in your body or simply points of tension or fixation in your mind. In the same way as before, as you breathe, allow the inhalation to focus your awareness

"Nature ever flows, stands never still. Motion or change is her mode of existence. The poetic eye sees in Man the Brother of the River and in Woman the Sister of the River. Their life is always transitions. Hard blockheads only drive nails all the time; forever. . . fixing. Heroes do not fix, but flow, bend forward ever and invent a resource for every moment."

—Ralph Waldo Emerson

within these regions of tension, constriction, or fixation. And as you exhale, allow the tension to relax, the constriction to release, and the fixation to dissolve into a sense of flow. Use the natural rhythm of your breathing to help you focus and flow. Continue in this way, seeking out any points of fixation in your body, thoughts, or emotions, and continue until your being feels deeply balanced, relaxed, vibrant, radiant, and open to the flow.

As you learn how to recognize and dissolve fixation into flow while you are sitting quietly, you'll be better able to carry this same awareness into activity. For example, if you are walking down the street and you notice your mindbody go into constriction around some thought, simply smile to yourself as you recognize the target. Then, inhale and gently draw your awareness into the region of holding or fixation, breathe, and let it flow.

If you are talking with someone and you notice the constriction of your mindbody—associated with rising apprehension, self-consciousness, or stress—as you continue to talk and breathe, simply allow the breath to help sweep your awareness into and through that region and once again release fixation into flow.

The more you practice this simple, yet profound method of balancing yourself, the more confident you will be in any situation.

Beholding the Space Between

We learned an interesting lesson from one of our Chinese friends. "Hold up your hand and spread the fingers," he said. "Now, what number comes to mind that best describes what you see?" Most of us said five. He went on to say, "If you are like most Westerners, you will say 'five' because you see five fingers, or maybe you will say one, because you just see one hand." He laughed. "When you ask people in my country to do this they will most likely say 'nine,' because they see five fingers and they also see and value the four spaces between the fingers. Without the spaces, how can we have the fingers, and without the fingers, what sense does the space make? Just imagine how many other important things you Westerners overlook."

"What vistas might we see if we were to understand the full power of the human mind? The human consciousness may prove the most inspiring frontier in our history, an endless wellspring of knowledge, and our means of liberation from all limitation... If we can find ways to awaken the full power of awareness, we could enter a new phase of human evolution and revitalize ourselves and our world."

—Tarthang Tulku

Look at one of your hands and spread the fingers apart a bit. Notice the hand as a whole, and each of the fingers, one by one. Then, shift your attention to notice the spaces between the fingers and around the hand. Focus back on the hand, then to the spaces. See if you can find the balance of mind that is able to hold both the form and the space equally at the same time. As you do this, what do you notice about your experience of the form and of the space?

Now, expand this exercise in balance by sitting quietly and observing the world around you. Notice trees, birds, people, buildings, cars, or telephone poles around you, and see each of them clearly and vividly.

After some time of noticing the forms, expand your mindful observation to notice the spaces within or around the forms. See the distances between trees, or between branches on a tree, or between the needles or leaves on a branch. Or notice the spaces above and between the buildings or the space that fills the hallways and rooms around you. Notice how the space between things actually connects everything, how the space between you and what you observe is a medium of connection, not of separation.

Now, see what it takes to attend equally to noticing the distinct and apparently separate objects, and at the same time to be sensitive to noticing the space that connects and pervades all things. Beholding this sense of infinitely expansive space that connects all things, can you view all objects as merely clouds of energy or standing wave forms filled with and floating in space?

This same principle can be applied inwardly to finding greater balance of mind. Notice how the objects of mind arise, change, and pass like clouds in the clear sky of your mind. Notice the tendency to observe only the thoughts or images and to miss the deep, clear sense of inner openness. You can anchor yourself in your thoughts or you can anchor yourself in the mind's open field of awareness. Learning to balance these two perspectives can offer profound peace of mind.

Sense the infinity and the unity of inner space and outer space. Sense how the radiance in all things distributes itself in space into a state of perfect balance and harmony. Discover how all forms, inner and outer, arise out of and within space, last a while, and then through movement and change they exhaust themselves and dissolve back into space. Learn how this marvelous dance of form and space reveals a profound sense of balance that is fundamental to your deepest being.

The Balanced Mindbrain State

Some of the most inspiring insights into how we can find greater balance in our lives can be gained by looking into how our brain works when our mind is in a balanced state. Over the years, we have had the good fortune to do extensive laboratory research using state-of-the-art technology to measure and observe the brainwaves of people while they were involved in a variety of self-mastery tasks.

One of the most amazing insights from our mindbrain research is that when the mind is in a balanced state, the brain functions in a measurably balanced way. As you watch the electrical activity of your brain displayed on a color monitor, you can see how moment to moment the mindbrain state flows in and out of balance. When the brain comes into balance, there is a "synching up" of the activity of both the left and right sides of the brain. It is like what happens when dozens of individual musicians stop tuning their individual instruments, or stop trying to drown each other out, and finally begin to actually play music together as one orchestra. This shift can be dramatic, instantaneous, and breathtaking, both for the person making the shift and for those of us in the lab watching the brain activity on the screen. By way of analogy, this shift from ordinary, distracted, turbulent mental activity to a more coherent, powerfully balanced mind-brain state is like watching the jumbled carbon atoms in a lump of coal organize and transform themselves into the coherent arrangement of the same atoms that we know as a bright, shining diamond. This shift toward a more balanced mindbrain state could also be described as like seeing a dim ten-watt lightbulb reorganize its energy into the coherence of a laser

"The greatest thing then, in all education, is to make the nervous system our ally, instead of our enemy."

—William James

"The only advantage over competitors is the brain power you have in your own organization."

—Ralph Styer

beam in which those same ten watts would have tremendous power.

Some examples of balanced mindbrain states were first recognized in rare and spontaneous moments that people describe as peak experiences, religious or mystical rapture, epiphanies, or illuminations. For many of us, these moments occur unpredictably and by chance at moments when we are wholeheartedly present with what we are doing—when we are filled with love, appreciation, or compassion; when we are cracked open in crisis; or when our attention is captured by beauty. For people who are well versed in meditation, prayer, martial arts, or other self-balancing practices, these powerful moments of profound grace and balance occur much more frequently and easily than for people who have invested little discipline in learning about themselves in a deeper way.

In terms of the brain power and performance of people in the laboratory, there is a striking difference between people who are highly disciplined in mental or spiritual disciplines as compared to others who have lived their life with little investment in personal development. Those who have trained in a disciplined way have measurably more brain power, greater concentration and mastery of attention, greater mental stability, enhanced tolerance for ambiguity, greater creativity, flexibility, and graceful fluidity in their mindbrain functions than those who have neglected to discipline and develop their minds. (Most of these qualities are ones we've been describing as useful for balance!)

When this unusually balanced brainstate was first discovered, numerous researchers attempted to identify the key method necessary to bring it about. After thousands of experiments, the data analysis revealed that the single most important element was an open focused quality of mind, sometimes described as "panoramic attention" or as "mindfulness of space." In this state of panoramic attention, the mind is balanced, peaceful, open, clear, and powerfully present. Brain activity is balanced left to right and front to back in a highly integrated, organized, coherent, and nearly superfluid state of responsive functioning.

Studies of people who are competing in extreme endurance

"The faculty of voluntarily bringing back a wandering attention is the very root of judgment, character and will. No one is really in control of themselves if they do not have this. An education which would improve this faculty would be the education par excellence."

—**William James**

sports show that when they are able to shift into an open-focused quality of mind, they are able to significantly increase their endurance and decrease their pain, when compared with competitors who are performing in a more narrowly focused and effortful way. Other studies show that open-focused people in stressful situations are able to think more clearly, make wiser decisions, process complex information more efficiently, and minimize stress when they are able to maintain a more panoramic or open-focused state.

The good news is that you don't need a brainwave machine or fancy techniques to do this for yourself. With practice, you can learn how to shift into this balanced mind/brain state whenever or wherever you like, even in the most stressful of situations.

The shift to an open-focused state does not happen by trying to make it happen. Trying just creates more tension, noise, or turbulence in the mind/brain. The shift toward balance takes place by simply relaxing and allowing the quality of mind and attention to rest naturally in its lucid, receptive, and alert state. You have already experienced a bit of this in the mindfulness practices in chapter four. Here are some steps to discover this balanced mindstate:

1. Because it is easier for the mind to open, equalize, and balance when your body is relaxed, take a few deep and easy breaths and release any tensions you may become aware of. To help you with this, imagine that your breath is like a warm and gentle wind. As you breathe, allow your inhalations to focus your awareness and breath into regions of tension or pain. Allow this warm and gentle breeze of the breath to melt any of the ice fields of tension or to soothe any pain. Then, as you exhale, allow the flow of the breath to help you to dissolve the tension, and to leave those areas feeling more internally spacious and open. Allow the natural flow of the breath to help you to focus as you inhale and to flow as you exhale. Take a few minutes to scan through your whole body and to let the breath help you to draw your awareness into any regions in your body that are calling for your loving attention.

"The Way is perfect like vast space where nothing is lacking and nothing is in excess. Indeed, it is due to our choosing to accept or reject that we do not see the true nature of things. Live neither in the entanglements of outer things, nor in inner feelings of emptiness. Be serene in the oneness of things and such erroneous views will disappear by themselves. When you try to stop activity to achieve passivity, your very efforts fill you with activity. As long as you remain in one extreme or the other you will never know Oneness."

—**Sengstan**

2. Deepen this same technique to help you focus your awareness into any sticking points of tension in your mind. Breathing in, focus in a deep and spacious way within the center of any thoughts. Breathing out, let the energy of that thought flow or dissolve like a cloud melting into the deep clear sky.

As you continue now, remember to smile to yourself so that you don't take this too seriously or try too hard to get this right. Also, let your eyes remain soft and relaxed. Everything up to this point is preparation.

3. Next, sense and feel your whole body like a big balloon that is completely open, unobstructed, and hollow inside.

4. Now, as you sit here, sense yourself sitting right at the very center of your universe. Consciously open and expand the field of your awareness to become aware of your unique place in space. Sitting here, allow the internal sense of openness and spaciousness to expand. Allow your attention to reach out now in an expansive way like a broad beam of panoramic awareness to see, sense, or feel everything that is in front of you. Let it reach out and become aware of whatever is behind you. Allow your peripheral vision to naturally expand and to effortlessly include everything to your left . . . and then to your right . . . Allow your field scanners to reach up to see, sense, or feel whatever is above you, and to reach down to sense and discover whatever is below you.

5. Now allow yourself to effortlessly maintain this evenly hovering, open awareness that attends equally to the flow of both inner and outer experiences. Find the balance of mind necessary to equally attend both to the things or people around you, as well as to the spaces between these things. Delight in dwelling within the equalizing spaciousness of balanced awareness. As your spatial acuity deepens and expands, regard space itself as a medium of

"Awareness is like a beam of light that shines endlessly into space. We only perceive that light when it is reflected off some object and consciousness is produced. . . Awareness is the light by which we see the world. . . We mistake the clear light of pure awareness for the shadows that it casts in consciousness. . . We forget that we are the light itself and imagine that we are the densities that reflect the light back to us."

—Stephen Levine

communication. Space, properly perceived, connects and unifies everything and everyone. Space pervades and supports all things; it doesn't separate them. It holds all things together. Remember that the new physics teaches that if you could expand the spectrum of your senses, the open spaces around you would be sensed as full of information waves. If you doubt this, turn on a radio or TV and remember how much invisible information bombards you all the time.

6. As you deepen and expand this quality of panoramic attention, effortlessly include the resonance of all the sounds filling the space within and around you. Balance this by including in your experience how these sounds emerge from silence . . . how they fill and move through space . . . and then how sounds dissolve again back into silence. In a similar way, sense everything within and around you that is in motion . . . and balance this with the mindful awareness of everything that is still and unmoving. Rest in this balanced awareness, allowing the flow of each breath to remind you to find a fluid, dynamic balance between focus and flow, forms and space, motion and stillness, silence and sound. Let this awareness extend equally to include all the experiences within and around you.

This deceptively simple practice for balancing the mind requires little or no effort. With panoramic attention, you simply rest at ease in the flow of experience while remaining lucidly aware. The benefits of using it, however, are far reaching, profound, and extensively documented. One key finding of studies shows that while ordinary focal attention is commonly associated with tension and fixation, this effortless quality of "panoramic awareness" shifts your mind-body/brain into a state that is often described as being transparent to stress. When you are balanced in this quality of mindbrain function, stress and tension don't "stick to you." Instead, the intensity of your experience and the flow of information is smoothly processed in an

". . . Right relationship means right relationship with the elements, the land, the sacred directions. . . The seed of pure mind is within all people. It is always there. It is not made impure. Our actions may be impure and set up a stream of reactions, but always we can come again to the seed of pure mind and right relationship. . . it is time now for people to choose. The first step is to see the power of your own consciousness. . . The common kernel is care for all beings, good relationship, cycles of reciprocity, generosity, giving of oneself, being an empty bowl so you can know what is."

—Dhyani Ywahoo

easy and effortless way, free of tension, fixation, and the accumulation of distress. Though the tendency of most people when under stress is to tense, narrow, or constrict their focus of awareness and to "try harder," you will find extra clarity, strength, efficiency, and endurance by shifting into this more panoramic state of effortless awareness. Many people when faced with new information shut down or become more stressed and effortful. Those who know how to shift into a more openly focused mindset are better able to accelerate learning, integrate more information, and access intuition more easily.

Preventing Information Fatigue

Enmeshed in this information age, we are bombarded with more information in a day than our ancestors received in years. Indeed, it is said that an average Sunday edition of the *New York Times* contains more information than the average person at the beginning of the twentieth century encountered in their whole lifetime! In our craving for knowledge and intellectual stimulation, it is common to devour vast helpings of sumptuous written and electronic material—only to wind up with a bad case of mental indigestion. When we take in more than we can absorb and integrate, the information drips off our minds like water off a duck. Few of us stop to soak on the ideas and implications of what we experience and get really "wet." Distracted and mentally moving fast, we don't have or make the time to be fully present, to ponder things deeply, or take our studies to heart.

In a report entitled "Dying for Information"—50 percent of managers surveyed reported feeling overloaded by information and worried about the stress-related problems associated with information overload. Respondents cited three factors in this overload: 1) They don't understand all the information they receive and don't have the time to figure it all out; 2) They worry about how to manage the sheer volume of information; and 3) They worry that they might put themselves at a disadvantage because they might miss important information.

"Most everybody is overwhelmed. And they respond with various defense mechanisms. Denial, isolation, increased greed ('I'll get it while I can'), righteousness ('It's their own fault'). There are a whole set of mechanisms that people use to keep from being open, because the quality of the human heart uncontrolled by the mind is that it will give away everything... We have to find ways to exercise the compassion of our hearts, and at the same moment learn how to know what the limits are and be able to say no without guilt."

—**Ram Dass**

For people working under these pressures day in and day out, it is common to experience a constellation of symptoms that has come to be called Information Fatigue Syndrome. Symptoms include:

- increased sense of frustration
- increased irritability that acts like a corrosive acid eroding the quality of working relationships
- inability to solve problems or make decisions
- tendency to panic, resulting in poor judgment, foolish decisions, and problematic consequences

Do these symptoms sound familiar to you? Take heart. If these factors are plaguing you, you can find greater mental balance in the following ways:

1. Increase your comfort and skills in working with information technology.

2. Increase your skills in accessing data through your eyes if you have the habit of subvocally reading information to yourself.

3. Learn to sort out the "urgent" from the "important" information by developing greater skills in prioritizing the flood of information in your life.

4. Build times to "unplug" or push your "clear" button. Remember the lessons from nature—waxing and waning, filling and emptying. If you want to develop the capacity to manage information overload, you need to periodically do an "information fast." Set aside times when you turn off the TV and radio, put aside your reading, and unplug your telephone. Be content to simply, quietly, deeply be with yourself and those who share your life. Ideally, take an information fast during a time when you can be in nature and let yourself bask in the wave forms of your natural world.

5. When it is time to once again enter the information

"To arrive at the simplest truth, as Newton knew and practiced, requires years of contemplation. Not activity. Not reasoning. Not calculating. Not busy behavior of any kind. Not reading. Not talking. Not making an effort. Not thinking. Simply bearing in mind what it is one needs to know...

Those with the courage to tread the path to real discovery are not only offered practically no guidance on how to do so, they are actively discouraged and have to set about it in secret, pretending meanwhile to be diligently engaged in the frantic diversions...."

—**G. Spencer Brown**

highway, begin mindfully and selectively. Be keenly aware of the impact of the intensity and volume of information that streams your way, and choose wisely which information you give priority to. As you re-engage in the many sources of information that are a part of your life, make a conscious effort to balance the information that you open yourself to. Challenge yourself to seek out as much good news as bad news, to harvest as much beauty as pain, and as much peaceful, soothing, harmonizing input as violent, agitating, and disruptive input. Realize that just like food, you do have a choice for what information you consume, and discipline yourself to turn off negative media that does little but disturb you.

6. Strengthen your intuitive intelligence by cultivating the strength of your quiet mind skills—mindfulness, attention, deep listening, and the physically felt sense of your aliveness. As you learn to trust your intuition, you will tap the wellspring of spontaneous and profound wisdom that is available to the open mind in a state of "not knowing." Most situations in which we want to be successful call more for the authenticity and spontaneity of our authentic presence, rather than the rote recitation of memorized data. Increasing your access to intuitive intelligence equips you with the skill, confidence, clarity, and peace of mind necessary for enhanced learning and creativity.

Balancing Doing and Being: Don't Just Do Something, Sit There!

Do you live your life more as a "human being" or as a "human doing"? Many of the people we meet comment that they have been so busy being a "human doing" that they have lost touch with their human beingness. They are often weary, and wound so tight that they exhaust themselves.

The business of doing takes many forms. We live in a culture

> *"The true state of affairs in the material world is wholeness. If we are fragmented, we must blame it ourselves."*
>
> **—David Bohm**

> *"A mind once stretched by a great idea or new understanding will never fully return to its original dimensions."*
>
> **—William James**

where we are heavily conditioned to be uncomfortable with ourselves and to feel like we have to have something or do something to be a good, worthy human being. This leads us to be compulsively driven into doing things because we are so uncomfortable just being who or how we are. You will notice that some people are so out of balance that they are uncomfortable sitting still for more than a moment before they have to do something. You notice them tapping their feet, fidgeting around, chewing gum, smoking a cigarette, jumping up to get something to eat, anything but just simply being with and enjoying the moment without having to complicate it. Even if we are more or less physically still, it is likely that our mind will be agitated and busy doing—thinking, imagining, or otherwise complicating the simplicity of the moment. When we can't tolerate it any more, we space out or fall asleep.

"Just to be is a blessing. Just to live is holy."

—**Rabbi Abraham Herschel**

Begin to recognize and appreciate when you are simply being and when you are necessarily, or unnecessarily, complicating things by doing. Gradually increase your capacity and tolerance to simply be with what is going on without having to change it. When it is time to shift, be mindful of shifting from being to doing, or from doing to being. Seek for the quality of internal strength and balance that ultimately allows you to maintain the integrity of your mindful presence of being, even while you are busy doing things.

EIGHT

Catching the Waves:
Balancing the Harmonics
of Subtle Energy

Because energy is defined as the capacity to produce effects, love
may be referred to as an energy; it is subtle, not because its effects or
subjective impact are subtle, but because it is ineffable to science,
or so it has seemed.

—JUDITH GREEN AND ROBERT
SHELLENBERGER

Just as musical notes have their primary
note and then a host of exquisitely subtle and beautiful overtones, the com-
plex instrument of your human body has its physical structure and a host of
subtler harmonic dimensions along a seemingly infinite spectrum of energies
and frequencies. While novice musicians may not have developed the refined
attention necessary to consciously hear, appreciate, and produce such exquisite tones, or may even lack the faith that they even exist, truly great musicians
are able to not only hear such harmonic overtones, but to fine-tune their
instrument to produce sublimely sweet music using such tones. The same is
true for the subtle energies within and around us. We may not yet be able to
sense them, but they are there and as we learn to tune into them, we are naturally better equipped to live a more beautiful, balanced, and creative life.

Insight into the world of invisible energies is offered by Buckminster Fuller, whose engineering genius inspired countless inventions and discoveries that have helped millions of people to live in greater balance upon the earth:

"The fact that 99 percent of humanity does not understand nature is the prime reason for humanity's failure to exercise its option to attain universally sustainable physical success on this planet... When I was born in 1895, reality was everything you could see, smell, touch, and hear. The world was thought to be absolutely self-evident. When I was three years old, the electron was discovered. That was the first invisible. It didn't get in any of the newspapers; (Nobody thought that it would be important!) Today 99.99 percent of everything that affects our lives cannot be detected by human senses. We live in a world of invisibles... I am confident that humanity's survival depends on all our willingness to comprehend *feelingly* the way nature works."

For many people, the notion of energy is an enigma. The greatest scientists of the world will readily admit that even energies that are taken for granted—electricity and gravity, for example—are still mysteries defying our full comprehension. The energies that we are talking about in this chapter are, at one level, related to subtle fields of life force that are bioelectromagnetic in nature and can be measured with a host of medical practices including X-rays, MRIs, CAT scans, electrostimulation, and acupuncture. There are also frequencies or qualities of energy that are more subtle and elusive in nature. They can be directly sensed, or even generated, with a high degree of precision by a sensitive person, and many of their effects can be measured. But the energies themselves are simply too subtle to measure with existing measurement technology, just as most ordinary electromagnetic energy was less than a century ago.

Every culture with a deep wisdom tradition has terms describing these subtle energies: life force, vital energy, or bioenergy; *prana* in Sanskrit; *chi, qi,* or *ki* in oriental medicine and martial arts; *lung* (pronounced 'loong') in Tibetan medicine and meditation; and *ruach* in Hebrew. In an excellent article recently published in

"At the heart of each of us, whatever our imperfections, there exists a silent pulse of perfect rhythm, a complex of wave forms and resonances, which is absolutely individual and unique, and yet which connects us to everything in the Universe."

—George Leonard

Bridges, the Magazine of the International Society for the Study of Subtle Energies and Energy Medicine," Roger Jahnke, a doctor of oriental medicine, illuminates the nature of subtle energy from the perspective of the healing discipline of Qigong:

"One description of Qigong is as a discipline to 'refine the body of pure energy.' When . . . the Qi develops and circulates . . . it spills out into all of the channels and circuits. This is called the circulation of the light. . . . As the practitioner's attention is fixed on the body of light, the dense body of substance becomes secondary. Rather than a physical body with a resonating energy field, the individual, from this perspective, is an energy field that has a small dense body of flesh at its center.

"Thousands of years ago, Chuang Tzu asked, 'Is it Chuang Tzu asleep dreaming he is a butterfly? Or is it the butterfly dreaming he is Chuang Tzu?' In the Qigong of transcendence it is asked, "Is the practitioner of the deep Qigong state a person in a moment of transcendent energetic experience, or is his manifestation in a physical body actually a brief exploration into substance by an entity whose normal state is one of highly refined resonating light energy?"

In recent decades, we have witnessed an increasing interest in the subtle energetic nature of human beings. This interest has been accelerating the evolution of medical science and fitness training to include progressively subtler and subtler dimensions of our human body. Gradually, we have come to recognize that within our physical structure are myriad vital biochemical, bioelectric, and subtle energy fields of influence that are essential to the state of dynamic balance that we call health. When the flow of energy at any of these levels is blocked, the quality of our health and vitality is compromised. Whenever the flow of energy at any or all of these levels is balanced, we move toward health.

The increasing awareness of subtle energies is due to a number of factors: the post-Einsteinian physics of the unified field has revealed that our world is composed of dynamic relationships of countless frequencies of energy. Advances in technology are revealing that our universe is indeed woven of myriad frequencies of

"Deeply, gently, from within, life unfolds. Blossoming into being as the radiant outpouring of unfathomable, immeasurable Mystery. Worlds of dense and subtle forms, unceasing and unobstructed radiance, pulsatingly vibrantly modulated by the subtle interplay of a myriad unseen forces. Each of us at our core are radiant beings. The outer forms that we behold are like transient, gossamer films, shimmering within the omnidimensional fractilian field, home, matrix of multispectral luminescence—life—awestruck with humility and wonder awaken to discover your self as clear, lucid, loving, radiant Presence."

—L'imagineer

energy, and that the health of living organisms is reflected in the flow of energy within them, and in the balanced exchange of energy between them and their environment.

The growing crisis in health care and the increasing density of electromagnetic fields in our environment are leading to advances in the number of studies related to life energy. Ultrasound, X-rays, MRIs, CAT scans, electrostimulation, acupuncture, and a host of modern and ancient approaches are increasingly being used in the diagnosis and treatment of disease and the promotion of health. Many of the hands-on treatments are proving to be highly effective, and free from the expense and side effects associated with pharmaceuticals or invasive technology.

As stress, complexity, and fragmentation in our modern lives continue to mount, more and more people are seeking knowledge and skills to restore their balance and to live with a greater sense of simplicity, connectedness, and wholeness. Increasing numbers of people are taking an interest in traditional and nontraditional spiritual pursuits, and are actively practicing various forms of contemplation, meditation and prayer, yoga, or healing and martial arts such as tai chi, chi kung (or Qigong), and aikido, all of which expand the spectrum of awareness to the natural flow of subtle energies within and among us. The effects of many of these ancient practices have been well documented in Western, Eastern, and indigenous traditions for thousands of years, and are now being confirmed by medical and scientific studies, increasing our collective faith in such pursuits.

Balance Equals Health

Many medical systems in cultures around the globe regard health as the expression of balance. Unlike Western medicine, which looks at "fighting" disease with antibiotics of all sorts, other traditions—Tibetan, Japanese, Chinese, Ayurvedic, naturopathic, homeopathic, and bioenergetic, to name but a few—use nonviolent models that seek to restore health by restoring harmony within the

" If a living system is suffering from ill health, the remedy is to connect it with more of itself."

—**Francisco Varella**

"Heaven is my father and earth my mother and even such a small creature as I finds an intimate place in its midst. That which extends throughout the universe, I regard as my body and that which directs the universe, I regard as my nature. All people are my brothers and sisters, and all things are my companion."

—**Chang Tsai, eleventh-century**

living system as a whole. These medical systems understand that all parts of a living organism are necessary and important components of its wholeness. If there is illness, it means that one of the parts or systems is out of balance with the whole. Healing, then, becomes a question of recognizing where there is too much of one thing or too little of something else, and applying appropriate treatments to reduce the excesses or build up the deficiencies.

Looking through the lenses of the acupuncture tradition, Professor J. R. Worsley, president of the College of Clinical Acupuncture in the United Kingdom, explains that health is determined by the balance within the subtle energy called life force:

"The body-mind-spirit of every man, woman and child desires health so that we may be at one with the energy of the cosmos, both within us and without. When there is disunity the human life force signals its distress. We see then many different symptoms: continual anger, migraine headaches, sexual problems, emotional instability, ulcers, arthritis pain... These life force signals tell us that our balance is disturbed, that the energy is blocked and must be released to flow smoothly through the human system. Our drug-oriented and suppressive attitudes toward illness often create additional imbalance because we have not yet learned to place the emphasis on health as unity which brings wholeness to the human condition."

The law of the five elements in oriental medicine follows a basic cycle: begin with Fire, Earth, Metal, Water, Wood, and return to Fire. This cycle describes the flow of life force energy, or *chi,* in every being and in the universe. According to this system of subtle energy balance, *chi* energy is characterized by its dual aspects of yin and yang, which form an inseparable wholeness. As Professor Worsley poetically describes it, "yin, the passive force—the negative, the night, the moon—is never separated from the yang—the creative, the positive, the day, the sun. The two are like poles of a battery. Without both poles, the battery will not function."

The five elements, like yin and yang, never stand alone. Each element governs and is governed by another. For example, according to this theory, Fire creates Earth and rules Metal, Earth creates Metal

"From health stems harmony, balance, and unity. From disease we suffer discord, chaos, and disunity."

—J.R. Worsley, President, College of Clinical Acupuncture

"Energy medicine attempts to reconceptualize patterns of information flow in the body in ways that differ from those of biochemistry and molecular biology."

—Brendan O'Regan

and rules Water, Metal creates Water and rules Wood. Water creates Wood and rules Fire, while Wood creates Fire and rules Earth. Each element is also understood to be related to a particular emotion, organ system in the body, and even season of the year and time of day. Learning to manage the energy of each of these interrelated elements is to participate in a dynamic dance of wholeness.

In practice, the cultivation of subtle energy awareness has to do with four areas of learning, each of which is related to balance:

1. Learning to relax and let go of unnecessary tension in the body or excessive turbulence and agitation in the mind.

2. Learning to balance the mind in order to access a state of intense calm and concentration without distraction (the panoramic mindstate described in chapter seven).

3. Practicing breathing exercises that link and balance the flow of mind/energy/body.

4. Learning to tap the wisdom and harness the power in rhythmic activity.

We have both done our share of traditional weight and aerobic training, and we've been amazed at the balanced power, strength, vitality, and suppleness achieved through the more subtle energy training. For nearly twenty-five years now, Joel has practiced and studied various styles of tai chi, chi kung, and aikido. As he recalls:

"When I was in high school and college, I worked as a stock boy and then salesman for a lumber company. In my early days in that job it was not uncommon for me to stack more than a ton of lumber a day. As a result, I got really strong, but not in a particularly balanced or flexible way.

"Later, between my undergraduate and graduate study, I studied and practiced tai chi for nearly three hours a day for about six months. In those days I didn't have a car and I rode my bike to get around town. When I started doing tai chi, I was amazed how much stronger and flexible I became, even though the movements were so very subtle.

"Since Universe is Energy, part of the process of understanding, at least as I experience it, is to learn to 'see' flows of energy and specificities of energy. Both are necessary. Because, you see, Universe is both Whole and Specific. Western science is beginning to understand this through explorations about particle and wave. Both particle/particularity/specificity of Universe and the wave/flow of Universe were aspects I was encouraged as a child to apprehend and understand. I was asked to 'see' the 'dancing points of light' and then to apprehend the shift from location to flow."

—Paula Underwood Spencer

"Then, in preparation for an intensive six-month training program we did for the U.S. Army Green Berets, I did a lot of well-engineered weight training, plus internal energy training with aikido, a Japanese-style martial art that works with bringing 'the energies of heaven and earth into harmony within the human being.' This produced yet another quality of balance that served me well during the arduous training we did for the troops.

"And finally, when we did a year of contemplative retreat, my only real exercise was sixty to ninety minutes a day of chi kung, the Chinese Taoist energy balancing system, and a variety of yoga postures. This was a good balance for the quiet sitting practice that lasted from fourteen to twenty hours each day. During the entire year, my health and spirits were excellent and coming out of retreat, I felt physically stronger than before and had amazing suppleness and endurance as I set out on a number of long hikes."

It seems that the more deeply we are able to cultivate inner balance, including energetic balance, the more dramatically it will be reflected in the "outer layers" of our lives. That's why we devote the rest of this chapter to energy practices.

Two Palms Talking

Palm to palm, rub your hands vigorously together as you breathe deeply for about a minute. Then, continuing to be mindful of your breathing, gently hold your hands about two feet apart and slowly bring them toward each other. Imagine that you are generating or gathering a spongy, luminous field of energy between your hands, and let your hands gently push in on this ball, and then bounce gently outward again. As you do this, remember to smile to yourself so that you don't try too hard, get too self-conscious, or take this experiment too seriously. After a short while, hold your palms facing each other and gently move your hands back and forth, noticing any subtle vibrations or sensations that may occur along your fingertips or palms. Maintain a sense of curiosity, and be open to discovery. Feel free to repeat stage one and to breathe and rub your

"...convert the body into a luminous fluidity, surrendering it to the inspiration of the soul. This sort of dancer understands that the body, by force of the soul, can in fact be converted to a luminous fluid. The flesh becomes light and transparent, as shown through the x-ray— but with the difference that the human soul is lighter than these rays. When, in the divine power, it completely possesses the body, it converts that into a luminous moving cloud and thus can manifest itself in the whole of its divinity. This is the explanation of the miracle of St. Francis walking on the sea. His body no longer weighed like ours, so light had it become through the soul."

—**Isadora Duncan**

hands together again if your sensitivity begins to fade. Experiment with the exercise at different times and see how your experience changes. Chances are you will have a direct experience of the subtle energies we are talking about.

Heaven Meets Earth

"All beings are embraced within one All-encompassing great energy. So I understood from the coolness Of this morning's passing breeze."

—Yamada Mumon

Another dimension of subtle energy balancing is the weaving together of above and below, of heaven and earth. Your ability to reach to the heavens is dependent on how deep your roots are in the earth. One especially powerful method of staying present in your power throughout the day is to experience yourself as a conduit for the energies of the earth and heaven. Because the electrical conductance at your feet and at your head have inverse properties, there's actually a basis in the bioelectrodynamics of your body to support this practice. Variations of this method have been used in countless cultures around the globe for thousands of years.

As you sit or stand quietly, imagine or sense a spiral of energy rising from the earth up through you and opening into the sky. Just be with this image or sense for a few moments, allowing it to emerge as naturally as possible into your awareness. Breathe in and draw the energy of the earth up and into you. Exhaling, feel this flow of energy rising up through your body and opening upward into the sky. Draw the energy of the earth up and into yourself, and then offer it up to the sky. As you begin to do this, you may find it helpful to use one of your hands to make an uplifting spiral, reaching up from the earth and spiraling up to the heavens. As you breathe and continue this image, imagine that this rising vortex of energy spirals through you with a deep and powerful cleansing action, dissolving any blockages to the free flow of the energy of your bodymind, and leaving you feeling clean and clear, vitalized and keenly aware, as though your energy and vibration have bumped up a notch.

If this kind of visualization exercise is difficult for you, just relax and give it your best shot. It's important to remember that, as with most of these exercises, you'll find that the more effortlessly you hold the image and allow it to happen, the more vividly you'll be able to actually experience its reality.

As you breathe, simply allow the flow of earth energy to continue to rise and flow in the background. Now, as you inhale, imagine drawing a vortex of energy or light down into you from the heavens above. Use all the special effects you can to make the visualization as vivid or as deeply felt as possible. Imagine that you fill yourself with the energy of the heavens, and that as you exhale, it spirals down and through you into the earth. Drawing in the heavens, bring that energy or light down through you into the earth like a wave of blessings. Let this shower of light and energy wash through you, cleaning and clearing your body and mind of any energies that get in the way of the flow. Feel your body and mind sparkling clean and clear in this balancing flow. Let the descending wave smooth, balance, and ground your energy, and deepen your sense of stability and rootedness in the earth.

Once you have established the ascending and descending flows of energy, simply rest in the flow of awareness of both of these two spirals flowing through you at the same time. Allow this vitalizing, harmonizing, healing flow of energy to totally dissolve any remaining tensions or concerns. As you rest easily in this counterbalancing stream, any energy that's blocked or frozen within you simply dissolves and melts into the flow. Let any sense of denseness or solidity in your mind/body dissolve and find its dynamic balance as a higher order of stability and strength that is pure flowing energy and light.

Though at first you may just get the idea of what this image suggests, with practice this will become a concrete and powerful experience for you. Be patient, don't expect fireworks or anything special. Just let your mind move like a magnet over a jumbled pile of iron filings and know that as your mind moves, all of the energies and particles within you will begin to align. Allow the energy that's already within you to flow more smoothly through you.

As with many of the methods you're learning, its actual form is very simple, but the power and insight that can be generated through practice over time can be quite profound. Throughout the

"When you walk across the fields with your mind pure and holy, then from all the stones, and all growing things, and all animals, the sparks of their soul come out and cling to you, and then they are purified and become a holy fire in you."

—Hasidic Saying

day, if it feels right to you, when you're sitting at your desk, on the bus, or walking down the street, you might activate your awareness of these spirals of energy and light flooding through you. As you do, awaken to and rejoice in your groundedness and connectedness to the strength, steadiness, and nurturing nature of the earth, and to the open, light, majesty, and vast potentials of the heavens. Realize that though you may not be aware of them, you're never separate from these realities even for an instant. Practicing in this way will quietly, powerfully, and invisibly equip you with a way of moving through the world in balance and in a way that leaves a trail of light, good vibes, and blessings wherever you go.

Circle Breath

In this exercise we'll introduce you to one more extremely useful strategy for balancing and focusing the energies of your mind/body. We use this technique often when we're walking or sitting quietly for a few moments. Initially we learned this from bioenergy healer Mietek Wirkus, and later learned variations from numerous teachers from other disciplines. As a child in Poland after the war, Mietek would accompany the local doctor in his visits to people who were sick or in pain. The doctor had no medications and few supplies, but he had found that his patients would often get better just by having Mietek be with them for a while or hold their hand.

Through prayer and meditation, the healing love of Christ, and years of training with elders who had developed their own healing gifts, Mietek learned much about the balancing and healing energy of love. In 1982, when bioenergy therapy was approved in Poland to supplement ordinary medical work, Mietek became one of the first professional bioenergy therapists to work in the Polish medical centers performing detailed diagnoses and treatments for hundreds of people each week. In 1985, Mietek and his wife, Margaret, a journalist who assists in his work, emigrated to the United States. They settled in Bethesda, Maryland, and have offered classes for more than

"The healer must feel and be the heart chakra... Heart center vibrations relate to unconditional love, and to treating other beings with love, understanding and respect... It is not thinking the word 'love', it is not a visualization process, it is the real sensation of pure love which brings warmth, delicate vibrations in your heart area."

—Mietek Wirkus

"The conclusion is always the same: love is the most powerful and still the most unknown energy of the world."

—Pierre Teilhard de Chardin

two thousand physicians, nurses, and other helping professionals.

Mietek has also participated in numerous research projects. We first met them at a special conference on energy medicine and healing at the Menninger Foundation, where Mietek was the focus of considerable interest. At one point, we were conducting an informal study on Mietek's brainwaves during a healing session. While he was working, one of the observing scientists stepped forward to get a closer look. "My God," the skeptical scientist exclaimed, "you can actually feel the energy he is generating." Stepping back and then moving forward with his hands outstretched in front of him, he excitedly pointed it out to the rest of us, "See right here, about four feet away from him, you can begin to feel the energy. It's like a very gentle breeze or an electrostatic field. And it grows stronger, or denser, the closer you approach. I've never experienced anything like this in my life." Intrigued by their notoriously skeptical colleague's discovery, dozens of other observers performed this simple experiment themselves, and most were amazed that they could actually sense a subtle and calming field of energy radiating from Mietek and his patient. One method that Mietek uses to keep his own energy balanced while he is working with people is the circle breath we're about to teach you. Here's one version of how the method we learned from him works:

Begin by becoming aware of your body and the natural flow of your breathing. As you inhale, draw your attention up along the back of your body, from the base of your spine to the top of your head. Then, as you exhale, allow your awareness to circle from the crown of your head down along the front of your body all the way to the base of the spine. Inhaling, again draw your awareness up from the bottom of your spine to the crown of your head; exhaling, allow your awareness to circle down along the front of your body to the base of the spine. The flow of the breath defines a circle rising up the back and then flowing down along the front of the body. The beginning and end point of the breath is at the bottom of your spine. At the peak of your inhalation, your attention is focused at the crown of your head for a moment. Practice until you establish an

"Researchers of so-called energy medicine are a curious lot. We unearth ancient practices, dust them off, clean them with modern solvents, and study them under the lens of high technology. All the while, we seek to distill simple truths about health and illness."

—David Eisenberg

"There is a light in this world, a healing spirit more powerful than any darkness we may encounter. We sometimes lose sight of this force when there is suffering, too much pain. Then suddenly, the spirit will emerge through the lives of ordinary people who hear a call and answer in extraordinary ways."

—Mother Teresa

easy, effortless, circular flow of energy around this orbit. Once you know how to initiate this flow of balancing energy and awareness, you will be able to rest in this circulation of energy while you are engaged in other activities.

Like many other exercises that ask you to direct your attention and energy in unfamiliar ways, this may at first feel awkward. As with all learning, as you become more familiar with organizing your energy and awareness in this new way, it will begin to feel more and more natural, and unfold in more and more effortless and deeply sensed ways.

The Drop and the Ocean

Sitting quietly and comfortably now, allow the breath to freely come and flow, effortless releasing and dissolving thoughts and tensions into space. As you inhale, imagine a bubble of light filling you from within. As you exhale, imagine this bubble expanding and opening out into the space around you. With each in-breath, be filled by this luminous energy, and with each exhalation, imagine this sphere of light opening and expanding, moving freely through the space, the walls, the buildings, the earth around you. Let everything open. Let your small sense of self expand and open to your surroundings. Allow all of the feelings, sensations, and vibrations within your body to expand, open and dissolve like a cloud melting into space. Use the breath to extend your sphere of energy awareness like the radiating circle of a pebble dropped into a still pool...

Ahhh... Opening in all directions... Filling the space above you.... Filling the space below you.... Expanding and opening out before you... Behind you... Opening and expanding as a sphere of energy life awareness all around you... Opening and expanding with each breath....

Now as you inhale, allow this light energy to take on a pleasing color and a pleasant feeling quality—perhaps blue and peaceful, or red and warm, or any combination that feels right to you. As you inhale, allow this feeling and color to fill you deeply and as you

"... When you want to enter a different aspect of Life, you wait for the point at which Particle becomes Wave. And just at that split second before the Particle is gone and the Wave takes over, you enter between, and you become Energy. At that point where the wave becomes Particle again, you enter between and you re-become who you were or you make a different choice. Which is also possible. I think it is that space in which healing occurs."

—Paula Underwood Spencer

exhale, allow this colorful, "feelingful" sphere to open and expand within and around you. Imagine flooding the space around you with radiant waves of warmth and well-being. Imagine generating an atmosphere of peace, balance, and harmony that pervades the world around you. Sitting quietly, simply allow this wellspring of inner energy to rise within you and to open and expand so that everyone around is bathed in this light.

Now, having established this expansive sense of well-being, imagine that as your sphere of energy awareness opens, there is an echo from the universe at large. Imagine that as your nucleus of energy expands outward, a vast ocean of peace, or warmth, or love converges and pours itself into you. Sense the incredible feeling of balance that emerges as you simultaneously experience this expansion and convergence—your tiny mind-drop opening outward, dissolving into a vast spacious ocean, and this ocean of positive energy vibration flowing and converging into your drop. Allow all of your limitations, pains, thoughts, and cares to be dissolved into this free-flowing convergence, resting in wholeness, connected and belonging to the world.

The Nine-Part Breath

The last technique in this chapter is an important one to add to your energy balancing tool kit. It's called the "nine-part breath" because it has the powerful effect of focusing your mind/brain in just nine breaths! Because of its effectiveness in optimizing the functioning of your central nervous system, it's often used as a preliminary practice for any activity that calls for clear thinking and focused concentration.

It's been interesting in our research to see how many places we've encountered this technique. We've found it being widely taught in medical centers around the world, and when we were working with NASA it was being studied to see if it might be helpful in preventing lapses into the hazardous states of inattention that lead to high-speed plane crashes.

Many schools of natural healing describe cycles of energy

"Slipping away from the cliff bush, dew drop plummeting, into the sea."

—R. Christopher Thorsen

"All things, material and spiritual, originate from one source and are related as if they were one family. The past, present, and future are all contained in the life force. The universe emerged and developed from one source, and we evolved through the optimal process of unification and harmonization."

—Morihei Ueshiba, O'Sensei

changes that accompany each hour of the day. In acupuncture they are associated with the activation of different meridians and the physical, emotional, and mental functions associated with them. According to the natural body clock discovered by the Chinese, each meridian has its own two-hour period during the day when it is at its peak energy. For example, 11 P.M. to 1 A.M. is the time during which the gall bladder has slightly more energy than any other meridian. A person with an imbalance in the Water element often finds that their energy wanes during late afternoon beginning at about three o'clock, reaching a low ebb at about five o'clock. This is due to the bladder's dominance from 3 P.M. to 5 P.M., and the kidneys' dominance from 5 P.M. to 7 P.M. Similarly, each of us has a time of day when we feel at our best or worst, depending on our unique life energy.

In the ancient Indo-Tibetan *Kalachakra* system of medicine and astrology, every second, minute, and hour of each day corresponds to subtle shifts in energy within the body and in the heavens above. The practice of meditation within this system is based on understanding the balance and harmony of these energies. Within the Judeo-Christian and Islamic traditions too, each section of the day has its own set of holy prayers and practices, reflecting an awareness of the different energies that each daily cycle brings. For example, in the Benedictine monastic tradition, monks and nuns observe a series of hymns, prayers, chants, rituals, and invocations for each hour of the day. The hours are regarded as the seasons of the day and are meant to be traversed in a mythical way in order to attune oneself to the elusive sacred Mystery that lies beyond time. Until the crazed pace of modern life set in, many wisdom traditions encouraged a way of life that was slow enough to nurture balance, harmony, and deep connectedness to these energies throughout the many activities of each day.

One simple way to re-establish this balance is to cultivate a mindful awareness of the natural cycles of your breathing throughout the day. Not only does the breath flow in and out, but day in and day out, your breathing shifts back and forth on roughly ninety-

"We consist of and are sustained by inter-weaving currents of matter, energy, and information that flow through us interconnecting us with our environment and other beings. Yet, we are accustomed to identifying ourselves only with that small arc of the flow-through that is lit, like the narrow beam of a flashlight, by our individual subjective awareness. But we don't have to so limit our self-perceptions... It is as plausible to align our identity with the larger pattern, interexistent with all beings, as to break off one segment of the process and build our borders there."

—Joanna Macy

minute cycles, alternating in its strength of flow between your nostrils like the ebbing and flowing of an inner tide. This natural cycle of energy flow is called the "nasal rhythm" in modern medicine.

Though outwardly this rhythm is reflected by the alternation of a stronger breath flow through one nostril or the other, inwardly the flow of the breathing affects, and is related to, shifts in dominance between the two hemispheres of your brain. At the mental level this cycle of alternating activation of the left and right hemispheres of the brain shows up as alternating periods of mental focus and mental diffusion throughout the day.

Learning to read your energy and to shift your energy from one state to another is an important key to personal balance. One of the most simple and direct ways to do this is to pay attention to the changing flux and flow of the breath from one nostril to another. Before we introduce you to two simple variations on this method, let's first do a little experiment to see how your brain is working.

When you begin, it's helpful to check and see which nostril you're breathing most strongly from. This can be done by simply observing the flow of the breathing, or by putting a small mirror, like a compact, under your nostrils for a couple of breaths. Then you can look to see which nostril has left the largest cloud on the mirror. This is the nostril that you're breathing most dominantly through at this moment. If you don't have a mirror handy, you can just lick the back of your index finger and hold it under your nose as you breathe. Now, as you breathe on your finger, whichever side you feel the most air flow from is the dominant nostril at this time. So what does this tell you?

At the times when you're breathing predominantly through the right nostril, the mental functions associated with your left hemisphere are activated, and activity of the right hemisphere is cooled or subdued. What this means is this is a good time to focus your attention on tasks that require sharp clear thinking and attention to details, such as writing a technical report or balancing your checkbook.

On the other hand, or brain if you will, if the breath is flowing

"What we call mystical experience occurs when there is a sense of oneness or harmony between the energy or power of our bodies, minds, and spirits and the energy of other beings and the universe itself."
—John Mack, Harvard psychiatrist

"You and I and everything in the universe exist as a part of the endless flow of God's love. Realizing this, we recognize that all creation is bound together by the same benevolence. To harmonize with life is to come into accord with that part of God which flows through all things. To foster and protect all life is both our mission and our prayer."
—Morihei Ueshiba, O'Sensei

most strongly through your left nostril, then the mental functions of your left hemisphere will be cooled and the functions associated with the right hemisphere will be activated or enhanced. This will facilitate the focusing of your attention on qualities that are more related to patterns and process. Thus, left nostril breathing reflects easy access to mental functions associated with right brain functions, such as creative planning and design. Functions like imagination, intuition, and relaxation are naturally enhanced when you're breathing through your left nostril and activating your right hemisphere. Researchers have also observed that the state of left nostril/right brain dominance is more conducive to receiving new ideas, while right nostril/left brain dominance is an advantage for speaking and giving a presentation.

If you watch carefully, you'll also notice that there are periods throughout the day when the breathing is naturally balanced between both nostrils. These points of balance occur at those moments of the "changing of the guard," when the breath flow is at the point of shifting from right side dominance to left side dominance or vice versa. At these times, there's an evenly balanced flow of breath through both nostrils. This translates over to an evenly balanced flow of energy and information processes between the mental functions of left and right hemispheres of the brain. So, whenever the breath flow is even between left and right you'll be better able to stay focused, and to balance alertness with relaxation, thinking with observing, and analyzing with creative imagination. Once you learn the nine-part breath, you'll be able to tune your system with your breathing so that you can balance your energy/brain/mind whenever you like.

The first variation in this approach teaches you the basic mechanics of the process, which is really very simple. Once you gain some mastery over this technique, it may quickly become your favorite balancing tool. This method has been described by many of our clients as the closest thing they've found to "mental floss" for clearing the noisy mind! First, inhale through your right nostril and exhale through your left nostril. This can be done by using the index finger of your right hand to close the nostril that you're not breathing through. As you inhale, close the left nostril, and breathe in through the right nostril. Then shift your finger to close the right nostril and exhale effortlessly and easily through the left nostril. Repeat for three full breaths. Then inhale through your left nostril and exhale through your right nostril three times. Finally, resting your hands in your lap, inhale and exhale through both nostrils three times, breathing as evenly as you can. Check in with yourself and notice any subtle shifts that have occurred in how your physical and mental energy is flowing.

Though at first this method may feel awkward, once you learn the moves and get into the flow, it's really very simple. The most important point to keep in mind as you do this nine-part, alternate-nostril breathing is to breathe easily and naturally. Avoid trying to breathe too deeply or forcefully. What works best is to simply relax and merely guide the flow of the breath through the floodgates of your nostrils as you breathe at your own natural rhythm and depth. You may be thinking, "Sure, I can just see myself now, sitting at my desk doing this one. I can just imagine what people will think." Well, keep in mind that once you learn how this works and what it feels like, you can simply guide the breath flow through the power of your visualization and intention alone, without needing the aid of your fingers. This will allow you to do this practice anywhere without anyone having a clue what you're doing.

Many people find that this is a useful technique to have in their pocket, kind of like a polishing cloth to shine up their mind in a spare moment here or there. One of our colleagues does this to get balanced for the day while she's warming up her car in the morning. Others we know will use the nine-part breath to clear their mind like a reset switch between intense meetings with clients. As you get to know yourself and your own natural rhythm, you'll find many useful times to plug this one in.

Now that you have the basics, let's add a second variation. Continue to breathe in the same alternating rhythms and add a simple visualization. In the space in front of you, envision a shining sun

"The Sioux idea of living creatures is that trees, buffalo and man are temporary energy swirls, turbulent patterns... You find that perception registered so many ways in archaic and primitive lore. I say that it is probably the most basic insight into the nature of things, and that our more common, recent Occidental view of the universe as consisting of fixed things is out of the main stream, a deviation from basic human perception."

—Gary Snyder

or a radiant source of the purest light and energy that you can imagine. Imagine the streams of light/energy filling you and flowing through you like a shower of light that washes you clean and clear from the inside out.

As you sit quietly in the presence of this source of light, tune in and remember that you are in essence a living, vital, field of energy. And that the quality of your life and health depends on how successfully you're able to receive, transform; and release energy. As you breathe naturally, imagine or sense yourself as a field of energy and light resting in and infused by a larger ocean of energy and light. Imagine that as you breathe you're able to light up your personal energy field and wash it clean and clear of any darkness or disease.

Holding this image in mind, begin the nine-breath sequence again. As you do the first set of three breaths, imagine that you can inhale this light through your right nostril, and that as you inhale it flows down through the right side of your body. As you exhale through the left nostril now, imagine that this pure, clear stream of light rises up through the left side of your body, totally flushing away or dissolving any tensions in your body or any agitation or disturbances in your mind. Once again, the stream of light and energy flows in through the right nostril filling you with the purifying, vitalizing light, and as you exhale, it streams up and out the left, washing your energy, body and mind, clean and clear. One more time now, *in right . . . pure clear light . . . out left . . . flowing clean and clear. Yes!*

In the second set, inhale and draw the light in through your left nostril, down along the left side of the body and then let it wash up and out through the right side of your body. *Vitalizing, purifying, energizing light in . . . washing the body clean and clear and dissolving any trace of dullness or sluggishness in your mind . . .* good. Once again, breath in through the left, mentally guiding the flow down through the body, then exhale up and out the right, breathing away any fogginess in your mind or any fatigue in your body. And a third time now, energizing and vitalizing, dissolving and releasing.

With the last three breaths, imagine two streams of pure clear

"There is a vitality, a life force, an energy, a quickening, that is translated through you into action, and because there is only one of you in all time, this expression is unique. And if you block it, it will never exist through any other medium and will be lost."

—Martha Graham

light streaming into you from the sun or your special energy source, filling you through both of your nostrils. The two streams of light come down through the left and right sides of your body to meet and flow together. As you exhale, imagine or mentally guide these streams of flowing energy together into a single stream that spirals up through the center of your body, filling you with a deep, bright, clarifying light. In through left and right, down... merging and flowing up together to your crown and out through the mid-point between your two eyebrows... lighting up your body and mind in a deep and quiet way. Allow each breath to bring your mind and body into balance and into flow....

Pause for a moment now and scan through your circuits to check for any subtle shifts in your energy or awareness. Like any new set of physical or mental moves, this may seem complicated at first. The essence of the nine-part breath is simple: in left, out right three times; in right and out left three times; and then in and out through both three times. Once you get the sequence, you can experiment with adding the visualization. As always, remember to smile, relax, and allow the breath to flow naturally without any effort.

"Perceive all conflict as patterns of energy seeking harmonious balance as elements in a whole."

—Dhyani Ywahoo, Etowah Cherokee

Energy Protection

Often we meet people who are afraid of being thrown off balance by other people's energy. They fear that they will be drained by others, or that they will pick up on other people's negativity. Their fearful anxiety, and the tension and toxicity associated with it, is honestly more detrimental than any incoming effects from other people.

In order to protect themselves, some people stay home behind locked doors, carry guns, drive cars with bulletproof glass, or live in gated communities. Others wear surgical masks or rubber gloves when they go out in public. Some people wear talismans, chant prayers, give to charity, or sprinkle holy water in order to protect themselves. Although each of these strategies may well have their appropriate application, each may also subtly reinforce a fearful mindset in relationship to others that would tend to make one even more vulnerable and out of balance.

In his book *Aikido, the Arts of Self-Defense,* the great aikido master, Tohei Sensei, speaks of a different quality of protective energy that we can invite into our awareness, one that connects us with a greater level of balance:

"Remember that you live always under the protection of some mysterious force. This force is nature. Therefore, true self-defense does not stop with defending oneself against others, but strives to make oneself worthy of defense by nature herself. It respects the principles of nature. True practice must be in consonance with the will of nature.... When your mind and your acts become one with nature, then nature will protect you. Fear no enemy; fear only to be separated from the mind of nature. If you are on the right path, nature will protect you ... and you need not fear anything. When an enemy wants to attack you while you are asleep, nature will awaken you. When an airplane has an accident, you will fortunately not be on that plane. Trust nature and do not worry. Leave both your mind and body to nature. Do not recognize friend or foe in your mind. In your heart let there be generosity as large as the sea which accepts both clean and unclean water. Let your mind be as merciful as nature which loves the smallest tree or blade of grass. Let your mind be strong with sincerity that can pierce iron or stone. Repay the forces of nature, work for the good of all and make yourself a person whom nature is pleased to let live. This is the true purpose of training."

The most effective protection field is to fill your heart with love and to let that love illuminate your world. For example, let the radiance of your heart reach out and bless people as you drive to work. Pray that they safely reach their destinations and find the happiness and fulfillment that they are looking for.

Seek to discover the natural radiance of this inner light of love within you. When you find it, then let it shine as a blessing to the world. Because this dimension of your being may be too subtle for you to sense at first, experiment with living as though it is really here within you and around you. Looking out into your world, begin to

"From a hidden place, unite with your enemies from the inside, fill the inner void that makes them swell outwardly and fall out of rhythm; instead of progressing, step by step, they stop and start harshly, out of time with you. Bring yourself back into rhythm within. Find the moment that mates with theirs—like two lovers creating life from the dust. Do this work in secret, so they don't know. This kind of love creates, it doesn't emote."

—Neil Douglas-Klotz (from the Aramaic of Jesus' words "Love your Enemies...")

notice and sense the radiance of everything—how sounds, smells, and lights radiate out through space, how the wind blows, yet is invisible. Notice how sounds travel through space and can be heard but not seen. Warming your hands by a candle or a stove, catch a glimpse of the radiance that shines through all things, especially living beings.

As you move through the world, imagine that you trace a pathway of energy through space and time. Imagine that anyone passing through the field of influence you have generated is drawn more toward balance in their own life. At stoplights, or at crossroads, on mountaintops, in churches, or meeting rooms along the way, pause, breathe, focus, and intentionally generate a large bright field of blessing energy that will refresh or inspire all those who pass through that space for a long, long time to come.

"Be lamps unto yourselves; be your own confidence. Hold to the truth within yourselves..."
—Buddha

"You are the light of the world."
—Jesus

NINE

Balanced in Spirit

There is something in all of us that seeks the spiritual. . . . The spiritual
is inclusive. It is the deepest sense of belonging and participation. We
all participate in the spiritual at all times, whether we know it or not.
There's no place to go to be separated from the spiritual, so perhaps one
might say that the spiritual is that realm of human experience which
religion attempts to connect us to through dogma and practice.
Sometimes it succeeds and sometimes it fails. Religion is a bridge to
the spiritual—but the spiritual lies beyond religion. Unfortunately, in
seeking the spiritual we may become attached to the bridge rather than
crossing over it.

—RACHEL NAOMI REMEN, M.D.

Bedazzled by the dizzying complexity
and breakneck pace of our modern
lives, our wobbly balance has exiled
us from the vitality of staying in touch with the deep core of our wholeness:
a spiritual connectedness with our world. Rushing to and from work, managing our investments, taking care of our kids and our parents, many of us
become distracted. We forget what we're doing and why we're doing it. We
forget where we came from and where we are going. Having wandered far
from our homeland, we may have a gnawing feeling that what is most essential in our lives has slipped away. Yet no matter how far we have wandered,
still it seems that something deep within us is calling us home. As the Sufi
mystics remind us, the main form of spiritual practice is remembrance of the
one reality in which all things have their being.

A story, attributed to Dan Millman, comes to mind about a little girl named Sashi. It reminds us that our search to remember, to find balance in spirit, may begin very young. Not long after the birth of her brother, Sashi began asking her parents if she could be alone with her new baby brother. Her parents were uneasy about this, worried that she might be jealous and might hurt him, so they said, "No." But Sashi was really a loving big sister and showed no signs of jealousy toward her brother. With time her pleas grew more urgent. Finally the parents consented. Sashi was overjoyed. She went into the baby's room, and shut the door. It didn't close all the way and was open a crack—just enough for her curious parents to listen in. What they saw was little Sashi walking quietly over to her brother's crib, putting her face really close to his, and saying, "Baby, tell me what God feels like. I'm afraid that I'm starting to forget."

Taking Refuge

We checked our maps as we crossed the Straits of Juan de Fuca to make the most direct crossing to a tiny bay where we could find shelter from the storm. Braving fairly heavy seas for nearly five hours through eight-foot swells and fifteen-knot winds, we bounded along on our twenty-four-foot sailboat. The three of us were a pale shade of green by the time we reached the southernmost of the San Juan Islands. Rounding the point into a tiny harbor sheltered from the wind, we were feeling extremely wobbly; it was all we could do to keep our balance while we pulled down the sails and dropped anchor for the night. We fired up the stove and brewed a pot of green tea to settle our stomachs. "A toast to safe harbors and shelter from the wind!" We raised our raku cups with a clink of sincere gratitude for our safe passage.

As we sat on deck talking under the stars that night, our conversation turned to our countless fellow travelers—people out in their tiny boats on the heavy seas of their life—who may be dizzy, disoriented, and fearful, feeling out of their league, alone, or in danger, or even blissfully unaware of how at risk they are. It seemed to us that we are all attempting to skillfully navigate our way across the great ocean that spans from birth to death, and that many of us are ill equipped. "Where can people take refuge from the stormy seas in their lives?" we wondered aloud together. On your journey across the changing seas of your life, where do you take refuge and seek balance? In your work? In your family? In your possessions or investments? In your network of support? In your faith in, and communion with, the Mystery, by whatever name you may call it?

The notion of refuge is a universal theme throughout the world's great spiritual traditions. One of the most beautiful references to it is found in the Koran, in this translation by Lex Hixon:

"With each breath may we take refuge in the Living Truth alone, released from coarse arrogance and subtle pride. May every thought and action be intended in the Supremely Holy Name as direct expression of boundless Divine Compassion and Most Tender Love. May the exaltation of endless praise arising spontaneously as the life of endless beings flow consciously toward the Single Source of Being, Source of the intricate evolution of endless worlds. May we be guided through every experience along the Direct Path of Love that leads from the Human Heart into the Most Sublime Source of Love."

A survey of the world's spiritual traditions reveals a common grounding in a trinity of refuges: First, is the living example of great teachers. Second, is the inspired body of spiritual teachings that gives practical principles, techniques, and advice on how to live a truly righteous and balanced life. And third is the refuge found in fellowship in the spiritual community of kindred souls who walk along the path with you and who are a source of companionship and support along the way. The presence, or absence, of any of these three refuges has much to do with your success in finding balance in your life. With this in mind, ask yourself,

- How have the spiritual beliefs and traditions you encountered growing up contributed to the quality of balance in your life?

- Who are the people—living or historical, whom you hold as

"We are not human beings having a spiritual experience. We are spiritual beings having a human experience."

—Pierre Teilhard de Chardin

"If for a moment we make way with our petty selves, wish no ill to anyone, apprehend no ill, cease to be but as a crystal which reflects a ray—what shall we not reflect! What a universe will appear crystallized and radiant around us!"

—Henry David Thoreau

the most inspiring spiritual role models or mentors? What qualities lead you to have faith in or devotion toward these people?

- What wisdom traditions speak most deeply to your soul and nourish you spiritually? Where do you find the most reliable, relevant, practical guidance and inspiration for living your life in a wise, compassionate, and balanced way? What principles or precepts guide your life, and what practices keep you in tune with the larger whole?

- Who are the members of your circle of spiritual friends—those who live with the integrity and values that you feel most in tune with, who are most supportive of the ideals you aspire to hold, who inspire you to stay true to a path worth walking?

- What other sources of spiritual inspiration do you rely on?

Reflecting upon and answering these questions may be the cause of either much heartfelt gratitude or grief. Many of us have busied ourselves with so many other pursuits that these supportive influences have been severely neglected, and their balancing presence is sorely lacking. If this is true for you, it would be a wise investment of time and energy to seek out or rebuild these connections.

We live at a time when the spiritual fabric of our society has come unraveled, leaving many of us looking for a way to put our piece of it back together. Many of us really didn't get much of a spiritual education growing up and now aren't sure how to balance our spiritual inclinations with the rest of our life. In many of our lives, spirituality is found more through communion with nature, in the arts, or in love for family, than in traditional religious institutions or weekly services. You may be one of those who grew up in a spiritual tradition but never really felt spiritually nourished by your religious upbringing, or perhaps you were at some point deeply disturbed by the incongruencies you encountered in the name of the religion you were raised in. Whatever the reason, you may feel uneasy when it comes to stepping out of your comfort zone to explore unfamiliar spiritual paths.

"Everyone who is seriously involved in the pursuit of science becomes convinced that a Spirit is manifest in the Laws of the Universe—a Spirit vastly superior to that of man, and one in the face of which we, with our modest powers, must feel humble."
—Albert Einstein

"There are a thousand ways to kneel and kiss the ground!" said Rumi, the great mystic poet, and now that is more true than ever before. The intensity of spiritual yearning of our time is matched by a sometimes dizzying diversity of approaches to fulfill it. In our search for balance, we may somewhat timidly step out of our comfort zone to explore old traditions that are new and unfamiliar to us. Stepping out across these boundaries generates an energy that can be interpreted as fear or excitement, or some blend of the two. On any given weekend you might go hear a sermon, or celebrate Mass at a parish different from your own. You might teach Sunday school or attend a Bible study class. A friend might invite you to a Jewish Renewal Shabbat meditation or to go Sufi dancing. You may be drawn to a temple or church where people worship in a language different than your own, where they may sit in pews, on cushions, or on folding chairs. You may sign up for a meditation retreat at a Buddhist center, yoga ashram, Jewish community center, or a Christian abbey; attend a symposium with teachers from diverse faiths; or attend services at a Unity church, a Church of Religious Science, a Unitarian Universalist Church, or Baha'i temple. Perhaps you'll study medicine ways with a Huichol or Siberian shaman, or participate in a sweat lodge prayer and purification ceremony with a Native American elder, or engage in one of countless other paths of practice. Along the way, perhaps you'll visit one of the growing number of spiritual bookstores. Given the number of options to choose from, it is easy at times to feel confused or overwhelmed. In search of balance and spiritual renewal, you may simply choose to putter in your garden, talk deeply with your spouse or friends, really play with the kids, be blissfully alone for a day, go for a walk in the mountains, volunteer at a senior center, or meditate in the simplicity of your own home.

No matter what you choose, be aware that, until you have found spiritual peace, you will never know true balance. Whatever path or paths you take up the mountain of Spirit will be learningful. If you do venture out in unfamiliar ways, go slowly, mindfully, and watch the signs. Don't rush. Walking in balance, feel the earth at

"And I have felt a presence that disturbs me with the joy of elevated thoughts; a sense sublime of something far more deeply interfused, whose dwelling is the light of setting suns, and the round ocean and the living air, and the blue sky; and in the mind of man; a motion and a spirit that impels all thinking things, all objects of all thought, and rolls through all things."

—**William Wordsworth**

"Our discovery of God is, in a way, God's discovery of us. We know Him in so far as we are known by Him, and our contemplation of Him is a participation of his contemplation of Himself. We become contemplatives when God discovers Himself in us. At that moment, the point of our contact with Him opens out and we pass through the center of our souls and enter eternity."

—**Thomas Merton**

your feet. Let your heart and mind stay open to seek the source of the light behind the many lampshades you see. Friendships with fellow travelers are precious; they can go deep and last a lifetime. Ask many questions. Celebrate the humanity, sincerity, and aspirations that you share. Let your heart be inspired and uplifted through prayer, chant, and rituals. Find unity in sharing sweet silence. As you learn from and appreciate diversity, balance differences with searching for common ground. Take courage in knowing that you can always return to the familiar paths, more mature in your wisdom, enriched by your explorations, and having discovered some new ways to "kneel and kiss the ground."

If you find that you are the type who is easily confused or bewildered by exploring many paths or studying with many teachers, it may be wise to simplify your spiritual pursuits. If diversity overwhelms you, do research until you find a path that is spiritually satisfying for you, and then through study, practice, and contemplation, drill that well deep until you come to the heart of balance.

If you are by nature a weaver and synthesizer, your temperament may better suit you to seek inspiration from study and practice with a diversity of different traditions. Seek to find the common heart and core around which they come together and appreciate how each contributes to deepening your wisdom and love and strengthening your faith. If you are a mature practitioner with a clear sense of your path and tradition, there is little to fear and much to gain through encounters with other traditions. These will likely serve to clarify and deepen your faith and insight. Keep an open heart, an open mind, and seek for a path that works for you.

Where to Begin

The spiritual journey toward balance begins with the first step: opening your heart to a sincere wish or prayer to renew the spiritual vitality of your life. Because it truly is a responsive universe, if you are sincere and keep your heart, mind, and eyes open, you will likely begin to see signs that point you toward your next step.

On your quest for wholeness, seek the wise council of those whom you respect or who inspire you with their authenticity and spiritual integrity. Ask them what paths they have taken, what churches, synagogues, or temples they are nourished by. Ask them what preachers or teachers they have found who live with the greatest integrity and spiritual vitality, and who offer the most practical wisdom, inspiration, teaching, and guidance. Ask what books, translations of scripture, and inspiring biographies have most deeply touched and inspired them in their lives. Seek out the company of well-grounded, sincere, and credible fellow seekers. If possible, meet once a week, or at least once a month with a circle of fellow seekers to share your discoveries and to discuss your questions.

As your search continues, remember that, in essence, you already have what you are looking for. The spiritual path is one of remembering the true depth of your wholeness. It is not about deserving, earning, or acquiring something you don't already have. Some say, "God loves you just as you are." Others express it as "All beings have the seed of enlightenment or full awakening within them," or "There is nothing that exists outside of God." How could you ever be separate from the wholeness that you are?

"When you search for the Beloved,
It is the intensity of the longing that does all the work.
Look at me and you will see a slave of that intensity!"
—Kabir

Perils of the Path

"How do you know your mother is your mother?" No, this is not a Zen *koan*. This was Joel's high school physics assignment on his first day of high school. Joel's teacher was an intense, brilliant scholar and social activist who had also at one time in his life been a Jesuit monk. "Write a paper," he said, "showing me your reasoning and proofs for your assumption that your mother is truly your mother. Question your assumptions about reality. How do you really know what to believe and where to put your faith?" "In some ways," Joel reflects, "I feel like I am still working on this homework assignment, and over the past twenty-five years it has helped me to continually uncover and examine my unchecked assumptions."

In search of balance through spiritual pursuits, there are many

"God is at home... It is we who have gone out for a walk."
—Meister Eckhart

perils of the path. Keep your eyes open and your discerning wisdom keen. There are teachers and traditions that are rare and precious beyond belief. If you are fortunate enough to be able to spend time with them, your life will be truly enriched. And, there are teachers and traditions that, quite honestly, we don't send people to. We find the practical advice from the Buddha very helpful:

"Do not believe in what you have heard; do not believe in the traditions because they have been handed down for generations; do not believe in anything because it is rumored or spoken by many; do not believe merely because a written statement of some old sage is produced; do not believe in conjectures; do not believe in as truth that to which you have become attached by habit; do not believe merely the authority of teachers and elders. After observation and analysis, when it agrees with reason and is conducive to the good and gain of one and all, then accept it, practice it, and live up to it."

How do you know if you are pursuing an authentic spiritual path, or if you have met a good teacher? If you are looking for a balanced approach, watch for: impeccable ethical and moral integrity; service to others; compassion; respect for discipline; personal accountability of both leaders and community members; faith; embodiment; groundedness; respect; joyfulness; fellowship with, or at least tolerance for, people of different faiths; an inspiring lineage of practitioners whose lives have been enriched; a community of kindred souls that inspires your respect and admiration; love; celebration; humanity; respect for silence as well as questions; an honoring of the mythical and the mystical; a path of clear reasoning that welcomes debate; a balance of prayer, contemplation, study, and service in practice; a reverance for the Mystery, by whatever name.

Avoid extremes. While discipline is important, a well-grounded, gradual, and steady approach to practice is more likely to develop balance than an overly austere or intense spiritual fast track. The diversity of spiritual paths is designed to fulfill the spiritual maturing of individuals of different temperaments. For example, if you tend to be overly indulgent, a path that offers some discipline and austerity can be helpful. If you tend to be a "control freak" or rigid

"The Light is One Though the lamps be many."

—**Anonymous**

"There comes a time in the spiritual journey when you start making choices from a very different place ... And if a choice lines up so that it supports truth, health, happiness, wisdom, and love, it's the right choice."

—**Angeles Arrien**

in your ways, a path with too much austerity or rigorous discipline may just add to your imbalance.

Spiritual communities, though potential havens, can also become escapes for the socially challenged. And teachers from other cultures, though masters in their spiritual disciplines, may lack the experience they need within their new culture to give realistic council to their students—and may even lose their own balance as they encounter the enticements of the West.

We wholeheartedly encourage you to keep your eyes wide open. Open-minded skepticism will help you to find a healthy balance between over-critical cynicism that may miss the real thing, and gullible naïveté that is easily duped into signing up for misleading or dangerous pursuits. Over the years, in search of a deeper understanding, our work, travels, and research have led us to encounter many different spiritual paths. Having also encountered many of the perils of the path—and having worked clinically with some of the casualties—we offer the following list of cautionary guidelines to check out before you "sign up" with a spiritual teacher or group. Though it is possible that, you may find some of the following warning signs on an authentic path, they are often associated with less trustworthy situations. It is always wise to observe the integrity of people's behavior carefully, and ask yourself these three essential questions:

- Does what I hear make sense to me?
- Does it conform to the golden rule?
- What is the intention? Is it to harm or to help? Is it for limited self-interest—"self"-improvement—or service for the good of the whole and benefit to many for generations to come?

If you are looking for balance on the spiritual path, beware if you encounter any of the following "red flags":

- teachers or circles of practitioners on your journey who are out of integrity, or who don't practice what they preach

"Whoever deeply searches out the truth and will not be deceived by paths untrue, shall turn unto himself his inward gaze, shall bring his wandering thoughts in circle home and teach his heart that what it seeks abroad, it holds in its own treasure chests within."

—**Boethius**
(A.D. 480-524)

The Four Reliances:
"First, rely on the
spirit and meaning of
the teachings, not on
the words;
Second, rely on the
teachings, not on the
personality of the
teacher;
Third, rely on real
wisdom, not superficial
interpretation;
And fourth, rely on the
essence of your pure
Wisdom Mind, not on
judgmental
perceptions."
—Buddhist teaching

- scenes where questions are not welcomed or answered in straightforward ways, or where raising concerns about conduct or ethical violations is frowned upon—especially if you are told you are being too judgmental when you do raise honest concerns

- anyone who claims that they can give "it" to you, especially for a price

- anyone who claims to be the only teacher or path that can deliver the goods

- if the price of admission excludes people who are truly sincere

- if you are expected to purchase lots of expensive merchandise or paraphernalia to get on board

- slick, extravagant trappings or heavily marketed, empire-building enterprises

- discrimination or attempts to turn your heart against others

- hidden agendas

- fanatical, narrow-minded sects

- a heavily authoritarian, paternalistic, sexist, or militaristic scene

- practices that work with intense energy manipulation or heavy breathing practices without having first established a strong foundation in ethics and personal grounding

- teachers, paths, or seminars that seem ungrounded, make outrageous claims, use coercion tactics, or hustle you to get others to sign up

Be discerning if you encounter people who seem to display unusual or extraordinary powers. People easily confuse psychic sensitivity with spiritual maturity, deluding themselves and others. Channeling, clairvoyance, or other entertaining displays may have little to do with anything spiritual. If teachers claim to be channeling disembodied beings, enjoy the show, and see if there are any messages of value to you. When in doubt use common sense and, if you stay around, carefully observe the ethical integrity and behavior of your traveling companions. Because some teachers misrepresent themselves, claiming spiritual authorizations, realizations, or backgrounds that are downright lies, you may want to check references or question their authenticity. If the biography of a spiritual teacher heavily emphasizes their attainments in past lives (maybe, but who knows?) we suggest that you stay focused on the integrity of the one you can see sitting in front of you.

In Search of Wholeness

We often hear people say that their wholeness as a human being is not welcome at work, and they are expected to leave their values, feelings, spiritual orientations, and even physical needs at home. These comments are as common from executives as from blue collar workers. To ignore or deny any of our many dimensions is foolish, dangerous, and unfortunately quite common in the institutions of our workaday world. What we ignore or disown we tend to waste or destroy.

As living whole systems, we are endowed with miraculous capacities for sensory discovery of our world, creative physical movement and communication, a broad bandwidth of emotions, an inconceivable capability for creative imagination, intelligence, and thinking, and a nervous system with an extraordinary ability for intuitive discernment of systems dynamics at a far greater breadth and depth than mere thinking or ordinary perception can ascertain.

At our heart and core, inseparable from the rest, is a quality of radiant and receptive presence—a creative and compassionate intelligence that defies description. In the English language we regard this as "consciousness" in the psychological sense, or "Spirit," the animating force within all things, if we assume a more spiritual view. Being universal in proportions, it transcends the narrow confines of our personal identity. To say that there is no place for spirit,

"Spirit... is the point of human transcendence; it is the point where the human is open to the Divine, that is, to the infinite and the eternal. It is also the point where human beings communicate. At that point of the Spirit we are all open to one another."
—**Father Bede Griffiths**

or consciousness, in a relationship or business is as foolish as saying there is no place for our body or mind. Let's get real. We are multi-dimensional human beings—all other arenas of human endeavor will be handicapped without drawing inspiration from the full spectrum of our humanity.

The truth is that we of course bring our spirituality everywhere we go, we just don't think of it in those terms. In his dissertation, "Spirituality and Transformational Leadership in Secular Settings," Dr. Stephen E. Jacobsen, a former business entrepreneur and now ordained minister, observed that though leaders in business had a difficult time clearly defining "spirituality," they still believed and spoke strongly about its vital importance in forming the values, ethics, and beliefs that they brought to work. This diverse group of business leaders of different genders, backgrounds, organizational settings, and locations shared a common belief that spirituality is at the heart of their business activity. They regarded spirituality as a means of integrating self and the world, and affirmed that life is a seamless whole system without boundaries between what is "spiritual" and what is "secular."

In Good Company: The Presence of Spirit At Work

One way to understand how the sacred reality of Spirit manifests in our daily lives is to invite a dialogue with people you work with to inquire, "When, or how, do we glimpse Spirit at work?" Responses we have heard include:

- in moments of appreciation, caring, kindness, and compassion
- in moments of deep listening, or in shared silence
- in moments of clarity, when we glimpse our place in the "big picture"

"While not everyone is religious, everyone is spiritual, because we are composed of mind, body, and spirit. Therefore, our spirit is already in the workplace, because our minds and bodies are. Spiritual principles are universal; they can and should be applied everywhere. Treating people the way you want to be treated is a simple yet profound spiritual principle, one which led to the abolition of one of the worst labor practices in history—slavery."

—Laurie Beth Jones, author of Jesus, CEO

- in moments of wonder, when synchronicities converge to confirm our intuition with a "yes!"

- in moments when we know to our core that we belong here

- in moments of creative collaboration, when we join forces to create a better world

- in mindful moments, when we are wholeheartedly present

- in moments of deep recognition of each other and of ourselves

- in moments of dialogue, when the deep listening of a group reveals a glimpse of truth larger than one person can hold

- in moments of forgiveness, when we let go of the past and focus on creating our shared future

- in moments of commitment, when our love and action blend into one

A growing interest in spirituality in the workplace is evident in recent polls and articles in *Industry Week, Business Week, Journal of the American Medical Association, Fortune, Newsweek, New Leaders,* the *New York Times, Leaders,* and the recent *International Workplace Values Survey,* which involved 1,200 people in eighteen countries around the world. Each year it seems that there are more major conferences for leaders in business that have a specific focus on integrating more soul or spirit into business. Confirming these trends, the Institute for the Future recently launched a project to document the increasingly important role of spirituality in business.

To get a feeling for the findings of the recent polls on how people find balance through spirituality, imagine yourself at work or at a work-related convention. See yourself surrounded by all of your coworkers, partners, customers, and suppliers. As you look around at all these people, keep in mind that the polls say two out of three of these people have a deep yearning for spiritual growth. Fifty percent of us have experienced a personal transformation in recent years. Eighty percent of us believe in God, more than two out of three of us (69 percent) believe in the presence of angels, and three

"... people living a practical life, who are very unselfish, very dedicated, probably experience God deeply without knowing it or seeing it. Because they go out of themselves and into the world around them in the people they are serving, they encounter this absolute, this One, though they may not name it explicitly that way. I believe that religious experience is far more common than people imagine it., They think only monks and nuns have it, but I think everybody is open to it in some way and most people get glimpses of it."

—Father Bede Griffiths

out of four of us believe that unexplainable miracles are a reality in our lives. Ninety percent of us reach out to the Sacred through prayer or meditation, with 57 percent of us praying daily.

There is considerable evidence suggesting that having a spiritual orientation toward life offers benefits for individuals and businesses as well. If you need more incentive for seeking balance through spiritual development, keep in mind that the growing body of research on health and high-level human performance shows that people who have cultivated a greater sense of their wholeness are more stress-resilient, creative, and productive. After five years of study in many leading corporations, Stanford University's pioneering Corporate Health Program, funded by the Rockefeller Foundation, concluded that a spiritual orientation toward life is one of five characteristics that are the basis for optimal health. The World Workplace Values Survey tells us that interest in spiritual development ranks ahead of physical development in its importance to people in business, which should lead us to rethink the facilities and perks that will best reward our staff. Clinical studies indicate that people who are sick are 75 percent more likely to become better if they have a spiritual view of life. And in alcohol recovery treatment, a "spiritual change" in a person is associated with a permanent sobriety rate of 93 percent.

If you take these thoughts to heart you may discover that you are more than the story you've been telling yourself. Much more. The reality of your soulfulness is here at work or play in every moment: it is here as the silence amid sounds and as the stillness within ceaseless motion; as the clarity within confusion, and the knowingness here at the heart of your unknowing. Each day the tides of hope and fear, beauty and pain, breakthroughs and breakdowns of life and work break our hearts and minds open and help us to wake up and remember who we really are.

For some of us, findings such as these inspire our faith that spirit is alive in our daily lives, even if we seldom discuss it. These findings are useful to seed conversations with your family, friends, and coworkers about the beliefs and core values that are truly at the heart of our lives. As more and more people are seeking for balance in their

> *"In the spacious mirror of reflective consciousness we begin to catch glimpses of the unity of the interwoven fabric of the cosmos and our intimate participation within the living web of existence. No longer is reality broken into relativistic islands of pieces. If only for a brief moment at a time, existence is glimpsed and known as a seamless totality. To explore our gradual awakening to the aliveness and unity of the universe… awakens the intuition that a living presence permeates the universe."*
>
> —**Duane Elgin**

lives, it seems that no relationship, family, business, or organization can afford to disregard or deplete the vitality and creative spirit of its people.

When I Am in Balance . . .

In our research for this book, a teacher of ours, Rabbi Ted Falcon, pointed out to us a Hebrew prayer about balance that can be used as a meditation. It goes, *"shiviti Adonai l'negdi tamid,"* (Psalm 16:8). One way of translating this ancient formula into English is, "When I am in balance, God is before me always." Taken to heart, this formula can be the seed of a profound contemplation on balance that can accompany you into every activity of your life. Reciting this prayer, in English or in Hebrew, let your mind grow more calm, clear, and balanced. Held in the same light, reciting the Rosary, the Lord's Prayer, or the *shema* prayer, or chanting a Sufi *zikr* or the mantra *Om Mani Pedme Hung,* will likely offer similar results. Sitting quietly, resting in the flow of your breathing, allow your recitation to carry you more and more deeply into a balanced, radiant peace. Looking out from deep within, letting your eyes truly be windows for your soul, behold the world as sacred and alive with spirit. Sitting, walking, driving, talking, alone or with others, allow your sense of inner balance to deepen and behold the mystery, sacred majesty, and presence of the world's radiance shining deep within and around you.

Spirit at the Threshold

In most traditional cultures of our world, the day begins and ends with some time of meditation, prayer, worship, or communion and thanksgiving that affirms a life of balance in relation to the larger whole. For those of us who make the time for such attunement on a daily basis, life takes on a different tone as we establish a reference point of deep balance to access throughout the turbulence of the day. Joel remembers witnessing his grandfather's approach to balance:

"Balance means responding to criticism and to applause in the same ways—not to be controlled by either."

—The Baal Shem Tov

"Rabbi Zusya used to say: "My mother Mirl, peace be with her, did not pray from the book, because she could not read. All she knew was how to say the blessings. But wherever she said the blessing in the morning, in that place the radiance of the Divine Presence rested the livelong day."

—Martin Buber

"Each morning before work, my grandfather, who was Jewish, would take time with his prayer book and skull cap to *davin*—say his prayers. I think he started this on a daily basis after his own father died. While he was praying, I'd often play in the kitchen at dawn with the sun streaming through the windows as it rose majestically over the Cascade Mountains to the east of our home. When he'd finish, we'd talk and have breakfast together, often oatmeal, or eggs and toast, and then he'd set out with his pickup truck to his shop and junkyard. Then again in the evening before bed, Gramps would read the Psalms and take some time in prayer. Though he never pressured me to follow in his example, in his wise and gentle way Gramps succeeded in transmitting an important message through his disciplined, reverent example: there is a larger reality worthy of my reverent supplication, and making time to commune with it on a daily basis is a wise way to begin and end each day.

"Years later, sitting on his deathbed together as we weathered the last raging storms of his life, we took refuge in his faith and the confidence that he had indeed lived a good life. When I first arrived at the hospital, he looked at me, saying in a serious tone, 'Son, something is really wrong, and I think I'm gonna die. And I'm just not sure what to do.' After being with Gramps in the hospital more than a dozen times before, I took his tone to heart. 'Well, I'll be here with you and we'll make this journey together, at least as far as I can go with you. And you know, you just can't do it wrong.' For days, his condition worsened until, writhing and moaning in pain, Gramps started pulling out his intravenous tubes. He seemed like a woman ten months pregnant—trying to give birth to himself. Weak and exhausted, he finally drifted off to sleep resting in my lap, and I sat with him on his bed. A deep quiet and peace seemed to radiate from his frail body, so unlike the unbearable turbulence and struggle of the previous three days.

"Then after about a half hour, Gramps opened his eyes peacefully. He looked transformed, renewed, and refreshed with a clear gaze like a young child waking from a peaceful nap. His eyes were deep and steady, and he seemed to gaze out from a clear, deep, loving pool. His presence was radiantly peaceful and I felt like I was looking into the eyes of a saint. 'Son,' he said, bemused and with a tone of discovery, 'My whole life has been a crazy *mashugana* dream!' (*mashugana* is Yiddish for "crazy"). Surprised by Gramps' radical transformation, I laughed, and replied, 'It took you eighty-nine years to figure that out, old man!' 'Yeah, I guess so!' he chuckled as he continued, 'My whole life has been a crazy dream, and ya know what?' 'What?' I leaned closer. 'I'm going to dream a happier dream next time!' he said. And then, with a twinkle in his eye of absolute wonder and amazement, he explained how he had just died and come back, and died and come back again and again, and that he was not afraid to die now and felt he knew the way.

Then looking around the room, he said, 'You know, son, I know there is only you and me here in this room, but I've got to tell you there are so many others here with me. My ma, and my dad, and Molly, and all my brothers and sisters [who had all been "dead" for many years]. They're all here with me and I can see them so clearly. Can you see them too?' I absolutely believed what he was saying, and looked hopefully around the room. With some disappointment I had to admit that I was unable to discern any angelic presences, 'No, I can't see them,' I admitted. 'But I absolutely believe that you are close enough to the threshold and that the door is open wide enough for you that you can see through.'

The impact of Gramps' close encounter had a profound effect. After three days of unbearable pain, his agony vanished, his fear evaporated, and the radiance of his peacefulness and joyfulness became a blessing for all who entered the room. Everyone who came into his presence left feeling more buoyant and balanced. The doctors were amazed at his transformation and thought he actually might live, but it became clear that his body was beyond repair. Two days later, on the last Sabbath of his life, and too weak to say any formal prayers, I played some Jewish music for him. He began to hum along. 'Gramps, do you know any Jewish songs?' I asked. He laughed and said, 'Oh sure I do. I know lots of songs,' and then he started singing. 'On Friday afternoon,' he began in Yiddish, and

> "The clear bead at the center changes everything.
> There are no edges to my loving now.
> I've heard it said there's a window that opens from one mind to another,
> but if there's no wall, there's no need for fitting the window, or the latch."
>
> —Mevlana Jelaluddin Rumi

then translated to English, 'We clean the whole house and everything is clear, bright, and beautiful, and when the Sabbath begins the whole house is happy!' he sang. 'Yeah, it goes just like that,' he laughed. As death approached, his peace, love, and joy deepened. The intense suffering and turbulence of the days before never returned. His strength and his breath gradually waned. At dawn on Memorial Day, his breath became more and more subtle until at last only his radiant smile remained. As the sun rose over Mount Rainier to the east and flooded the room, Michelle and I sat quietly and peacefully in meditation and prayer. What a beautiful end to Gramps' 'crazy *mashugana* dream,' and perhaps what a beautiful beginning to his next one!"

> *"It is as if God planted a great big kiss in the middle of our spirit and all the wounds, doubts, and guilt feelings were all healed at the same moment. The experience of being loved by the Ultimate Mystery banishes every fear."*
>
> **—Father Thomas Keating**

Grace: The Balance That Brings Tears to your Eyes

Can you remember those precious moments in your life when you felt so ecstatically whole and in balance that it brought tears to your eyes? The great poet Kabir says, "between the conscious and unconscious, the mind has put up a swing; all earth creatures, even supernovas, sway between these two trees, and it never winds down. Angels, animals, humans, insects by the million, also the wheeling sun and moon; ages go by, and it goes on. Everything is swinging: heaven, earth, water, fire, and the Secret One is slowly growing a body. Kabir saw this for fifteen seconds, and it made him a servant for life."

At rare and precious times in each of our lives, we catch a glimpse of the exquisite balance we call "grace." If you are an athlete, you might describe this experience as being in "The Zone." For others, such an event is regarded as a "peak experience." And for those with a more spiritual orientation, such rapturous moments of unity and wholeness may be reverently regarded as "moments of grace" or as "spontaneous communion with the sacred Source"—by whatever name you call it. These are times when balance is realized in its fullness across all dimensions of our being.

Kabir saw this for fifteen seconds, and each of us in our own ways—in the rare and precious moments in our lives—have also caught a glimpse of unity and wholeness beyond description. In one of our favorite accounts, Mary Austin remembers, "I must have been five or six when this experience happened to me. It was a summer morning, and the child I was had walked down through the orchard alone and come out on the brow of a sloping hill where there were grass and a wind blowing and one tall tree reaching into the infinite immensities of blueness. Quite suddenly, after a moment of quietness there, earth and sky and tree and wind-blown grass and the child in the midst of them came alive together with a pulsating light of consciousness. To this day I can recall the swift inclusive awareness of each for the whole—I in them and they in me and all of us enclosed in a warm, lucent bubble of livingness. . . .

"I remember the child looking everywhere for the source of this happy wonder and at last she questioned: 'God?' because that was the only awesome word she knew. And then, deep inside, like the murmurous ring of a bell, she heard the answer, 'God, God.' "

Can you remember a time when your tiny bubble of Self cracked open, dissolved, or expanded, when your inner and outer worlds touched, communicated, and unified? Can you remember the exquisite moments of love, peace, and wholeness when boundaries dissolved, and you beheld yourself and your world as radiant and alive with a sacred Presence?

- What stands out to you when you recall them?

- What qualities of being were most alive for you then?

- What inner or outer factors seem to make you receptive to this sublime balance?

- What inner or outer factors seem to reduce your availability to such grace?

- How have these timeless moments lived on for you or influenced how you have chosen to live your life?

- How did those experiences influence how you relate to other people or other living creatures?

". . . I was taking a walk in the garden by myself, I felt that a golden spirit sprang up from the ground. . . my mind and body turned into light. I was able to understand the whispering of the birds, and was clearly aware of the mind of God. . . the spirit of loving protection for all beings. Endless tears of joy streamed down my cheeks. Since that time I have grown to feel that the whole earth is my house. . . . The training. . . is to take in God's love, which correctly produces, protects and cultivates all things in Nature and assimilate and unite it in our own mind and body."

— Morihei Ueshiba, O'Sensei

Grace is found in both intense peace and activity. Polls tell us that fully one-third of us—your friends, family and coworkers—have had a profound or life-altering religious or mystical experience. In reality, this unnamable mystery is as close to us as water is to waves. Even if we don't talk about it, even if we don't have the vocabulary to discuss it, there have been moments in most of our lives when, for a timeless moment, the fabric of the story we tell ourselves dropped away to reveal that, in truth, we are both particle and wave, wave and ocean. As Saul demonstrated on the road to Damascus, and as countless others have experienced giving birth, playing sports, in nature, in love, or driving down the road on the way to work, we are utterly unable to protect ourselves from spontaneous moments of grace.

Often when we lecture on this topic, we will sometimes conduct an informal poll. "How many of you have experienced moments of grace when you were alone?" we'll ask. "How many have touched or shared such a moment with another person? With an animal? How many have experienced such exquisite balance in a moment of safety or peace? How many in moments of danger or intensity? How many of you have experienced a moment of profound balance while in nature? How many while at work? How many when you were very young? And how many when you were older?" Our poll has made it crystal clear that any time, any place, with the next step, or the next breath, we may tumble out of the chaos and confusion into the spiritual balance of grace.

In these precious and timeless moments, it is as though a key is turned, unlocking, and opening a quality of being and experience that is both profoundly familiar and wondrously liberating. Something inside of us releases, lets go, and says yes in its belonging to the Mystery. These moments of grace have much to teach us about the true nature of balance. We learn about living more effortlessly, with a sense of flow and a joy that at times may be profoundly peaceful, though often intense beyond imagination. What emerges is an exhilarating sense that whatever this larger reality is, it is here in its wholeness with us in every moment.

"The man who comes back through the door in the wall will never be quite the same as that man who went out. He will be wiser, but less cocksure, happier but less self-satisfied, humbler in acknowledging his ignorance, yet better equipped to understand the relationship of words to things, of systematic reasoning to the unfathomable Mystery which it tries forever vainly to comprehend."

—Aldous Huxley

What is unusual is not these moments of grace themselves—we are multidimensional beings, who live mostly unaware of the totality of ourselves. What is unusual is that we seem to live in a culture that, until recently, has been very shy about speaking openly of experiences that lie beyond the stifling confines of our status quo reality. Yet as the stress and pressures in our busy lives increase, and more and more people are feeling unbalanced, in ill health, or out of control, and as we watch our children and parents growing older, these instances are signposts reminding us of our deep belonging and the sense of profound inner peace that is only a breath away.

Moments of grace deepen our faith that it truly is possible to live in balance with the spirit of wholeness that is the source of all life. And they strengthen our aspiration to live our lives in a way that is likely to bring more balance into our turbulent world. As Brother David Steindl-Rast reminds us, "To those among us who have entered into this mystery through faith it need not be explained; to others it cannot be explained. . . . But to the extent to which we have given room in our hearts to gratitude, we all have a share in this reality, by whatever name we may call it. . . . All that matters is that we enter into that passage of gratitude and sacrifice, the passage which leads us to integrity within ourselves, to concord with one another, and to union with the very Source of Life."

When we touch times of profound balance we are given a glimpse of who and how we are at the core of our being. Even if only glimpsed for a few seconds, they may guide and inspire a lifetime that seeks to bring wholeness alive. "Everything is swinging: heaven, earth, water, fire, and the secret one is slowly growing a body." When we find ourselves in balance and see this, like Kabir, it makes us a servant for life.

Remembering to Remember!

On the spiritual path there are three main steps to remember:

1. You never follow a spiritual path alone. Spiritual practice, by definition, is a path of deep relationships within the

"Oh Thou Who art the Perfection of Love, Harmony, and Beauty, The Lord of heaven and earth, Open our hearts that we may hear Thy voice which constantly cometh from within. Disclose to us Thy Divine Light, which is hidden in our souls, that we may know and understand life better. Most Merciful and Compassionate God, give us Thy great Goodness; Teach us Thy loving Forgiveness; Raise us above the distinctions and differences that divide men; Send us the peace of Thy Divine Spirit, And unite us all in Thy Perfect Being. Amen."

—The Khatum prayer of Hazrat Inayat Khan

wholeness of your life. Begin each day, or even each activity, by pausing to remember a sense of belonging and connectedness, or by affirming your heartfelt relationships to the mentors, spiritual principles, and circle of spiritual friends who support you along the way.

2. Within this context of deep supportive relationships, do whatever you do wholeheartedly, with as much mindful, loving presence as you possibly can. Hold the intent or prayer that through your actions, your words, even your thoughts, you will move toward a greater balance and contribute to greater harmony in the world.

3. Reaffirm and celebrate your connection to all beings, and dedicate or share the potency generated through your actions. Imagine that as you breathe, you can gather the vital charge of all your good deeds into your heart, and convey it heart to heart to those you love, and to all living beings. Imagine streams of light or love flowing from your heart to the hearts of others. Or let it be like the light of a candle that is effortlessly reflected in the heart-jewels of countless beings in the vast constellation of your relationships. Let your love light up the lives of all who share your life. Let this light shine as an offering to the Source of All the Light in your life that it may continue to guide you and all others in a beautifully balanced way.

Taken to heart, this simple framework will help you to weave your spiritual journey deep into the fabric of your daily life. Upon awakening, remember step one. During the day, recall step two. At the end of the day, take step three. At the beginning of a session of prayer or meditation, or at the beginning of a meeting or presentation, initiate step one. As you continue, remember step two. As you conclude and rejoice in your accomplishments, energize step three. Practiced in this way, a deeper core of balance will surely come alive through your life, no matter what else you do.

Expanding the Circle of Balance: Home, Play, Work, and World

"The first day or so we all pointed to our countries. The third or fourth day we were pointing to our continents. By the fifth day we were aware of only one earth."

—SULTAN BIN SULMAN AL-SAUD,
SAUDI ARABIAN ASTRONAUT

NOW THAT WE HAVE GOTTEN THE basics of inner balance, it's time to expand the scope of our focus to include the world outside our individual selves, because, obviously, our interactions with others can either enhance or diminish the sense of wholeness we're seeking to cultivate. Though there are many different dimensions of relationship—parent-child; student-teacher; romantic and life partnerships; friends; siblings; playmates; and community relationships, to name a few—our intention is to focus on the aspects of balance that are common to all relationships. We'll be sharing ideas and methods that apply equally to people you know as well as people you don't know, and also present some specific guidelines for raising the balance quotient in some of your special relationships.

In the second part of this section, we'll examine the challenge of bringing our workaday world into greater balance with the rest of our lives. We'll start by appreciating the scope of the dilemma and then survey a variety of creative solutions for restoring life/work balance.

⑥

TEN

All My Relations

When we seek for connection, we restore the world to wholeness.
Our seemingly separate lives become meaningful as we discover how
truly necessary we are to each other.

—MARGARET WHEATLEY

At its essence, to be in balance means to be a whole person in relationship. That's because life is relationships—relationships between the many subtle fields and flows of energy that weave the fabric of our being; relationships with other people and with other living beings; relationships between ourselves and the rest of the universe. If you look deeply into any living being, a universe of intricate interrelationships will be revealed. Life is *all* about relationships.

Balance in relationships can mean many things: the balance of giving and receiving; of speaking and listening; of being alone and being together; the balance realized by resolving tensions or extending love and caring. As paradoxical as it seems at times, the more deeply balanced we are within ourselves, the more sensitive, objective, empathetically attuned we can be with others, and the more we can help others move toward, rather than away from balance in their own lives. That's why the work you have done so far in this book has been a crucial preparation for interpersonal balance.

Network of Support

In recent times, advances in science have helped to expand our collective understanding of what ensures the health, vitality, longevity, and sustainability of an individual or a species. Our current understanding is that those most likely to survive and thrive are actually the ones who are the most cooperative, communicative, connected, and mutually supportive in relationship to the world.

This brings to mind the image of a bridge that spans a great chasm. The heavier the load it must bear, the more supportive elements are required to keep it from crumbling under the weight. As each of us struggles to manage the heavy load of pressures upon us, those of us who offer support and who are most supported by others stand a much better chance of holding up rather than caving in or suffering under the stress.

The bottom line is that to live a healthy, well-balanced life, it is essential to have a strong network of supportive relationships. Your network is made of all the people, places, or things that in some way nurture the quality of your life. It may include not only friends and family, but people at work or those we know through community, sports, or religious groups, professional associations, or special support groups that you join for a variety of reasons.

A growing body of research in clinical medicine and the social sciences affirms the vital importance of building a strong network of support. It has been consistently demonstrated that people with a strong support network live longer, are less vulnerable to getting sick, and tend to live happier, more fulfilling lives. In numerous studies, children who have strong, supportive relationships with their families were less prone to getting sick, and less likely to turn to drugs, get pregnant, or be involved in crime. Another study has shown that women with breast cancer who are in support groups have a life expectancy four times longer than women in the same situation who are not in support groups. In a study of men suffering with painful angina attacks, men who reported that they lived in supportive primary relationships experienced six times less chest pain than men who were not. And people who have suffered from a heart attack are far less likely to suffer a second if someone calls them once a week, even for thirty seconds, and lets them know they are cared about. Old folks who have a pet, or even a plant, to care for

"If we think about it, we find that our life consists in achieving a pure relationship between ourselves and the living universe about us. This is how I 'save my soul'—by accomplishing a pure relationship between me and another person, me and a nation, me and a race of people, me and animals, me and the trees or flowers, me and the earth, me and the skies and sun and stars, me and the moon; an infinity of pure relationships, big and little.... this, if we know it, is our life and our eternity: the subtle, perfected relation between me and the circumambient universe."

—D.H. Lawrence

live longer than their counterparts who do not feel needed by others.

Especially as the pace and complexity of our life/work increases, the importance of support increases, though the time to develop and maintain it often seems to disappear. That's why it is crucial that you begin to see support as a vital component in the creation and maintainence of balance. We simply do not do well without it!

Make the Support Conscious

Here's a way to enhance your support network and to articulate to others their importance to you. On a piece of paper make three columns. In the first column, list the names of the people who have most supported you over the past six months. In the second column, list the people who will be looking to you for support in the months to come. Finally, in the third column make a list of the people whose support you will most need in the next six months. Over the weeks to come, seek out each of these people. Thank them for the support they have given. Request continued support, or let people know you're ready to help them in the future. Then ask them, "How can I support you better as we continue our life or work together?" Talk openly about what you have learned from the past and what your hopes or concerns are for the future. Work together to come to the understanding necessary to offer greater support to help each other find more balance as your life continues.

The Support Map

In the center of a piece of paper, make a doodle that represents yourself. Now, around the "you" doodle in and write the names of everyone that makes up the network of support in your life. Surrounding you will be your friends, your parents, children, spouse or significant other, the members of your spiritual community or sports teams, your mentors and coaches, and perhaps your pets. Include here whoever offers support to you in your life in any way—materially, emotionally, morally, spiritually, informationally—

"I am coming to believe that anything that promotes isolation leads to chronic stress and in time may lead to illnesses like heart disease. Anything that promotes a sense of intimacy, community and connection can be healing."

—Dean Ornish

"Spiritual practice is really about weaving a network of good relationships."

—Dhyani Ywahoo

doodle them in on this map of your network of support.

Then pause for a few moments to contemplate the unique role that each of these people plays in helping you to find balance and harmony in your life. Give each relationship two ratings. On a scale of one to ten, indicate how important each relationship is in your life—if it is very important, give it a ten; if it is not very important, give it a lower number. In a similar way, give a rating for how strong that relationship currently is in your life: if it is very strong, or taking much of your time, give it a 10; if it is currently neglected or feels distant, give it a lower number.

Then step back and reflect on the balance or lack of balance revealed through this analysis. If you notice that your spouse is a "10" in importance and yet you only gave him/her a "5" in the strength of the connection you currently feel, what does that tell you? If you find that you are giving 9 points' worth of attention to a relationship that did not get a very high rating in its importance to you, then you may be well advised to seek for balance by resetting your priorities or talking with others to reset expectations.

If you are like many people, you may find as you do this rating that you have been neglecting some relationships that are deeply important to you. In fact, you may have drifted so far from some of them that you have actually lost track of people, or they have died without ever hearing from you how much you cherished them. If this is the case for you, harness the power of any grief you may feel to help you examine your values, and reset and reaffirm your priorities. Let this truth-telling strengthen your commitment to devote the quality of attention necessary for your important relationships. Make calls, send letters or gifts, say prayers, or plan a trip to let people know how much they really mean to you.

Balance in the Field of Relationships

Now, let's expand your thinking about your field of relationships. In the center of a piece of paper, once again draw a symbol, or a circle, that represents yourself. Around your circle of self, draw

"If I am I because you are you and you are you because I am I, then I am not I and you are not you. But if I am I because I am I and you are you because you are you Then I am I and you are you."

—Menachem Mendle of Kotsk

other circles, or symbols, that represent all the people who are, or have been, most significant in your life—for better or for worse. If you feel close to a person, draw their circle close to you. If you feel distant from someone, draw their circle farther away.

Then, draw the quality of connection or relationship you have with each person. This may be a bold, strong, direct line connecting the two of you, or it might be a faint, broken, knotted tendril, or a telltale vestige of a once-deep bond. Some of these relationships may carry a positive or negative charge with them. To some you may feel physically drawn while toward others you prefer to keep your distance. Some relationships will reflect a true meeting of minds while others are more of a soul connection. Pause to reflect on this field of relationships:

- In which of these relationships do you experience the most harmony and balance?

- Which relationships seem most out of balance to you?

- What are the specific experiences, feelings, thoughts, desires, or assumptions that lead you to feel that this relationship is in or out of balance?

Stepping back to view the larger picture, think about what factors in your life are supportive of balance in those relationships that are working well, and what is getting in the way of finding balance and harmony in other relationships?

Focus now on two or three of your most significant relationships. Take some time to reflect upon and write down some insights regarding each of these relationships:

- What is working to create as much balance as there is in each of these relationships?

- What do you know in your heart, soul, or gut is needed to bring each of these relationships more toward balance?

To move toward a more mutually fulfilling balance in each of these relationships, meditate on what you are most grateful for in

"Love for a person permits him to unfold, to open up, to drop his defenses, to let himself be naked not only physically but psychologically and spiritually as well. In a word, he lets himself be seen instead of hiding himself. In ordinary interpersonal relations we are to some extent inscrutable to each other. In love relationships, we become 'scrutable.'"

—**Abraham Maslow**

each relationship, that which you wish to carry forward into your future. What no longer serves in these relationships that it is time to let go of? What new ways of being together would you like to see emerge through these relationships?

Reflect also on what limits or boundaries need to be honored:

- What are you willing to do?
- What are you willing not to do?
- What are you not willing to do?

Next, consider your special roles in the different relationships of your life—as a friend, a lover, a spouse, a parent, a child, a peer, a professional, a leader, an employee. Ask yourself in which roles do you find yourself living most in balance? In which roles do you feel the most challenged to find or keep your balance? For example, do you sense yourself to be out of balance as a spouse, yet experience balance in your role as a parent? If you find yourself in the roles of both a parent and a child, in which role do you feel most in balance or out of balance? What is the level of balance you currently feel in your professional role? At work, do you feel most in balance when you are in the role of a leader, a peer, or as someone who is being led?

It may also be revealing to notice which roles and relationships you have completely forgotten. Be honest with yourself and acknowledge those people and functions you have avoided writing down. Open your heart and mind to reflect on what this tells you about the issues you need to address in order to find greater balance within yourself and in relationships with others.

The Paths Toward and Away from Balance in Relationship

By learning to recognize the many invisible patterns of relationship, you may come to a wealth of valuable insights regarding how to find more harmony with the people in your life. From our experience, it seems clear that we are more likely to find balance in rela-

"... how few understand what love really is, and how it arises in the human heart. It is so frequently equated with good feelings toward others, with benevolence or nonviolence or service. But these things in themselves are not love.
Love springs from awareness. It is only inasmuch as you see someone as he or she really is here and now, and not as they are in your memory or your desire or in your imagination or projection, that you can truly love them. Otherwise, it is not the person that you love but the idea that you have formed of this person, or this person as the object of your desire, not as he or she is in themselves."
(continued on page 205)

tionships of all kinds—parent/child, life partners, friends, family, coworkers—when we:

- stay honest with ourselves and with others about what is really true for us;
- communicate what is true for us with authenticity and compassion;
- listen from the heart, and for the heart, in what is being communicated;
- make the invisible visible by recognizing and clarifying assumptions and expectations;
- know our options, and make conscious rather than compulsive choices;
- show respect by being willing to "look again" or "look more deeply" into ourselves and others;
- remain patient, tolerant, and keep our sense of humor;
- have confidence in ourselves and nurture trust in our relationships;
- treat ourselves and others with kindness, caring, and compassion;
- see our relationship as a mutually supportive vehicle for realizing our highest potentials and for discovering a wholeness greater than our individuality and;
- view the relationship as serving a larger sphere than just ourselves.

The training ground of your relationships will continue to offer moment to moment feedback on the quality of balance in your life. Receive this feedback with a sincere wish to learn, and the quality of your relationships will noticeably improve over time.

Conscious Relationships

Most relationships are formed unconsciously through the

"The first act of love is to see this person or this object, this reality, as it truly is. And this involves the enormous discipline of dropping your desires, your prejudices, your memories, your projections, your selective way of looking... a discipline so great that most people would rather plunge headlong into good actions and service than submit to the burning fire of this asceticism. When you set out to serve someone whom you have not taken the trouble to see, are you meeting that person's need or your own?"

—Father Anthony de Mello

interplay of our habits, mindless behaviors, and unacknowledged and unspoken expectations and assumptions. Is it any wonder that so many of our relationships seem so problematic and so far out of balance?

When you invite yourself and others to be more conscious in your relationships, you create the opportunity to let your relationship become more choiceful and creative. The artist Vincent van Gogh once said, "To live, to work, to play are really one. If you ask me, the most creative thing we can do is to love people." To turn our relationships into works of art takes a high level of honesty, objectivity, patience, and commitment. Mindful moment to mindful moment, the choice is always yours: succumb to the momentum of unconscious habits, or intensify mindful awareness to understand what is really going on and creatively, compassionately enhance it.

You can cultivate the artistry of any relationship even if your partners have no interest or inclination to raise their own level of consciousness, compassion, or creativity. Ultimately, this is work that only you can do on yourself. No one can do this for you, nor can you make changes in someone else's life without running a risk—at some level—of being disrespectful or of doing violence to them. Moment to moment, in every relationship you are in, you are making choices based on your habits, values, priorities, and the quality of awareness present. You can endure the situation as it is; you can withdraw from the relationship—physically, mentally, or emotionally—or you can search for ways to make that relationship a creative work of art.

Remember, learning is led by questions and fed by feedback. Questions organize and focus your attention. Feedback provides vital information necessary for learning: no feedback, no learning. Therefore, from time to time, it is helpful to check in with yourself and with the people you live or work with most closely. Ask yourself, and then ask others:

- How are we doing in our relationship?
- What signs of balance or imbalance do you notice in how we are living or working together?

"You know, there are three kinds of friends in the world.
An ordinary person sees only who you are; for that you don't need a friend.
Then there's a friend who sees in you what you can be.
And then there's the real holy Friend, and the presence of this Friend you are already."

—Reb Shlomo Carlebach

- What conscious or unconscious expectations or assumptions do we need to test, clarify, or reset to develop the quality of relationship that we both want to have?

- What is working well in our relationship that is worth celebrating?

- How are we feeling fulfilled or frustrated in this relationship?

- What do you think would help us to find greater harmony or balance in our relationship?

- To ensure the vitality and strength of this relationship, what seems like the next stage of our learning and growth?

Reflecting upon these questions will help you to bring more clarity and truth into your relationships. Sharing these reflections with those you live and work closely with can stimulate the dialogue and learning necessary to deepen your relationships. If you are honest with yourself and others, you will recognize that there is often much to celebrate and much potential for further learning. Though this realization is seldom comfortable, neither is the buried dissatisfaction, frustration, and resentment that can come when we don't develop enough balance in our relationships to embrace and learn from the truth.

The Mirror of Relationships: We Are What We Behold

The cardinal rule in bringing harmony to your relationships is to remember that your work is on yourself. It is not about changing, coercing, or manipulating others. Over the course of a lifetime, we have the opportunity to learn from and grow within the context of many different relationships. Lessons learned in one relationship will often offer valuable clues for other relationships. As we learn and grow, we change, and as we change, our relationships change. On the other hand, many of us have learned by now that though we may leave a relationship with someone, the same difficult issues we had

"The only reason we don't open our hearts and minds to other people is that they trigger confusion in us that we don't feel brave enough or sane enough to deal with. To the degree that we look clearly and compassionately at ourselves, we feel confident and fearless about looking into someone else's eyes."
—Ane Pema Chodron

with that person may keep showing up in other relationships until we work it out in a balanced way. If you have a lesson to learn and you don't learn it in one relationship, it will certainly keep resurfacing until you get it.

So it is crucial in all relationships that we ask ourselves again and again: what issues or qualities in my own life, attitudes, or beliefs are being reflected back to me in the mirror of this relationship? Is this relationship asking me to be more patient, more honest, more mindful, more loving, more lighthearted, more focused, more present, more caring, or more generous with my time and attention? Look, listen, and feel into the relationship for what is really being asked for in order to realize harmony and balance between you. Deepen your empathy to know and understand both what is true for you, and, as best you can, what is likely true for others. Balance both reasoning and intuitive intelligence to discover what is most alive in each relationship.

With this in mind, when certain themes arise in your relationships, if you are mindful enough, you can chuckle to yourself and say, "Oh, I get it. The irritation that I'm feeling around this person is asking me to look at and work with my impatience. The important message here is for me, not for them. Thank you for offering this mirror for me to recognize what I need to work on. Let's see how well I can do this time!" Or, "Ah, I get it, this isn't about your fashion preferences. You are really reflecting back to me valuable information about my own judgments and intolerance. I'm more comfortable focusing on what's wrong with you than taking a hard look at what could be working better in my own life." Or perhaps, "My withdrawal from the intensity of your love and caring for me is challenging me to open my own heart, to feel worthy of your love, and to accept myself, rather than rejecting you as I have tended to reject myself." You can see how, at the simplest, most basic level, our relationships are about teaching us how to deeply listen to, understand, befriend, and love ourselves, and then how to deeply listen to, understand, appreciate, and love each other.

In extending love to others, the key point to remember is this:

"I tell you one thing—if you want peace of mind, do not find fault with others. Rather learn to see your own faults. Learn to make the whole world your own. No one is a stranger my child, this whole world is your own."

— The last words of the Holy Mother Sri Sarada Devi

"When you see a man of worth,
Think of how you may emulate him.
When you see one who is unworthy,
Examine your own character."

—Confucius

208   Living in Balance

though the people with whom we live and work maintain an air of having it together and having their life in control, just like us they all carry deep wounds from previous experiences that lead them to act in ways that are difficult for us to understand, even if we think we know them. This simple yet challenging fact of life creates a learning laboratory in which we are constantly being invited to learn more about ourselves and one another as we dance together in life.

Inner and Outer Balance in Communication

An important dimension of balance in action is how you communicate with others. As you practice mindfulness, you've probably begun to notice that, even as you engage in conversations with people throughout the day, you have a fair amount of background conversation going on in your own mind as you constantly interpret, evaluate, and judge your experience. Although this mental activity is useful in making sense out of your experience, it may actually be reducing the clarity of your experience itself. If we're talking together, for example, it'll be impossible for you to really hear what I'm saying if you're talking at the same time—and that includes thinking about what you're going to say next. Because so many of the breakdowns in our personal and professional relationships come about because people are not being listened to, or not feeling listened to, learning to listen better is really an important skill. Perhaps if people could calculate how much poor attention and listening habits cost us in rework, frustration, accidents, and heartache, we'd be more motivated to invest the time, energy, and attention necessary to improve the quality of our awareness and communication skills.

Most breakdowns in communication could have been prevented if people were really listening to themselves as well as listening to each other. Begin listening to the listening as much as to what is actually being said. Understanding this, you might find some value in applying the following four principles to your communications with people.

"If you want to be truly understood, you need to say everything three times, in three different ways. Once for each ear... and once for the heart. The right ear represents the ability to apprehend the nature of the Whole, the wholeness of the circumstance, the forest. The left ear represents the ability to select a sequential path. And the heart represents a balance between the two."

— **Paula Underwood Spencer**

Centering. Whenever possible, before you enter into a communication with someone, pause for a moment to get centered. Scan through your own circuits and, as you breathe, notice, loosen, and release any tensions that you may be holding. As you inhale, focus your attention right here in the moment, in the place where your power is, and as you exhale, let your awareness flow and open.

Intent to Stay Present. Generate the firm intention to be as fully present as you can with the person you're about to talk with. Imagine yourself using your breathing to stay present, open, and connected to them, and to simply listen wholeheartedly to what they're communicating. Think to yourself, Staying completely present, open, and connected with you, I breathe in... staying completely present, open and connected with you, I breathe out...

Or simply, Present... open... connected...

Generous Listening. As you begin your conversation, listen attentively to what's actually being said. Be mindful of your own internal conversations about what others are saying, but quiet your thinking by gently saying to yourself, mentally, *Listen*. Use your breathing to help you stay focused and relaxed.

Active Listening and Feedback. Use active listening skills to briefly paraphrase for the person you're talking with what you've heard them say. If the message you are hearing from someone carries a strong emotional charge to it, remember to acknowledge that you have heard two important things. First, let them know that you understand the issue or concern that is important to them. Second, communicate that you are sensitive to their feelings about the situation. For example, "That's great that you made the finals in the competition. You must feel honored and proud to receive such recognition from your peers." Or, "It sounds like when your mom told that story about your first date, you were really embarrassed." Or, "I can understand how worried you were when your daughter wasn't home by 2 A.M.—I bet you were upset when she finally got home, and were grateful that she was all right." Keep in mind that people need to hear feedback that you understand their issues, their feelings, and their often unspoken needs. Use active listening to reflect back to them what you've heard and to check that you understood their communication to their satisfaction.

Beyond Words

Balance in communication is about more than the interaction of what I say and what you say. Studies of effective communication have shown that 55 percent of the message is conveyed through body language, and 38 percent is carried by voice tonality. Nonverbal cues, then, account for as much as 93 percent of the total message that we receive, while only 7 percent comes from the words we hear or say! Taking this to heart, we come to understand that to improve our communications we must learn to listen carefully to numerous streams of information.

Let's look first at finding a balance between our internal dialogue and the actual words that we are hearing. It is helpful to understand that the speed of thought is many times faster than the speed of talk. Even a fast speaker would be lucky if they spoke 150 or 200 words per minute, while your thoughts zip by at nearly five times that speed. For every page of words you speak, I generate five to seven pages of my own internal script. It is as though we are communicating with modems that run at different speeds, which is measured in the number of bits of information that they can process in a second. The words we speak to each other flow relatively slowly, analogous to an old-model modem that could only process information at a rate of 2,400 bits per second. In contrast, your thinking process is more like a DSL which is thousands of times faster. Given the heavy competition of our internal background conversation, is it any wonder that people so often do not feel heard or understood! Once again, mindfulness is the key. By learning to be mindfully attentive to both of these conversations at the same time, you'll be

"If for every time I loved you, words could disappear, then silence, oh yes silence, would be all that you could hear."

—"Silence" by Emily Matthews

able to focus on what's really being communicated to you and to sort out your thoughts about what you have heard.

Here is a useful and fun exercise to apply mindfulness to finding balance in communications between yourself and others. Take a piece of paper and draw a line down the middle so that you have two columns. At the top of the right-hand column write, "What's actually being said." And at the top of the left-hand column write, "What my internal conversation is saying about what's being said."

Once you get a sense for this exercise, you can expand your mindfulness in communication to include additional conversations that are going on simultaneously in every conversation. Add to the stream of words you hear, and the stream of thoughts that you think to yourself, the third stream of communications: the flow of nonverbal information generated by your partner. As they speak, "listen" attentively to the cues offered by their gestures, posture, facial expression, and the tonality of their voice, all of which carry valuable clues about the emotions associated with the words they are speaking.

Also be attentive to a fourth stream of communication, the message that you are communicating through your body. Be mindful of what you are saying in words and in silences, in your posture and gestures, and through your facial expressions, voice tone, and the energy of your presence.

The fifth stream of communications to monitor is your internal intuitive sense, which is active during the exchange of more tangible auditory and visual communication. Notice what you feel in your gut, what your body is telling you about this communication. Also be mindful of the mental images, emotions, and the clear intuitive insights that stream into your mind throughout your communications.

Remember that communication takes place on many different levels. As you learn to be mindful of how these five different streams of information weave together into your communications, your insight, intuition, and empathy will deepen. The ability to monitor your mental, emotional, and physical state *while* you're engaged in outer activities and interactions, is the real key to finding balance in the midst of dynamic interaction with others. As you become more

"In human relationships, as mutual love deepens, there comes a time when two friends convey their exchanges without words. They can sit in silence sharing an experience or simply enjoying each other's presence without saying anything. Holding hands or a single word from time to time can develop this communication. This kind of relationship points to the level of interior silence..."

—Father Thomas Keating

"Language is primitive telepathy."

—Terence McKenna

aware of these multiple streams of information and how they inter-act, you will recognize many opportunities to find more balance while you are communicating with others.

Aloneness and Togetherness

One useful measure of balance in your life is your level of com-fort in relating to others versus being alone with yourself. These two aspects need to be in balance because the more you understand and are comfortable with yourself, the more authenticity and depth you will be able to bring to your relationships.

Some people are so uncomfortable just being with themselves that they are compulsively driven to be with others. They are afraid to be alone, so they call others or distract themselves with mindless activities or entertainment. We live in a culture that has invested heavily in trying to convince us that we are incomplete without being in a primary relationship or without being a parent. Although none of us can be fully complete outside of the network of our rela-tionships, a healthy balance in our life is reflected by our comfort in being alone, that is, "all one," with ourselves.

Michelle really cherishes her quiet, alone time. She often says she must have been a Gypsy in a previous life, because she read once that Gypsies learned how to be together in such close quarters in their caravans by taking time every day—before eight o'clock in the morning—when they didn't talk to each other. She thought that sounded like a great idea! After sixteen incredible years together, the two of us often say that one of the greatest strengths in our relation-ship is that we really know how to be "alone together." We love to do things together, and we work, write, spend time in retreat and in nature, and play intensively together! However, to maintain this intensity of relationship, it's essential for each of us to also have time to ourselves. It is not uncommon for us to walk, hike, or drive for miles together without saying a word to each other, or to sit and meditate or work around the house without interrupting each other for long periods of time. Then when we do reconnect, we bring a

"I must conquer my loneliness alone. I must be happy with myself, or I have noth-ing to offer. Two halves have little choice but to join; and yes, they do make a whole. But two wholes when they coincide...
That is beauty.
That is love."

—Lillian Darr

greater depth and insight to share with each other. We aren't disturbing and distracting each other out of our discomfort with ourselves, or out of our own sense of incompleteness. We are sharing insights, joys, discoveries, or questions that are really meaningful for us and that may enrich each other.

Balance and wholeness in relationships depends on feeling whole both when we are alone and when we are with others. If you are comfortable being alone, but uncomfortable with others, stretch yourself to seek greater balance by increasing your social skills and comfort in relationships. If being alone is uncomfortable for you, move toward balance by gradually increasing your capacity to enjoy being with yourself. Begin with short periods of time, perhaps 10 or 15 minutes a day when you are undistracted by others. To accomplish this you may need to renegotiate your time commitments or reset the expectations that other people have of you. If you can help others understand that the quality of your time with them will be enhanced if you have time to find balance and wholeness with yourself, you will be more likely to enlist their support of your alone time.

In your own life, be mindful of what drives you to engage or disengage from others. Do you initiate conversations compulsively, or do you check in to see if your partner is in a mindset receptive to what you have to share? Do you withdraw into aloofness or take time to be alone out of fear, anxiety, shame, or frustration, or because you really do enjoy being by yourself? Are you in touch with what is really true for you and do you let others know what your needs and wishes are? Do you let others know when you would like to have some quality time together with them? Do you communicate that you really need time alone to find your own internal balance, time that will ultimately help you to be with them in a more complete and wholehearted way? Don't assume that your invisible thoughts, feelings, intentions, or needs are readily understood to people around you. It is necessary to both know what is true for you, and to communicate it!

Making time to simply be alone with yourself is actually an offering to everyone you live in relationship with. Only by under-

"Grant me the ability to be alone;
May it be my custom to go outdoors each day
among the trees and grasses,
among all growing things and there
may I be alone,
and enter into prayer to talk with the One that I belong to."
—Rabbi Nachman of Bratzlav

standing yourself—your inner thoughts, hopes, fears, aspirations, and spirit—can you know what is really true for you and convey that to others in a way that brings harmony and balance to your relationships. Though at first it may be awkward, begin to explore ways to create some alone time to develop a stronger, deeper, more intimate relationship with yourself. During your time alone you might:

- take a walk and just be with and discover the miracle of yourself
- sit quietly and mindfully explore what you sense and feel, what you think and want
- take time to write in your journal
- sit, stand, move, or dance in front of a mirror
- talk or sing to yourself, or play music
- meditate, deeply listen, feel and know what is true for you
- make a list of the questions that are important to you in your life
- spend time in nature exploring the mysterious boundary between yourself and the universe; see if you can find where you end, and the rest of the universe begins
- mindfully bathe or shower, brush your hair, or massage your body
- eat a mindful silent meal

Harmony in relationships is found in balancing the attention we give to ourselves with the attention we give to our loved ones, friends, and coworkers. If we invest too much attention outwardly and get out of touch with ourselves, we lose our balance and may end up feeling resentful, get into fights, or pull away. If we get too preoccupied with ourselves, we can fall into isolation, narcissism, or loneliness. Ideally each day—or at least each week—will reflect a balance of some time to be with ourselves and some time to be with others in a nourishing and quality way.

"Great ideas... come into the world as gently as doves... if we listen attentively, we shall hear, amid the uproar... a faint flutter of wings, the gentle stirring of life and hope. Some say that this hope lies in a nation; others, in a man. I believe rather that it is awakened, revived, nourished by millions of solitary individuals whose deeds and works every day negate... the crudest implications of history. As a result, there shines forth fleetingly the ever threatened truth that each and every one of us, on the foundation of our own sufferings and joys, builds for all."

—**Albert Camus**

Play: The Giving and Receiving of Love

At a conference at the Menninger Foundation, we had the opportunity to watch a documentary about play behavior in animals that was made by a colleague of ours, Stuart Brown. One memorable bit of footage shows a hungry polar bear approaching a husky dog that was chained up in a yard on the outskirts of an arctic settlement. The bear approached, crouched down, with its ears back in a gesture that the dog recognized as an invitation: "Would you like to play?" Seemingly without fear, the dog assumed a responsive pose that communicated, "Sure!"

And play they did! Indeed, their play was so vigorous that the bear at one point actually tossed the dog way up into the air. They had great fun and played together until they were mutually fulfilled and exhausted. Panting and sweating, they concluded their playtime with gestures of completion and mutual satisfaction. Amazingly, the next day, the bear returned, and the dog and the bear continued to build their playful relationship with each other.

Years ago, after one of many mass killings in Texas, the state government commissioned a study to identify the psychological profile of people who were most prone to acts of brutal violence. After extensive testing and interviews with the killers, their families, siblings, and former teachers, one factor stood out as most significant: as children, they had never really learned how to play with other children.

A play dysfunction can dramatically impair the quality of our health and relationships with others. Numerous studies suggest that societies who indulge in large amounts of play are healthier. Play is vital to the healthy development of our nervous systems, and it has been suggested that it brings balance to our waking life in the same way that dreaming and REM sleep does for us in our sleeping hours.

Genuine play is about giving and receiving love. It is about discovering the extraordinary within the ordinary. Play is found in the creative ways that emerge between infants or octogenarians. It can unfold between preverbal children and speakers, between people of different cultures, and between creatures of different species. Play is not about who is best or most skilled, and definitely not about winning or losing. Play is about mutual discovery, learning, and delight. In play there is no advantage to being big or small, old or young. Play is not about manipulation or deception. It is not about forcing your will or body on others or about causing discomfort for one of your playmates. Play is not about tickling, which is an excellent example of abusiveness masquerading as play, and which often leaves emotional scars similar to other forms of abuse.

At the heart of play is love and a deep sense of wonder and mutual discovery. Play is about balance, mystery, belonging, inclusion, trust, sacredness, fearlessness, touch, reciprocity, love, kindness, openness, and joy. It is about awareness, joining, blending, following, and contributing of energy. It is not about humiliation, rejection, competition, mocking, exclusion, admiration, defensiveness, or fear.

We can approach our lives with either a work ethic or a play ethic. The work ethic approach encourages us to be goal oriented, and to pursue "management by objective" approaches to work. Victory signals the end of the game. The play ethic takes a different approach to life, one that is about continuous inquiry and discovery that could go on forever.

Play is not about playing a game in which one person wins and another loses, it is not about one person dominating or imposing their will on another. Based in cocreative mutual discovery, play teaches us how to learn and explore relationships in mutually respectful ways. A measure of our success in playing with someone is that when we finish, we feel a close bond, a deeper trust, and, given the opportunity, we'd welcome the opportunity to play together again. Play behavior, in its purest sense, is mutually fulfilling, self-fulfilling, noncompetitive, interactive exploration. It is essential to developing quality balanced relationships.

Do you have enough play in your life? Do you play, *really* play as defined here, with your spouse, your children, your friends, your coworkers? One of our most inspiring friends and playmates, O. Fred Donaldson, author of *Playing by Heart*, is a true master of the

"When original play was abandoned, life ceased to have meaning and we discovered purpose. When ethics arrived, we played fairly—to win at any cost. When kindness dissolved, we played for keeps."

—Fred Donaldson

All My Relations   217

high art of play. In his inspiring book, Fred offers the following six "Play Principles" you might want to consider in order to bring more play into your relationships:

1. Be not afraid of life.
2. Be quiet.
3. Touch is our primary language.
4. Be a beginner.
5. Smooth moves follow a clear heart.
6. Expect nothing, be ready for anything.

These six principles are actually six ways of beholding the unity of mind, body, and spirit. They are facets of the same jewel of balanced relationships. To understand one of these is to understand them all. To misuse one is to misuse them all. In the actual practice of play in relationships, these principles translate into action as follows:

1. Get down, touch the earth.
2. Be quiet.
3. Pay attention and be present.
4. Let go.
5. Release thoughts.
6. Be in touch.

As Fred reminds us, "We must feel it in our flesh and bones. We must touch and be touched. Then we will earn the integrity and wholeness of our lives by every act we do."

In your own life, when were the times when you discovered the joys of true playfulness? During those precious moments, what actually happened that drew you into play? How were you left feeling during and after those encounters? How might you make yourself more available for such close and meaningful play encounters in the future?

"Nobody sees a flower—really— it is so small—we haven't time— and to see takes time. Like to have a friend takes time."

—Georgia O'Keefe

In search of balance, invite yourself to consciously and intentionally seek out opportunities to play more in your life. Welcome the chance to learn from and play with children who still remember how to play—even if it's just for a moment in a checkout line at the market, or while standing at a street corner waiting to cross the street. Be ready for times when you can take a more playful stance and remind others of the joy to be found in living and working in a more creative, loving, open, and learningful way. Stretch yourself to assume a more playful attitude in at least some of the many situations you encounter. Remember, each encounter offers a treasury of extraordinary possibilities for you to choose from in weaving the balance of your life.

"In love there's no pure identity because love involves two and yet the two become one. That's the great mystery."

—Father Bede Griffiths

Shared Awareness

Play offers us a glimpse of what it is like to give and be given undivided attention. Learning to play and to love expands our capacity to truly give our attention wholeheartedly to our lives. If we have learned these lessons well, being fully present in relationship comes easily. If not, we may have to apply more discipline to staying focused when we are with others.

Giving your complete attention to someone is a rare and precious gift. This next exercise provides yet another doorway that can open you to build this capacity and experience a deep connection, sense of balance, and flow with another person. We often teach this core practice when we work with caregivers, hospice volunteers, parents' groups, or other helping professionals. As you do this exercise, let your awareness hover equally within yourself and with the person you are attending to.

To begin, invite your partner to find a comfortable place to lie down while you pull up a chair or sit down next to them. The person lying down needs only to deeply relax, and stay aware of the presence of their companion sitting by their side. When you are the person sitting close by, your role is to watch carefully and notice the breathing rhythm of your partner who is lying down. As you sit

"Whenever the rabbi of Sasov saw anyone's suffering, either of spirit or of body, he shared it so earnestly that the other's suffering became his own. Once someone expressed his astonishment at this capacity to share in another's troubles. 'What do you mean "share"?' Asked the rabbi. 'It is my sorrow; how can I help but suffer it?'"

—Martin Buber

with your partner, tune in and become aware of their breathing, and observe the rise and fall of their abdomen or chest. Then begin to synchronize the rhythm of your own breathing with theirs. Each time that your partner inhales, you silently inhale. Each time he or she exhales, make a soft but audible "ahhh" sound. Inhale silently, exhale softly. Ahhhh... The sounds you make let your partner know that you are completely there with and for him or her.

If you are the person who is lying down, let yourself simply receive the gift of this person's undivided loving attention. Do your best to stay receptive and feel the bond that grows between you. Patiently stay with this process through times of discomfort, self-consciousness, boredom, or distraction.

After 15 or 20 minutes, silently stretch, and then switch roles so that each of you has the opportunity to give and receive the gift of each other's complete attention. Then take some time to talk about how this experience has touched you.

- What did you learn about finding balance and flow in relationships through this experience?
- What insights have you gained about yourself in relationships through this exercise?
- Was it easier for you to be in the active or the receptive role?
- What feelings or thoughts did you notice?
- How was your perception of yourself or of your partner impacted through this exercise?
- What factors made this process easy or difficult for you?
- What did you learn about giving or receiving loving attention?

This exercise provides a safe and often profound opportunity to experience without words what it is like to fully be present with another person, and to have someone be totally there for you. This experience may provide a fierce mirror for us to see how self-conscious, self-critical, or easily distracted we are. It also offers us a

"Out of my experience... one final conclusion dogmatically emerges: There is a continuum of cosmic consciousness against which our individuality builds by accidental forces, and into which our several minds plunge as into a mother sea."

—William James

"Love doesn't make the world go 'round. Love is what makes the ride worthwhile."

—Franklin P. Jones

glimpse of a quality of connectedness, safety, intimacy, and caring beyond words that is deeply rewarding and affirming. As we develop our capacity to deeply listen to, care about, and give our full attention to ourselves and to others, we are more likely to discover what true balance in relationships can mean for the quality of our life.

Balancing Rituals for Couples

If you want to keep your intimate relationship alive, it's essential to give some time on a regular basis to connect deeply, even if it's only for a few wholehearted minutes each day! Here are some balancing rituals that can be easily integrated into your schedule. You can use these on a daily or weekly basis, and the time you give to them can be adapted to fit in with the changing rhythms of your lifestyle: if there is no time for it one day, that's okay. Just find what works best for you and keep trying.

Remember the fundamentals of balance: you will lose it, but you can always find it again! That is just as true for interpersonal relationships as for inner balance. The point is to mindfully notice that you haven't had time for deep connection and then return, forgiving of yourself and your partner, to deepen the connection once again.

Hairbrushing. One of our favorite quick ways to reconnect is to brush out each other's hair. Michelle particularly loves this. It seems to nourish the "roots" of balance in our joint psyche, linking us back to tribal days when people regularly shared moments of tender loving care through grooming each other. Bioenergetically, it also helps clear our energy field of accumulated static electricity, which is especially important after long days in front of a computer monitor.

Foot Rubs. In this same category of physical rituals that move us toward balance is the special gift of giving each other a foot rub. This is a great one for quiet moments after a hard day's work or play—or

"The secret of my song though near, none can see and none can hear, Oh for a friend to know the sign, And mingle all their soul with mine!"

—Mevlana Jelaluddin Rumi

anytime! The soles of the feet have receptors connecting to all the organs and structures of the body. Foot rubs are one of the best ways to give and receive a balancing and revitalizing mini-massage, especially if you use some aromatic essential oil like lavender or juniper. You don't have to be an expert on reflexology to give your partner a deluxe treatment (though there are many guidebooks available on the subject, and even little cards that map out the terrain of each foot in detail). Just trust the inner guidance of your heart and let your hands "go for the sole."

Get Wet. Anything to do with water is a helpful strategy for balance—bathing or showering together, swimming, washing one another's feet, listening to the soothing sounds of a waterfall or ocean waves on recorded environmental music tapes, or even going for a walk in the rain (especially if you live in Seattle, as we do), are all wonderful ways to reconnect in a balancing way.

Read to One Another. Two friends of ours experimented with unplugging their TV and reading poetry to each other in the evenings instead. Another couple we know are working their way through *The Hobbit* and can't wait to jump into bed to get to the next chapter.

Take a Walk. Friends of ours decided to go for a walk after work around the reservoir in their town as part of their daily routine. This strategy proved immediately beneficial, both for their own individual sense of health and vitality, and for their health, vitality, and balance as a couple. People with children can bring the kids along too!

Morning Tea and Meditation. Another couple we know found that reestablishing an old family custom of "morning tea and meditation" in bed made a major difference in the quality of their relationship and the energy with which their day got off to a start. For other couples, praying together in the morning or evening has become an integral element of staying balanced together.

The Four Rivers of Life. One couple whom we worked with started to incorporate a time of deep reflection and truth-speaking each evening. Using a simple process we'd introduced them to, which involves four questions as a tool to give structure to their contemplations, they each take turns listening and speaking deeply as they share what is true for them. Here are the four questions:

- Where today was I inspired by something or someone?
- Where today was I surprised?
- Where today did I find myself being challenged or stretched to grow or think in new ways?
- Where today was I touched or deeply moved by something that came into my life?

We first learned this series of contemplations from Angeles Arrien, who received them from her Basque ancestors. In the Basque tradition, these four questions honor the Four Rivers of Life: the river of Inspiration, the river of Surprise, the river of Challenge, and the river of Love. According to the wise elders of this tradition, it's impossible for us to truly stay in balance without jumping in and bathing in these four rivers on a daily basis.

Recognizing Each Other

Here's another practice to deepen your connection. Sit quietly across from one another. Like mirrors deeply reflecting each other, see in each other your parents, grandparents, and ancestors. See too the generational cascade of traditions, attitudes, beliefs, customs, and habits that help or harm. See in yourself, and in each other, the miraculous moment of your conception. See yourselves swimming in the wombs of your mothers. See yourselves as tiny children, wide-eyed in a wonder-full world. See in yourself and in each other the potentials for becoming a wise old man, or a wise old woman. See in yourselves and each other the seeds of influence that will bear fruit in the lives of others for countless generations to come.

"... the energy between us was communicated [through our] eyes, and made me begin to cry. We were both feeling the same thing, without any words being spoken. It was as though we recognized one another... as though we were one entity, one field. There was no obstruction or delineation between us. My heart felt like it had burst open... [my] whole body was breathing, in a sense. I was perceiving through my heart, not just through the eyes. It was like the etheric being was in resonance with my husband's etheric being. Somehow this alignment occurred, and we were not limited to the flesh..."
—**Anonymous**

Quietly, connectedly, come into harmony within this place where your two streams of being meet. See and feel the connection. Then, from this place, share your visions for the future, your hopes and your fears, your life's greatest joys, and your sorrows. Perhaps you might simply want to exchange the following: *What is true for me right now is . . .*

The Precious Moment We Share

Because it is so easy to get caught up in the business and busyness of life and forget how important the people in our lives are to us, the sudden death of someone we love can be one of life's most powerful teachers on living in balance. In the clear light of this stark reality, the preciousness of the moments we have to share with our loved ones becomes sharply etched in our hearts. The intensity and shock of losing a friend can also help us get clear on our values and our priorities, and can renew our commitment to giving more balanced attention to what really matters in our lives and relationships.

So if you are serious about finding balance in your life, consider using on a daily basis the following powerful reminder: in each encounter this may well be the last time you are together with this person. The winds of change are fierce and unpredictable. As you tuck your kids in, kiss your sweetheart good night, or lay thee down to sleep . . . who really knows what comes next?

Living half awake, our sense of false security dulls the keenness of our awareness, and leads us not to treasure as deeply as we might the extraordinariness of each "ordinary" encounter. As we begin to realize how tenuous our precious lives and relationships are, we discover a vivid clarity that wakes us up and brings us more alive. In the moments when we realize we have just been going through the motions of our lives, that we have been checked out more than checked in, and that we really haven't been loving as deeply as we are able, we touch a grief that can bring us wholeheartedly back to life. Thich Nhat Hanh offers a powerful antidote to such forgetfulness in relationships. He suggests that when we are in the midst of a quar-

"Walk around feeling like a leaf. Know you could tumble at any second. Then decide what to do with your time."
—Naomi Shahib Nye

"You cannot do a kindness too soon because you never know how soon it will be too late."
—Ralph Waldo Emerson

rel with our beloved ones, we take a time-out for a moment to look deeply into their eyes and consider where we will be in 300 years.

Let each encounter be the most important thing in your life at the time. For the few fleeting moments that you are together, exercise the discipline necessary to give this person your complete, undivided attention and love. When your attention wanders to memories of the past or fantasies of the future, smile to yourself, and reel yourself back into this precious moment alive together. Really listen. Really care. Be real. Let yourself love and be loved. Be with them in such a way that if they were never to see you again, they would be moved to comment how meaningful their time with you was. Be with them so that if you were to never see them again, you would know in your heart that those last precious moments of life that you shared were really good ones. Remember, when you deeply touch someone's heart, you change their life forever.

"Thus shall ye look on all this fleeting world: A star at dawn, a bubble in the stream, A flash of lightning in a summer cloud, A flickering lamp, a phantom, and a dream."

—The Buddha

"Man comes from dust and ends in dust; he wins his bread at the risk of his life. He is like the potsherd that breaks, the grass that withers, the flowers that fade, the shadow that passes, the cloud that vanishes, the breeze that blows, the dust that floats, the dream that flies away."

—Hebrew Prayer

ELEVEN

Life-Work Balance

No one else can tell you what your life's work is, but it's important that you find it. There is a part of you that knows—affirm that part . . .

—WILLIS W. HARMAN

It's difficult to feel we are living our lives in balance if we feel overworked and burned out. Yet for many of us, this is a fact of life. In 1991 average Americans had to work the equivalent of roughly two hundred hours more a year—that's one month!—in order to maintain the same standard of living they enjoyed in 1973. As a result, we have seen an increase in the number of dual-income families, more people working longer hours, and record rates of moonlighting and extra jobs.

We live in a strange and stressful time, when about one-third of us are overworked and looking to cut back, and another third of us are looking for meaningful employment. Although some economists say that we are addicted to work, and that people want to work more hours, many others understand that in today's highly competitive work environment there is simply more pressure and higher expectations on the people who do have jobs. Aware of this difficult situation, many students are now preparing for at least three careers!

The U.S. Department of Labor reports that over the last decade, nearly half of American businesses have downsized, causing tremendous stress for both their former and retained employees. Estimates show that overtime is at an all-time high, averaging 4.7 hours per week, and that today's employees are routinely expected to do the work of 1.3 people—for the same pay and in less time. When we read in the *New York Times* that 43 million jobs have disappeared since 1979, is it any wonder that so many people are afraid of losing their jobs, and that as a result they are willing to put up with the strain of working longer and harder?

Among full-time employees, 40 percent say that their employers expect an unreasonable amount of overtime, and with increasing numbers of unemployed, highly educated people, many people with jobs are anxiously overworking themselves at the cost of finding balance in their life and work. Working long hours, especially in jobs that we don't find fulfilling, leaves little time or energy to spend quality time with our families and friends, or to do things that renew, revitalize, and develop ourselves. As a result, many people feel frustrated, depressed, or resigned to just hang in there until some major wake-up call—an illness, accident, a threatened marriage, or life catastrophe—amplifies the internal screams: *Help! Let me out of here; there must be a better, wiser, kinder way!*

Given these mounting pressures, when we hear that 75 percent of firms that have downsized report no appreciable gains, plus huge problems with survivors, is it any wonder that so many people feel high levels of frustration and anger within and beyond the workplace?

Many factors motivate us to strike a better balance between the personal and professional dimensions of our lives. For nearly half of the people we've asked, a wish to give more quality attention to their children is a key motivating factor. One man described how he had made a major shift in his work habits 17 years ago when his second grader came home from school with a picture he drew of the family. "There were four of us in the family," he said, "but there were only three figures in the picture—mommy, daughter, and son, the artist. When my wife asked, 'Where's Daddy?' my son replied, 'He's at work!' In response to this wake-up call, this man got off the fast track he was on at U.S. West Communications and avoided taking jobs with extra hours and lots of travel. Though he says that the decision dashed his dreams of having a big house or driving a Porsche,

"The minute you begin to do what you really want to do, it's really a different kind of life."

—Buckminster Fuller

he has no regrets about having rearranged his priorities to spend more time with his family.

Contrast this decision with the current situation in Japan where the second leading cause of death after cancer is called *karoshi:* "death from overwork." Estimates are that over thirty thousand people have died from it thus far. In Tokyo, there is a hotline, set up by a group of lawyers to help victims file compensation claims with the government. The most common victims of karoshi are between 34 and 61 years old. They often die at their desks or commuting to work, dropping dead after a blood vessel in their heart or brain explodes. In Japan, time for anything besides work is so extremely limited that many people in young families don't have the time to go visit their elderly family members. To meet this need, an ingenious business has emerged called "Rent-a-Family," that hires actors and sends them out to visit lonely parents. The company is so popular that it has a waiting list of nearly one thousand people—elders are so lonely that they are profoundly grateful for the opportunity for seemingly meaningful interaction with other people, even if they are only actors paid to "really care for them."

In Japan, there's a popular TV commercial with a jingle that says, "Can you battle twenty-four hours a day?" We're told that everyone in Japan knows it, and that some companies sing it together every morning. While younger generations are more quick to say, "My time after five," older corporate warriors are more likely to stay out late drinking because to come home early is a sign that something must be wrong at work. To combat these trends, unions are actively promoting a shorter work week with the slogan, "Let's have a Japan where families can eat dinner together." They are also seeing an increasing number of young Japanese who frown on overtime and prefer reduced time at work over increases in pay.

In the United States, the problem may not be as severe as in Japan, but it is still a huge issue. The amount of paid vacation time is rapidly dwindling for many people, and many of us are afraid to even take the vacation time we do have. In these times of downsizing, we are afraid of being seen as replaceable or expendable,

"All this systems thinking stuff has no meaning without understanding that we're part of something larger than ourselves ... We've depleted the earth and we're fragmenting our spirit. We live under a massive illusion of separation from one another, from nature, from the universe, from everything. It's the great liability we have inherited from the Industrial Revolution back through Reformation ... The human species is profoundly out of balance. If our work has an impact, it will bring us back into the natural order of things."

—**Peter Senge**, in *Fortune* **Magazine**

or our department has been so downsized that there is no one to cover for us. For the increasing numbers of people who are self-employed, time off is often directly equated with money lost, challenging the self-employed to make tough and tangible boundaries to establish or maintain some semblance of balance in their lives.

Other indicators of the scope of the problem: stress-related workers' compensation claims in the United States have increased by 300 percent during the early '80s, and a vast majority of people experience some sort of stress-related illness. Ninety percent of private sector workers say their job is either *very* or *highly* stressful. As many as 80 percent report suffering from work stress–induced exhaustion, insomnia, depression, muscle pains, ulcers, and other stress-related disorders. Add to this the startling finding that most heart attacks occur between eight and nine o'clock on Monday mornings, and you have a graphic picture of just how our work is killing us!

Women and Work

When it comes to life-work balance, it seems that women are particularly suffering. Indeed, it is heartbreaking to see so many working women drained and depleted by the stress of trying to maintain not only their own sanity and balance, but also to promote the well-being and success of their families, households, careers, coworkers, and oftentimes their bosses' sanity and success as well! The toll is often telling and quite costly in terms of compromised health, strained relationships, emotional exhaustion, and spiritual starvation. Once in a while one of them breaks free, like Beth, who recently quit her well-paying job as an information technology specialist to realize her lifelong dream of opening a bed-and-breakfast in Martha's Vineyard, or Janice, who joyfully made a career change in mid-life to study horticulture and begin a small landscaping business.

However, most of our female friends and coworkers continue the ongoing battle with fatigue and the life-work pressures that assail them daily. Some keep at their stressful jobs purely for financial rea-

"There is no chance for the welfare of the world unless the condition of women is improved. It is not possible for a bird to fly on only one wing."

—**Swami Vivekananda**

sons, in hopes that they will be able to discover a way to balance it all one day. Others truly enjoy the challenges and opportunities of their work, and view the benefits as far outweighing the perils.

A survey by the Families and Work Institute shows that 55 percent of employed women bring in half or more of their household income, and that 53 percent say they don't want to cut back on any of their responsibilities at work or at home. Surprisingly, 48 percent of the women surveyed say they would choose to work even if they already had enough money to live as comfortably as they like, indicating that employment affects self-esteem, and that women who work full time are more likely to feel valued at home. Forty-six percent of women cite work-family balance as something they worry about "a great deal." Though life-work balance and other family concerns are viewed as peripheral issues by many corporate managers and politicians, these are core issues to many women. More than a quarter of women report lack of time together with their family as their greatest family concern, even more than neighborhood crime and safety.

"You don't get to choose how you're going to die or when. You can only decide how you're going to live."

—**Joan Baez**

According to Washington pollster Celinda Lake, women's top concern is having enough time and energy to get everything done that needs to be done. Women juggle their time among household, family, career, and community volunteerism. Fifty-six percent of the women polled by Lake Research said that they worry about balancing and juggling work and family very often or often. Their next major concern was retirement security, followed by "making ends meet." Moving ahead was much less on the minds of women than men. Lake's results suggest that most women are feeling challenged to make time for all the things they have to do now, without looking ahead to a better job.

Although 43 percent of those polled said that women are better off than they used to be, with job options and choices about work outside the home, half of those polled said that women don't necessarily have more choices, because economic necessity dictates women's work. As the labor market has restructured and many men have lost jobs because of downsizing and layoffs, women's earnings have become more important. More and more women are the sole support of their families, and many are the primary wage earner.

The only women we've seen who really seem to thrive and keep their spirits alive, despite the barrage of demands at work and at home, are the ones who have supportive relationships, are doing something they really love to do (at work or outside of work), and stay committed and connected to nurturing their physical and spiritual needs in healthy ways. Although most would appreciate a lighter and more balanced load, they enjoy their work and want to continue to grow in and through it.

In a study examining career women who successfully balanced career and relationship demands, Dr. Luann Linquist found that:

- no woman was willing to give up her career entirely;
- self-esteem appeared to increase with career success;
- they knew how to delegate;
- they found relief from stress by getting involved in their work;
- if they were in an intimate relationship, they tended to have supportive significant others; and
- they tended to see their career success as enhancing themselves and their significant-other relationships.

Sustained success in balancing career and relationships is a creative and dynamic process. It requires at least three primary elements: 1) a high degree of personal honesty and self-awareness; 2) skill and willingness to communicate what is true for you to others; and 3) a willingness to creatively collaborate, explore possibilities, and reach mutually satisfactory compromises with others.

If you are a working woman, pause here to look back over the ideas in this section and underline the key points and questions that speak most directly to your situation. Ask yourself what shifts you need to make to find a greater balance among work, family, and the rest of your life. What unspoken needs and requests for action do you have that you can communicate to others, to increase their under-

"Work is an essential part of being alive. Your work is your identity. It tells you who you are. It's gotten so abstract. People don't work for the sake of working. They're working for a car, a new house, or a vacation. It's not the work itself that's important to them. There's such joy in doing work well."

—**Kay Stipkin**

standing of your search and struggles to find balance in your life?

If you live or work closely with a working woman, take these ideas to heart and consider talking with your partner to see how you can help her to be more successful at finding balance in her life work.

The Toll on Our Children

Fortune magazine recently ran a provocative cover story entitled, *"Is Your Family Wrecking Your Career? (and vice versa)."* The article paints a disturbing picture of the conflict between corporate values and family values, and highlights the devastating impact on many of the children of dual-career parents. It includes statistics from a report by the Carnegie Council on Adolescent Development, which found that kids spend significantly less time in the company of adults than they did a few decades ago. About one-third of all adolescents have contemplated suicide; half are at moderate or high risk of abusing drugs, failing in school, getting pregnant, or otherwise seriously damaging their lives. The report stated, "In survey after survey, young adolescents from all ethnic and economic backgrounds lament their lack of parental attention and guidance." Elementary school teachers are debating whether they should quit assigning homework because working parents are too tired or busy to handle it. More than two thousand *Fortune* readers surveyed in 1995 said they spent, on average, fifty-seven hours a week working and commuting.

Because travel has become a critical component of many jobs in global companies, one parent—or both—may often be gone from home on short notice, and the family dinner has regularly disappeared in many homes as parents work late hours. In addition, many households have unstable child care situations, with a vast array of babysitters and parents needing a flow chart to keep it all straight. Even ten-year-old kids are carrying little datebooks to help organize their fully crammed schedules! In the last twenty years, daycare has been the highest soaring cost for families—up 202.7 percent—while the median income of families rose only 6.7 percent! One

"The work will wait while you show your child the rainbow, but the rainbow won't wait while you do the work."

—Patricia Clafford

elementary school teacher quoted in the article said her students seem needier than those in years past; they are more easily distracted and more often fatigued. "Just as adults get scattered, children get scattered," she commented.

Unless something gives in the way the workplace is organized, pressures on working families are likely to continue. In his book, *The End of Work*, trend watcher Jeremy Rifkin suggests that the work week should be shortened and the nonprofit sector expanded to rebuild the "social economy."

The criticality of the current situation demands our collective creative thinking, action, and investigation. What are the effects on our children and future society if families continue to require two wage earners to make ends meet? What role can government play to bring about a workplace transformation that would promote a saner society? What role can you play in modeling strategies for greater inner and outer balance? These are just some of the vital questions that we need to be asking as we contemplate life-work balance.

To Succeed in Life, You Don't Have to Get Caught in the Rat Race

If you need still more incentive to create a healthier life-work balance for yourself, then consider an important recent study. This study, conducted by professors at the Wharton School of Williams College, set out to determine whether people pay a price in workplace success if they give priority to family concerns. Taking a unique approach, it looks at data collected from the same people at two stages in their lives. It begins with responses offered by the participants in 1972, when they were high school seniors from across the nation, at which time they responded to a series of "life interest" questions. These were then compared with the respondents' earnings in 1986.

What the researchers found was that men who had placed high importance on building a good marriage and having a strong family life earned more than those who didn't, after accounting for educa-

"Because work addiction keeps us busy, we stay estranged from our essential selves. An aspect of that estrangement is that we cease asking ourselves if we are doing our right work. Are we actually doing our true work, performing tasks or pursuing vocations that are good for us, for our families, for the universe?"

—Diane Fassel

tional differences, tenure with current employer, and total job experience. Women in the study showed a similar trend, though less consistently. The researchers also found that placing an emphasis on success in work, or having money and steady work, really had no effect on earnings.

The researchers concluded that time invested in family life actually makes workers *more,* not less productive, and enhances overall health, well-being, and corporate performance. On the other hand, it was clear that having a poor family life creates more stressful demands on an employee's time and attention, causing enormous negative consequences in the workplace. Developing a good family life seems especially important early in careers, which is the time when many problematic relationship patterns are set up. The people who didn't build a strong foundation for their family life often paid the price for years, spending considerable time "putting Band-Aids on family problems."

The Wharton study suggested that employers who are authentically concerned about life-work balance, and the quality of work that people offer to their businesses, would be wise to give their employees as much support as possible to spend time with their families. Though this may require allowing for extra time out of the office, supporting people in finding life-work balance that works for each person's unique situation will pay significant dividends for employees, their families, their employer, and likely for those they serve.

But even if your employer doesn't share these values, the Wharton study should help you see that, in the long run, you can have a productive, successful work life even if you make your family a top priority.

Signs of Progress

Despite all the setbacks, stresses, and cutbacks, many companies are beginning to re-evaluate the stressful demands that they put on their employees. In recent years we have seen an increased valuing of *life-work balance.* Note: *work-life balance* is a term often frowned on

> *"As winning companies find they must engage workers' hearts as well as their minds, this increasingly emotional aspect of business is destroying the old corporate machismo that once allowed us to keep our feelings hidden and our inner lives mysterious, even to ourselves ... To the degree that individuals are successful at plumbing their depths, those people should be better off, and the companies that employ them may gain competitive advantage. In fast-shifting markets, the unexamined life becomes a liability."*
>
> —'The Learner Within', *Fortune* Magazine

as indicating a priority toward work over life. When we do exercises on values with corporate teams and executives in vastly differing industries, the number one value we see emerging over and over again is—you guessed it—*balance.*

Numerous factors have led to this emphasis. It is partially spawned by concern over sky rocketing health care rates—40 percent of over a trillion dollars per year takes a major toll on business. If health care costs continue to rise, the annual health care bill for America will eclipse the total after-tax profits of all the Fortune 500 companies combined! Another incentive is an attempt to develop greater allegiance of valued employees. A third reason is the growing recognition that these options allow people to live and work in ways that are not only healthier and happier, but more productive.

Alternative work styles and schedules that promote greater balance and satisfaction in employees' lives have been shown to pay off both business-wise and health-wise. There is abundant data that correlates supportive, satisfying conditions at work and good health, while low job satisfaction, a perceived lack of support, and a sense of "joyless striving," are recognized as major health risk factors. Dr. Suzanne Couellette Krobasa, professor of psychology at the Graduate School of the City University of New York, found that people who felt they had the backing of their boss were half as likely to get ill as people who lacked that support. One enlightening study of 3,200 people at Boeing showed that workers who stated that they "hardly ever" enjoyed their job were two and a half times more likely to report a back injury than subjects who "almost always" enjoyed their job. The study also showed that the most important factor in determining an employee's successful rehabilitation and the length of time it would take for him or her to return to the job was the employee's perception of the company's empathy for them.

In a business world where people are stressed, reactive, and not prone to deep reflection or clear thinking, it is not uncommon to hear statements like, "We're in business to make money, not to run a social center or a playground!" when such ideas are first presented. Though there is some validity in such a statement, hopefully the

> *"The individual is forcing the change. People are shopping around, not only for the right job but for the right atmosphere. They now regard the old rules of business as dishonest, boring, and outdated. This new generation in the workplace is saying, 'I want a society and a job that values me more than the gross national product. I want work that engages the heart as well as the mind and the body, that fosters friendship and that nourishes the earth. I want to work for a company that contributes to the community."*
>
> **—Anita Roddick, Founder of the Body Shop**

results of these and many other studies will temper this with the deeper recognition that creating a work environment where people feel valued and cared about, enjoy their work, and are excited about coming to work is not only tremendously practical and rewarding, but it is also likely to be profoundly profitable.

Study after study shows that companies with cultures that empower their employees by giving them proper leadership, support, and all the information that they need to make wise decisions, are actually far more likely to outperform competitors who function in a more top down, autocratic, "command and control" manner. For many companies, encouraging people to work from their homes reduces the overhead of providing so many offices and services at work.

When Joel was speaking at a recent meeting of the International Facilities Managers Association, the future of offices and office space in a networked and decentralized society was very much in question. One example, from our own experience, is of a high-powered training and consulting firm that had palatial offices in a downtown office building. At one point, a major reorganization led the offices to shrink, driving most of the consultants into offices in their homes. Because most of the consultants were on the road leading training programs around the globe, not only did the company save considerable money, but it gained tremendous flexibility. Though the staff missed the "clubhouse downtown," many of them honestly didn't miss the commute and hassle of parking downtown. And they still had a strong sense of community and camaraderie while they weren't on the road.

In recent years, dozens of major companies have launched programs to help their employees find a greater balance of life. Citibank is encouraging its employees to work out, spend time with their families, and take classes. We have heard that Wells Fargo has offered personal growth leaves, and that Xerox has offered social service sabbaticals. Increasing numbers of business leaders are coming to recognize the value of supporting their people in creatively constructing schedules that allow longer but fewer days in the office, or that offer more freedom to work at home. These options offer a

"There is a great need to bring spiritual values into the corporate setting. Persuading your organization to shift from a paradigm of competition, exploitation and self-interest, to cooperation, empowerment and the common good is one of the greatest gifts you can give to society."

—Richard Barrett, at the World Bank

greater likelihood of living a balanced life, especially for people with children.

One inspiring example comes from the legal profession where, according to a 1991 American Bar Association report, the quality of lawyers' lives has been rapidly deteriorating—partly due to a "macho image, which keeps lawyers from admitting they have personal problems (or) are unhappy with the profession's workaholic pace." Attempting to break the mold, Peabody & Arnold, a Boston firm with more than one hundred lawyers, downshifted to require only eighteen hundred billable hours a year from each attorney, in contrast to the two thousand or more at most other firms. Understanding that enhancing the culture keeps and lures top talent, it has also offered a series of lunchtime parenting seminars, flexible work options, and other opportunities for their staff to find a more balanced way of living and working. When one lawyer made a habit of working till 10 P.M. seven days a week for months at a time, several partners intervened to ask, "What kind of help do you need?" Over the past seven years, the firm has doubled in size and the Harvard Law School student guide now lists them as a firm "where it's possible to succeed while sustaining a personal life." Speaking to the long-term benefits, one managing partner said, "This isn't just about making Peabody & Arnold a nicer place. It's about not wearing down your machinery. Over the long run you'll get more productivity out of lawyers if you can just keep them happy." The same applies in many other organizations we have worked with.

When General Motors announced that they would automate in an extraordinarily thorough fashion at their plant in Flint, Michigan, where it was virtually the only employer, Frithjof Bergmann opened the Center for New Work there in 1984. In his first major proposal, he advanced the idea that instead of splitting the town into two dysfunctional halves, one desperately unemployed, and the other working overtime, why not let everyone work six months in the factories and during the other six months, make it possible for the workers to do something that they passionately wanted to do? Although Bergmann was not able to launch all of the

"Organizational change begins with leaders who walk the talk by transforming themselves."

—*Fortune* **Magazine**

"You have to force yourself to spend some time away from the hustle and bustle of your job in order to get down to reality again. If you don't spend enough time doing that, you can lose hold of the reins and get into all kinds of trouble."

— **Richard Abdoo, CEO, Wisconsin Energy**

initiatives he proposed, he did work with thousands of people helping them to discover what they really wanted to do. Some went back to school, others started new businesses, and many decided that they really wanted to spend more time with their families and children.

In Japan, the KOA Denko corporation, an extremely successful electronic components plant in the Ina valley, became so efficient that the organization was considering laying off nearly half of its employees. Instead, they took an inspiring path toward balance. Each morning, the employees would come to work in their uniforms and dust masks in one of the most technically sophisticated plants in Japan. After lunch, they would change into another set of uniforms and work in the fields growing produce that was then used to feed hungry people in their community and to sell to neighboring towns. People so enjoyed this unique form of balanced work-life that productivity further increased and people were much happier.

Other Wiser Ways of Working

A number of other companies are leading the way toward helping their employees strike a better life-work balance. Our friend Herman Maynard was a manager in DuPont's cable division. In 1988 his business unit's desire for performance had reached the point where high levels of stress were having a detrimental impact on employees' health, performance, and families. With a clear understanding of the relationship of stress on individuals' and businesses' health, the division worked together to develop a way to reduce stress, improve performance, and develop a healthier life-work balance. What they established were three overriding priorities that guided the decision making and work for the members of the division. Perhaps they can help guide you too. These were:

1. Safety, health, and family

If there was a question of whether or not to drive at safe speeds, get the needed amount of exercise or sleep, attend a child's school function, or work on business, the individuals were expected to first

"As long as we operate within this old paradigm, we are separated from our heart and values and feel powerless. We cannot suspend our values during the workday and think we will have them back when we get home. We're all interconnected. There is a spiritual dimension to business just as to individuals."

—Ben (Cohen) and Jerry (Greenfield)

care for their own and their family's physical and psychological needs.

2. Learning

The second priority was for each employee to spend a minimum of 20 percent of their at-work time learning. Learning could involve *any subject* the employee chose, and any learning process the employee selected.

3. Realizing the business mission

Though many people in the division believed this was a wise plan, it was so radically different than the cultural norm that it was still met with a high level of disbelief and skepticism. After allowing a three-month settling-in time for employees to fully believe that leadership was actually serious about this, the organization began to more closely measure the impact of the new strategy. What they found was that there was a dramatic increase in creativity, innovation, and productivity. The up-front price was for management to give up control and risk anarchy. Yet in the long run, the results were inspiring, and employees acted even more responsibly in how they used their time and spent money. The division sent a clear message that each individual was valued and trusted first as a person, and second as a contributor to the business. And people lived up to this trust.

Another approach to implementing greater life-work balance is being explored at Hewlett-Packard, whose leadership has formally endorsed alternative work schedules. At the company's financial services center in Colorado Springs, thirty-eight people out of a team total of sixty chose to work a four-day, ten-hour schedule instead of their regular eight-to-five, five-day schedule. Their experiment showed these results:

- Overtime was reduced by 50 percent.
- Productivity—transactions per day—exceeded that of colleagues who remained on the typical five-day, eight-hour schedule.
- Customer satisfaction and employee satisfaction increased.

> *"Work-life balance improves employee retention and yields much greater employee initiative and commitment. We know that it helps to reduce stress and burnout, and we are learning that it increases employee productivity ... we can provide the tools for people to balance their lives, it's not up to management to do the actual balancing. Employees must take initiative to do that. We can't make the job easier, but we can add significant flexibility to the way our people work."*
>
> **—Lewis E. Platt, CEO, Hewlett-Packard Company**

These results speak for themselves. Not only are Hewlett-Packard schedules flexible, but so are work locations. As technology continues to advance, working from almost anywhere has become possible. At present, between 10 to 15 percent of the company's employees telecommute. According to Lew Platt, Hewlett-Packard's CEO, who has most outspokenly supported Hewlett Packard's life-work balance initiatives, this means that, "the focus really does have to be on accomplishments and meeting objectives. It's no longer on 'face time,' and I think that's good. It suits the world in which we live."

This is not to say that companies will not resist such changes. As Platt acknowledges, "Cultural change is the most difficult change of all, especially in organizations that are led by a generation of managers who had at-home spouses and were willing to sacrifice much of their personal lives for their careers." He tells the story of one senior manager who had a meeting with his staff to discuss work-life balance. The meeting started at 5 P.M. and ended at 9 P.M.—and he didn't see the irony! Platt believes that though change is slow, it is happening, and he is championing the vision of "an environment that encourages employees and managers to work together to achieve common company objectives for business success, *while creating opportunities for balancing work with other life activities.*"

> "*There is an important link between deep change at the personal level and deep change at the organizational level. To make deep personal change is to develop a new paradigm, a new self, one that is more effectively aligned with today's realities. This can occur only if we are willing to journey into unknown territory and confront the ... problems we encounter.*"
>
> —Robert Quinn

Culturally Shifting Life-Work Values and Norms

On June 17, 1744, the commissioners from Maryland and Virginia negotiated a treaty with the Indians of the Six Nations at Lancaster, Pennsylvania. The Indians were invited to send their sons to William and Mary College. The next day they declined the offer for the following reason, as recorded in T. C. McLuhan's *Touch the Earth:*

"We know that you highly esteem the kind of learning taught in those Colleges, and that the Maintenance of our young Men, while with you, would be very expensive to you. We are convinced that you mean to do us Good by your Proposal; and we thank you heartily. But you who are wise must know that different Nations have different Conceptions of things and you will therefore not take it amiss, if our ideas of this kind of Education happen not to be the same as yours."

"We have had some Experience of it. Several of our young People were formerly brought up at the Colleges of the Northern Provinces; they were instructed in all your Sciences; but, when they came back to us, they were bad Runners, ignorant of every means of living in the woods... neither fit for Hunters, Warriors, nor Counsellors, they were totally good for nothing. We are, however, not the less obliged by your kind Offer, tho' we decline accepting it; and, to show our grateful Sense of it, if the Gentlemen of Virginia will send us a Dozen of their Sons, we will take care of their Education, instruct them in all we know, and make Men of them."

As the American Indians remind us, the kinds of skills we value and the ways in which we work are not divinely determined, but rather reflect evolving values. In medieval England, it is estimated that holiday leisure time occupied about one-third of the year—we now have fifty less holidays each year than our foremothers and fathers in England had. In Papua, New Guinea, it used to be that if people worked one day, they wouldn't dream of doing any labor on the next day. For the !Kung Bushmen only two and a half six-hour work days per week is the norm.

Until very recently, humans lived and worked according to natural seasonal cycles. Can you imagine the rhythm and pace of human life and work before the invention of clock time became accepted in the late seventeenth century? Or before the work "day" was expanded far into the night by the advent of electric lights and efficient internal heating systems in the early twentieth century?

For a truly rebalancing holiday, you and your family might want to experiment sometime with resetting your biorhythms by going with only natural light for a week or so, regulating your activities by the natural cycles of the sunrise, sunset, and moonlight patterns. See what effect simply eliminating electric lights for a week can make in your energy! Women might find this artificial-light

"Fame or integrity: which is more important? Money or happiness: which is more valuable? Success or failure: which is most destructive? If you look to others for fulfillment, you will never truly be fulfilled. If your happiness depends on money, you will never be happy with yourself. Be content with what you have; rejoice in the way things are. When you realize there is nothing lacking, the whole world belongs to you!"

—Lao Tzu

"fast" especially healing, both biologically and psychologically.

Until the nineteenth century, labor patterns were seasonal, intermittent, and irregular. With the industrial revolution, the information technologies revolution, and the increased mobility of the workforce, work styles have shifted radically. Even today's norm of steady employment for fifty-two weeks a year is a fairly modern invention, and vacation policies vary widely around the globe.

In Europe, where vacation policies are generally set by the government, workers get far more paid time off than in America. Traditionally, the norm has been four to six weeks of paid vacation with fifteen paid holidays, and eighteen days of sick leave. Recent efforts to cut vacation time back to only three weeks have been met with outrage by many European workers. For example, Austrians get thirty days of vacation after one year on the job, Finns and Swedes get twenty-five, Germans, twenty-four.

By contrast, a recent survey of over one thousand U.S. companies that set their own vacation policies showed that 82 percent allowed employees only ten days off after a year of service. And as we've seen, many people don't feel secure enough in their jobs to take even that. We hear from so many people who we work with that vacations often add to their stress. Even in the best of circumstances, due to the exhaustion most people carry into a vacation, there is barely enough time to truly rest and renew oneself.

Not all cultures reinforce working more to keep jobs. With the rise of high unemployment, many European nations are seriously considering legislating shorter work weeks. In Italian workplaces, a common slogan is *Lavorare meno. Lavorare tutti,* or "Work less. Everyone works." And the French Senate has recently approved a measure that would promote experimentation with a thirty-three hour work week, which, if instituted, would make room for two million new jobs.

Around the globe, many companies aren't waiting for the government to legislate work time; they are taking the initiative. At various foreign subsidiaries of Hewlett-Packard and Digital, when faced with the choice of major layoffs or a sweeping reorganization

"If you experience pain along the way, consider it a signpost of progress. And if you gradually become more comfortable in your skin, if you feel a spreading sense of oneness with all creation, don't fight it. There's more to us than the sniveling, snarling organism that craves power and approval. The clarity and contentment we seek lies deep inside us all."

—**Strateford Sherman, 'Executive Life', Fortune Magazine**

of work schedules, the companies opted for the latter. As a result, no employees at those Hewlett-Packard sites work more than a four-day work week, even though the plant is in operation seven days a week. When Digital offered its four thousand employees a choice of a four-day work week with a 7 percent pay cut, 530 employees supported it, saving 90 jobs that would have otherwise been cut.

Here in the United States, talk of a shorter work week is taken less seriously. As one spokesperson for the AFL-CIO noted, until a forty hour week without forced overtime is established as a norm, there's not much point in pushing for a thirty-two hour week. Yet, as new jobs are slow to appear, many union bosses are saying that a shorter work week is getting higher and higher on meeting agendas. For example, the United Auto Workers recently dusted off a slogan from the 1970s—"seven hour day for eight hours pay"—in their negotiations with a Chrysler minivan plant in St. Louis.

New Choices

Since 1948, the productivity of a U.S. worker, we are told, has more than doubled. This means that we can now produce what we could in 1948 in less than half the time. Or, if you like, you could now live at a standard twice as high as in 1948. This means, logically, that if you were content to live at the modest, but comfortable standard afforded by 1948 productivity, you could choose to:

- work only a four-hour workday;
- work only six months each year;
- take every other year off from work—with pay.

Instead of these options, however, most of us have made other choices in our lifestyles. Since 1973, the amount of free time people have has fallen nearly 40 percent from a median of 26 hours each week to under 17. With all our productivity and progress, with all our new technology and time saving savvy, it seems that few people are actually happier than in earlier years. Indeed, the number of people who reported being "very happy" peaked in 1957!

So, if there is really a growing number of people feeling stressed and yearning for more time and more balance in their lives, why aren't more people making decisions to step out of the rat race? One poll, conducted by one of the nation's largest telecommunication companies, showed that 69 percent of the people say they'd like to cut back on the hours they work but they simply can't afford to. Reasons commonly cited for not making a shift toward a more balanced lifestyle include job insecurity, lack of flexibility at work to change schedules, and the inertia of personal habit. The most common reason, however, was debt. Only 29 percent of the people in the study pay off their credit card charges each month. As a culture, we are driven by the addiction to buy more things and live in debt. Many people are doubly addicted to their work and to shopping, leaving little free time or extra money. This seems to be a uniquely American predicament—people in the United States shop three to four times more than their counterparts in Western Europe.

Polls show that less than one-third of the public are debt free (not including mortgages), and estimates are that for the rest of us, nearly 70 percent of our spendable income goes to pay the interest charges on our accumulated debt. If we compute that against a forty hour work week, that would mean that most of us work from 8 A.M. Monday morning until Thursday noon just to pay the interest on our debts! That leaves us to wonder how much of what we make between Thursday noon and the end of the day on Friday goes toward purchases that put us more into debt?

It's a vicious cycle. The more we work, the more tired and exhausted we feel. The more out of balance we get, the more prone we are to make unwise, impulsive decisions, and to buy things that we really don't need. The more we buy, the more we have to work to pay off our debts, and slowly the heavy wheels of the consumer machine grind us down.

Indeed, one major indicator of imbalance in people's lives is the addictive norms of consumerism found in our society. Eighty-nine percent of women polled and 75 percent of men agree that as a

"Finding the right work is like discovering your own soul in the world."

—Thomas Moore

"The highest reward for a person's toil is not what they get from it, but what they become by it."

—John Ruskin

nation we are addicted to shopping. Eight-eight percent of the women and 83 percent of the men strongly agree that "Americans are too materialistic." More than two-thirds expressed concerns that today's young people are too concerned about money and material success, and that in general people spend too much time shopping. Consuming is a "substitute for what's missing in our lives," say 75 percent of women and 69 percent of men.

We seem to understand this, but can't seem to stop. Exhausted and drained by the lifestyles we work so hard to maintain, it is easy to be sold the illusion that real satisfaction is just as close as the nearest mall or only an 800-number call away. It takes self-awareness, self-discipline, and commitment to invest quality attention and time necessary to savor the precious and fleeting moments of life's simple pleasures.

Learning to make wise choices and developing skill in selective prioritizing are essential for balanced living. Remember, choice follows awareness!

> *"My experience working ten years with auto workers is that they get so frustrated in their jobs that once every four months, in a rage, they go off to the nearest mall and fill up their pickup truck with anything they can find."*
>
> —**Frithjof Bergmann**

Curing Our Collective Craziness

Schizophrenia is a mental imbalance that mistakes one's dreams or fantasies for reality. With this in mind, let's look at the so-called American Dream. If you are an average American, each year you are bombarded with roughly twenty-five thousand TV commercials (not to mention the actual program content). The "American Dream" is so deeply programmed into your psyche that it is has likely forged an insidious link between who you think you are, your self-image, self-worth, and self-esteem, and the material goods that you own—or rather that you rent at a high price, if you buy on credit.

The unsettling and intentional impact of this is clear in a comment by retail analyst Victor Lebow, who actively promoted consumerism as vital to our economy during the post war period. According to Lebow, "Our enormously productive economy demands that we make consumption a way of life, that we convert the buying and use of goodies into rituals, that we seek our spiritual satisfaction and our ego satisfaction in consumption. We need things consumed, burned up, worn out, replaced, at an ever-increasing rate."

Unthinkingly, many of us have been so inundated with the televised version of the fantasy of the American Dream that we may just possibly be in danger of trying to live in a dream and missing reality. It seems that as a society we're in danger of going collectively crazy. In a recent Merck poll, the schizophrenia we're talking about seems quite evident. Among those surveyed in this poll, 71 percent said they have more possessions than their parents did, but only 49 percent described themselves as "happier"; 77 percent agreed with the statement, "If I wanted to, I could choose to buy and consume less than I do," but 53 percent also said that they spent nearly all their money on the basic necessities of life.

We know on one hand that we need to learn to do with less, that continued consumerism and materialism have, and will, outstretch and dangerously unbalance the physical and social resources of our world (and perhaps ourselves as well). Yet, on the other hand, we are forever being encouraged to buy and consume more, to never be satisfied with what we have, or even with who we are. Moving too fast to think deeply, our very sense of ourselves is constantly being confused with what we have rather than with who we are.

What is perhaps saddest is that we have given so much attention to our outer things, and so little attention to understanding ourselves, that many of us have only a shallow, superficial, and incomplete knowledge of the unique, vast, and profound beings we truly are. As a result, many of us have never discovered our beauty and strengths, but instead focus on the painful symptoms of the frustrations and unskillfulness that comes from living so out of touch with the deeper foundation and wholeness of our lives.

So what is the cure for our schizophrenia of having one piece of our mind living in the adman's fantasy world, and the other not believing it, not buying it, and deeply yearning for a more sane and balanced quality of life, and the satisfaction that money can never buy for us? The cure has to do with yearning for, and actively pursuing, greater balance in our way of life. As you follow a path toward a more

"...where I work, jobs become more demanding every day. Technology is accelerating at a dizzying pace. Product life cycles are shorter. Consumer power and expectations are escalating and competition is relentless. We're continually expanding activities through partners, forging alliances, always looking for a variety of survival strategies. It's a constant push, pull, and shove. Put these things together and you'll see why a tremendous amount of stress builds up on our jobs. These realities are what make it so tough to balance work and life..."

—**Lewis E. Platt, CEO, Hewlett-Packard Company**

balanced way of living, it may seem like you are waking up from a bad dream and discovering, perhaps for the first time, that you are a remarkable person living in a wonderful, though crazy, world. You can make choices and set priorities for a saner and more satisfying life.

Simpler Living

Simple living has been preached as a wise way of life for thousands of years. Jesus urged his followers to get their priorities straight and advocated the virtues of a simple life. Likewise, the Buddha recommended a middle way that avoided problems caused by overindulgence or by extreme deprivation or asceticism. The Taoist sage Lao Tzu reminds us that "He who knows he has enough is rich." In recent times, Gandhi reminded his followers, "Civilization, in the real sense of the term, consists not in the multiplication, but in the deliberate and voluntary reduction of wants. This alone promotes real happiness and contentment."

The ideal of simple living is not new even to American culture. It dates back to the self-reliant lifestyles of the Puritans, the Shakers, and to Henry David Thoreau in his two-room cabin at Walden Pond. In this century, the concept of "voluntary simplicity" was first introduced by Richard Gregg in 1936. A Harvard graduate, Gregg was inspired by his time with Gandhi and defined voluntary simplicity thusly: "Voluntary simplicity involves both inner and outer conditions. It means singleness of purpose, sincerity and honesty within, as well as avoidance of exterior clutter, of many possessions irrelevant to the chief purpose of life. It means an ordering and guiding of our energy and desires, a partial restraint in some directions in order to secure greater abundance of life in other directions. It involves a deliberate organization of life for a purpose."

In more recent decades this notion has been expressed in various ways, as "down-shifting," "right-sizing," or just plain simple living. The Trends Research Institute, a think tank in Rhinebeck, New York, named "voluntary simplicity" as one of the top ten trends of the coming millenium. Evidence from other polls and experts in

"To live content with small means; to see elegance rather than luxury, and refinement rather than fashion; to be worthy, not respectable, and wealthy, not rich; to listen to stars and birds, babes and sages with open heart; to study hard; to think quietly, act frankly, talk gently, await occasions, hurry never; in a word, to let the spiritual, unbidden and unconscious, grow up through the common— this is my symphony."

—William Henry Channing

the field shows that the movement of people toward a more balanced lifestyle is mushrooming. This is due to many factors, some of which we have been exploring in this chapter.

Foremost among the recent polls is a survey commissioned by the Merck Family Fund entitled "Yearning for Balance." This study showed that 72 percent of people age forty to forty-nine agree with the statement, "I would like to simplify my life." A full 28 percent of all the respondents in the study reported "making voluntary changes in my lifestyle that resulted in making less money"—not including those who had taken a regularly scheduled retirement.

Such people are sometimes described as "downshifters" or "domos"—downwardly mobile professionals—who are typically under fifty and who have abandoned a successful or promising career to pursue a life of greater purpose or spiritual focus.

People who have made the decision to downshift are more likely to have children than the population as a whole. They span all economic ranges and are not all necessarily well off. Most, 56.6 percent, make less than $34,000 per year, with 37 percent having an annual income of less than $10,000, and 24 percent make more than $100,000 per year. The gender gap is revealing: overall, 32 percent of all women in the United States and 23.5 percent of all men are downshifters. Not surprisingly, 60 percent of the downshifters are women. Nearly as many men as women, though, one-third of the total population, would prefer to work part-time. This far exceeds the availability of good part-time jobs.

The downshifters offer many reasons for making this shift in their lives. The most frequently mentioned reasons are:

- wanting to live a more balanced life (72 percent of moms, and 74 percent of dads)

- wanting more time (66 percent)

- wanting a less stressful life (70 percent of moms, and 58 percent of dads)

- wanting to spend more time caring for their children (87 percent of moms, and 72 percent of dads)

"To laugh often and much; to win the respect of intelligent people and the affection of children; to earn the appreciation of honest critics and endure the betrayal of false friends; to appreciate beauty, to find the best in others; to leave the world a bit better, whether by a healthy child, a garden patch or a redeemed social condition; to know even one life has breathed easier because you have lived. This is to have succeeded."

—Ralph Waldo Emerson

Would you guess that people who have downshifted are happy with their decision, or that they regret their decision? The study shows that those who have chosen to downshift are overwhelmingly happy about the changes they have made in their lives. Only 6 percent of the women and 13 percent of the men say they are unhappy with their decision, while 81 percent are happy with their decision and believe that lifestyle simplification leads to more balance and joy in life.

These findings are not isolated. A growing number of polls show that many people are beginning to shift toward a more balanced way of life. These polls agree in their reports that 75 to 80 percent of the public are saying, "We need to make major changes if we are going to live in a sustainable way on this earth." The recent International Worklife Values Survey tells us that 65 percent of the people interviewed from around the globe have experienced a major transformation in their lives in the past five years. Add to this that about 60 percent of us say, "Not only do we need to change, we want to change." Though for many this notion is still in the realm of ideal, most people really are sympathetic to the changes needed to live a more balanced and sustainable way of life.

According to the Merck Poll, people commonly say that three things will bring their lives more into balance and make their lives more satisfying: 1) spending more time with family and friends; 2) reducing stress; 3) doing more to make a difference in their communities.

People are not only aware of what will bring their lives more into balance, but many people are actively making changes in their lives to bring this about. Some "pro-balance" life-work strategies that are being promoted include:

- flex time
- job sharing
- working at home
- telecommuting

- early retirement
- simple living
- co-housing
- "urban village" industries
- sabbaticals
- exploring what has meaning and purpose for you in your job

Getting Started

So, what can you do to begin making changes toward greater balance in your life? Some clues can be gained by rethinking how you spend your money and time. The following three exercises can be helpful to organize your thinking.

1. Make a three-column form on a piece of paper. In the first column, record each purchase you make, and in the second, note how much you spend on it. In the third, note the level of satisfaction you gain from that choice. If you like, you can use a scale of -10 to +10, indicating the level of dissatisfaction or satisfaction that you experience. For example if you spend $10 to go to a movie that you didn't enjoy, your level of satisfaction might be -8. If you buy a jacket that you really enjoy and that keeps you dry and warm, perhaps your return on that investment will be a +9. Make similar notations for every purchase you make.

2. Keep a similar log of how you spend your time, noting the quality of satisfaction you gain from experiences that you have that don't really cost any money. For example, watching the sunset, talking with a friend, playing with your child, holding a loved one in your arms. How much fulfillment do you gain from how you spend your time in these ways? (This is a great exercise for finding more time in your life for things you want to do—it's amazing how much time we fritter away on things we really don't care about.)

"The price of anything is the amount of life you pay for it."

—Henry David Thoreau

"Most are engaged in business in the greater part of their lives, because the soul abhors a vacuum and they have not discovered continuous employment for man's nobler faculties."

—Henry David Thoreau

3. Take some time to figure out your hourly earnings, after taxes and other deductions. Once you've done this you will know how much your "life-time" is really worth. With a clearer sense of what your "life-time" is worth to you, you will be in a better position to evaluate how you invest your time, energy, and attention. For example, if you make ten dollars an hour, then a movie ticket or a meal out for $10 is equivalent to investing one hour of your life. Remember, the choice is always yours, and to the degree you are aware of what the real costs are, you will be more likely to create balance in your life by spending your time in more fulfilling ways.

Stepping back to analyze how your investments of time, energy, attention, and money create balance or imbalance in your life can offer valuable insight into how your choices create or detract from the quality of life you want to live. Many people notice that as the cost of maintaining their lifestyle falls, the amount of free time in their lives increases. The decision to slow down and simplify often adds quality time to your life. With more time you will be more likely to discover and explore what truly satisfies you in your life. It gives you the opportunity to improve and strengthen your relationships, and to focus on the values and life priorities most near and dear to your heart.

Soulshifting

There is another significant phenomenon happening around the world that deserves attention in this chapter. This is the multitude of people who are taking the yearning for balance even more deeply to heart. Currently estimated at about 10 percent of adults in the United States and climbing, the "upshifters," as they are commonly known, or "soulshifters" as we prefer to call them, are the ones who are learning to live more out of an eco-logical and spiritual awareness than a self-centered, ego-logical way of being. We

"I am done with great things and big plans, great institutions and big success. And I am for those tiny invisible loving human forces that work from individual to individual, creeping through the crannies of the world like so many rootlets, or like the capillary oozing of water, yet which, if given time, will rend the hardest monuments of human pride."

—William James

prefer to call them "soulshifters" to avoid possible confusion with the idea of downshifting. Soulshifters are spearheading a new way of life that is ultimately more satisfying, more sustainable, and more spiritual. A typical soulshifter would say, " I'm more than merely a dissatisfied consumer here to be entertained. I hold a larger sense of myself as a spiritual being committed to personal discovery, growth, learning, and meaningful work. I dedicate myself to living a meaningful life with my family, making meaningful connections and contributions to my community, and finding a meaningful sense of spiritual identity and development." This 10 percent of the American public is about twenty million people, and is almost two-to-one women to men.

Researcher Paul Ray of American LIVES, Inc., has looked through another set of lenses at a similiar transformation. In his study on U.S. culture, Ray found that a full 24 percent or 44,000,000 U.S. adults fall into a group described by him as *cultural creatives,* who are concerned with values that are more likely to promote balanced lifestyles. These values include ecological sustainability, spiritual transformation, altruism, stewardship for the earth and its people, and valuing the feminine and relationships.

Cultural creatives are called that because they are the innovators giving rise to new ideas and operating on the leading edge of cultural change. They tend to hold a self-fulfilling optimism regarding the future, and are actively involved in building healthier personal, social, and global conditions that are more conducive to harmony and balance. These people tend to be more middle to upper-middle class, and though they are a bit more common on the West Coast, they are found in all regions of the country. Cultural creatives comprise 50 percent more women than men, and the overall male-female ratio is 40:60. The commentary on this study holds that in these people lies a great hope for a critical mass of people necessary to make the cultural shift toward a norm of a more balanced and ecologically sustainable way of life and work. In other words, you don't have to do it alone—there are many other people out there who are advocating for similar changes.

"It does not need to be a choice between head decisions and heart decisions. An organization that balances head decisions and heart decisions has a far greater potential for achieving and sustaining success than an organization that doesn't have heart."

—Bill Maynard and Tom Champoux

Given that two-thirds of the economic activity in America is related to consumer purchases, it is clear that even a small shift caused by these folks, whether we call them downshifters, soul-shifters, or cultural creatives, will make a tidal wave of reverberations throughout the whole economy. In recent years, whole new industries are emerging to support the ecologically and spiritually minded. Look at the explosion of concern with making products recyclable, the radical shift toward healthier diets that rely more on pastas and fresh whole foods, rather than on animal products and their devastating health and environmental consequences. Likewise, the rise of the hemp fabric industry, and the fashion trend toward nontoxic dyes. As more and more people shift from yearning for balance to actively making the changes that create it, both the game and the paying/playing field will also change.

> *"Let us take care of the children, for they have a long way to go. Let us take care of the elders, for they have come a long way. Let us take care of those in between, for they are doing the work."*
> —**Traditional African Prayer**

Three Dimensions of Balance: Sustainability, Satisfaction, and Soulfulness

We are at a critical turning point as a global culture. If we as individuals, families, communities, and societies are to learn to live in balance, we must learn to assume a more ecological view of life. To do this, we need to seek balance within and among three primary ecologies—the physical, social, and spiritual. Duane Elgin, director of Choosing Our Future, and author of *Voluntary Simplicity* and *Awakening Earth,* reminds us that these three spheres are related to the three Ss of sustainability, satisfaction, and soul or spirit.

The path of the first S leads us to live a more sustainable way of life by learning to live in harmony with the physical ecology of our world. Pausing to reflect on how you relate to the physical world, ask yourself the following questions:

- How often do I consider the impact of my shopping habits, and my lifestyle on the sustainability of the physical environment?

- What are three things I can begin to do today to improve my impact on the environment?

- What reminders to do this can I create for myself?

- What are some food choices for the benefit of the planet and my own physical well-being that I can make three times a day?

The path of the second S leads us to consciously cultivate a more satisfying way of life. This is one that helps us to learn and discover how to live in harmony with our social ecology, that is, our relationship with other people, organizations, and communities, as well as with people of other countries and cultures, different races, genders, and mindsets. Again, pause to ask yourself:

- What do I most enjoy about my life? About my work?

- Who are the people whose presence and support I am most grateful for in my life? Who are the people who most look to me for inspiration and support? Who are the people or groups of people I am most comfortable with? Most uncomfortable with?

- What are some steps I might take to expand my comfort zone in order to enhance my social ecological wisdom, and cultivate more satisfying relationships?

The path of the third S invites us to discover how to live a more soulful or spiritual way of life—one that seeks to build harmony and awareness with the spiritual ecology of ourselves in relation to the larger, more mysterious and multidimensional Whole, however we might describe it. Pause again now to reflect or to write down your answers to the following questions:

- How do I nourish and inspire myself spiritually?

- Who are the people whose examples most inspire me as the embodiments of my spiritual ideals? Who are the people who most support me in my spiritual growth?

- What literature, media, or scripture do I find spiritually uplifting and inspiring?

- What would it mean for me to bring more soul and spirit into my daily life? How can I deepen my spiritual understanding and express that wisdom, compassion, love, and creativity in my life and work?

Balance is found in wholeness, not fragmentation. Taken to heart, these three paths braid together in a balanced and beautiful way. Remember that living in a way that honors our wholeness is truly the path of balance, and discover how these three paths to wholeness actually merge into one.

The Law of Progressive Simplification

From his analysis of the rise and fall of twenty civilizations, the great historian Arnold Toynbee offers us insights into our search for a balanced lifestyle, and a larger perspective on the current shifts in values and ways of life. Summarizing the principles of civilization growth, Toynbee formulated the Law of Progressive Simplification, which provides some clues to the shift needed toward greater balance in our civilization as a whole. The law reminds us that the growth and vitality of a civilization is not a function of power over land or power over people, and it is most certainly not related to how much we sell or how many resources we buy, sell, or consume. Rather, the measure of a civilization's growth is in its *ability to transfer increasing amounts of energy and attention from the material side of life to the psychological, cultural, aesthetic, and spiritual side of life.*

This startling and profound idea has much to teach us about finding life-work balance that is truly satisfying and meaningful. What it means is that the more mature a civilization is, the more people will invest their time, energy, and attention in activities and relationships that offer not merely material goods and gratification, but the satisfaction gained by a high quality of relationships, authentic and meaningful communication, the sharing of valuable infor-

"There is a greater reality which encompasses individual life experiences. It is a learning, a blending and a centering. When you take all of your experiences and blend them, you create a new color, a new symbol, a new vibration. The obvious reality has been transformed."

—David Chethlahe Paladin

mation, and by the sublime satisfaction of authentically inspiring spiritual experience.

If we take this principle to heart, it is clear that our civilization is still early in its evolution. Hopefully the strain we feel, and the multiple signs of burnout, distress, and imbalance we witness, will be viewed in retrospect as growing pains that are helping us to individually and collectively wake up, and to shift our priorities and commitment toward living life in a way that is truly in balance.

You can call yourself a cultural pioneer to the degree that you take this wisdom to heart, and begin to increase your ability to transfer your own energy and attention from preoccupation with the things of your life, toward the more sublime fulfillment offered by developing quality relationships, and by nurturing the creative, aesthetic, compassionate, and spiritual dimensions of your life. Perhaps this could be said to truly be your real work.

"The key to our inner resources is self-knowledge. Self-knowledge is gained by personal development... This comes close to being the meaning of life. Consequently the raison d'être for a company is to supply an environment in which personal development of human beings involved in the company can best take place... What a precious gift to humanity and our planet it would be if the remarkable knowledge we have achieved should be united with wisdom. Then our planet would be the paradise it is meant to be. Business life has the opportunity to bring that gift forward."

—Rolf Osterber, Founding Member of World Business Academy

TWELVE

Finding Yourself in the World

Within each of us, in the ground of our being, powers reside for the healing of our world. These powers do not arise from any ideology, access to the occult, or passion for social activism. They are inevitable powers. Because we are part of the web of life, we can draw on the strength—and the pain—of every creature. This interconnection constitutes our 'deep ecology': it is the source of our pain for the world as well as our love and appetite for life.

—JOANNA MACY

O ur search for balance is not a solitary affair, nor one that we need to work out solely with family members or other intimate relationships, nor even just between our work and home life. For the sense of belonging to a larger whole is a fundamental force in the search for balance, one that begins in our need for connection to a larger community, extending out to encompass the entire human family and, ultimately, to all of nature. Acknowledging our place in the greater whole helps us round out our experience, fostering our ability to see our part in the wheel of life and ultimately, creates a deep sense of balance and peace.

Glimpses of Community

It is only natural that we yearn for a sense of community. As bio-psycho-social creatures, we long for recognition, mutual support, and shared interest with other people—beyond the need for family ties. The fulfillment, in the sense of belonging, that one may find in being a member of a high-performing team, a spiritual community, or even a street gang can be immeasurable.

For millions of years we primates have faced the chaos of our world by taking refuge in community. Just as our ancestors huddled together for warmth, banded together for protection, teaching the young, gathering provisions, we gather today to seek out warmth, nourish ourselves, and find safe passage and clear direction in the company of others. From recent research in the natural sciences it is clear that cooperation is a more cogent force for balanced survival and sustainability than competition. Feeling ourselves as members of a community seems essential to our well-being and our health. As former health care providers and medical researchers—and corporate consultants for 15 years—we can assure you that the "disease" of loneliness is one of the most common and devastating illnesses of our time and culture.

People are starving for meaningful, nourishing, supportive relationships. In a culture where more than 75 percent of the population do not know their neighbors, people are longing for connectedness, belonging, and for the assurance and fulfillment that comes from being in the midst of a circle of deeply committed friends. The malaise seems largely due to a lack of knowing people more deeply, and failing to discover a common sense of purpose, meaning, vision, and values that are vital to community life. Remember, the root meaning of *community* implies "with unity!"

Communities may develop intentionally, as in intentional housing developments, or in membership in organizations and clubs. Or a sense of community may emerge more informally, by sharing interests in a neighborhood, or having kids on the same soccer team or carpool. As the pressures on individuals and families continues to increase, and as people spend such large amounts of time on their job, we hear increasingly frequent comments about the importance of developing a sense of community both at work and beyond. For example, a recent *Industry Week* survey of business managers from

*"The Way is long—
let us go together.
The Way is difficult—
let us help each other.
The Way is joyful—
let us share it.
The Way is ours
alone—
let us go in love.
The Way grows
before us—
let us begin."*

—Zen Invocation

around the globe suggests that people in business feel a deep sense of isolation, and over two-thirds of them, 69 percent, expressed an interest in having a greater sense of belonging in the workplace.

A 1993 Lou Harris and Associates survey asked a sampling of people what was most important in their lives. More than half of the people interviewed—56 percent—responded that their family and friends were most important. Next most important was religious faith (21 percent), followed by doing something to make the world a better place (12 percent), career fulfillment (5 percent), and monetary success (5 percent).

The roots of community are basic to life balance. In terms of humanity, remember that our bodies were shaped through countless generations of tribal communal living. The templates for our body, mind, and language were shaped by moving, touching, and living in close connection with others. We were born not merely to work, but to dance, to sing, to create art, to find, prepare and eat food together, to tell and listen to stories, to care for each other, and to be close to those we love, to ponder, to discuss, and to commune together with the awesome mysteries of life that we associate with the spiritual reality that extends beyond the horizons of our ordinary knowing. The pulse of our lives weaves us together into a larger circle of community with those we walk, dance, and pray with, those we eat and sleep with, those we work with and for, and those we learn from.

As the millennia passed and social groups increased in size and complexity, the need for community has become increasingly fulfilled through relationships with people at work and play, and through political parties, religious communities, clubs, sports teams, or neighborhood groups.

But as the fabric of our society continues to unravel, many of us still struggle to find a sense of community and belonging. Often, we are too busy for it, too tired, or too cynical to even look for it. Or we honestly have no sense of where to begin if we were to mount the search. In the absence of close family, the drive for belonging and community in many of our children may be satisfied through loyalty to local gangs. Countless lonely, exhausted adults alienated from

"A too highly developed individualism can lead to a debilitating sense of isolation so that you can be lonely and lost in a crowd ... Ubuntu has no equivalent in any of the Western languages ... Ubuntu speaks to the essence of being human. The solitary individual is, in our understanding, a contradiction in terms. You are a person through other persons. Ubuntu speaks about the importance of communal harmony ... speaks about warmth, compassion, generosity, hospitality, and seek to embrace others."
—Archbishop Desmond Tutu, Nobel Peace Prize Laureate

their families and neighbors settle for the illusion of community by pledging allegiance to a sports team with which they may have virtually no direct contact. Others adopt a media community populated by characters whose flickering fantasy lives assume great, but unfulfilling importance. Our displaced need for nurturing leads Americans to own more stuffed animals than any country on earth and to spend a fortune on our pets.

Speaking from years of experience in community building, feminist author Starhawk reminds us of the felt sense of community: "Somewhere there are people to whom we can speak with passion without having the words catch in our throat. Somewhere a circle of hands will open to receive us, eyes will light up as we enter, voices will celebrate with us whenever we come into our own power. Community means strength that joins with strength to do the work that needs to be done. Arms to hold us when we falter. A circle of healing. A circle of friends. Someplace where we can be free."

While Phil Jackson was head coach of the Chicago Bulls, they were the winners of three NBA championships prior to breaking the all-time record for the number of season's victories in April 1996. Speaking to the heart of their success as a team, Jackson offered an insight into community in his book *Sacred Hoops* when he said, "Working with the Bulls, I've learned that the most effective way to forge a winning team is to call on the players' need to connect with something larger than themselves. Even for those who don't consider themselves 'spiritual' in a conventional sense, creating a successful team—whether it's an NBA champion or a record-setting sales force—is essentially their self-interest for the greater good, so that the whole adds up to more than the sum of its parts."

So, in your search for balance, be sure to include the element of community. Think about the presence or absence of community in your life, and ask yourself:

- What have been the most fulfilling experiences you have had?

- What communities welcome you with the greatest sense of belonging?

"The community stagnates without the impulse of the individual. The impulse dies away without the sympathy of the community."

—William James

"We are visitors on this planet. We are here for ninety, one hundred years at the very most. During that period, we must try to do something good, something useful with our lives. Try to be at peace with yourself, and help others share that peace. If you contribute to other people's happiness, you will find the goal, the true meaning of life."

—The Dalai Lama

- What gifts do you bring to these communities?

- What do you find most fulfilling in participating in these communities?

- How would involvement in community best play in bringing greater balance into your life?

The complex relationships formed in community offer us the opportunity to draw inspiration from a larger whole. As Anne Hillman, author of *The Dancing Animal Woman: A Celebration of Life,* perceptively explains;

"As we weave our own stories into the tapestry of life around us, we begin to develop a wholly different perception of what it means to be human. This larger identity is formed in a group. It cannot be formed in isolated nuclear families, as our first identity was. We need the combined energy and wisdom of larger numbers. 'So many are required for the truth!' Perhaps this is the strong pull to community and group life that many of us feel in these last decades of the twentieth century. Perhaps a new archetype of the group is coming into being.... This resonance is a presence that may become a kind of 'knowing together,' (con-sciousness). Might then some higher intelligence begin to move our species as a group so that each of us becomes an instrument, attuned to the whole flock?"

On the path of balance, remember that you are never alone. Continue to seek out kindred souls and allies with whom your journey can be truly shared in a mutually fulfilling way. As with the other chapters in this book, the Resource Guide at the end of this book will offer some further clues for finding balance through community building.

> *"In a real sense all life is inter-related. All persons are caught in an inescapable network of mutuality, tied in a single garment of destiny. Whatever affects one directly affects all indirectly. I can never be what I ought to be until you are what you ought to be, and you can never be what you ought to be until I am what I ought to be. This is the inter-related structure of reality."*
>
> **—Rev. Martin Luther King Jr.**

Global Family

While attending a conference in India, our friend Joan took some time to visit some of the outlying villages. Seeing the poverty around her, she felt self-conscious of her fine clothing and jewelry. In one particularly poor village, she encountered an old woman with a peaceful gaze who, though dressed in a tattered sari, carried herself with great dignity. "Is it really true," the old woman asked, "that in your country people live in large buildings close to each other and that they don't know each other or talk to their neighbors?" "Yes," Joan said, "This is true."

"And, is it true that in your country, people pay strangers to care for their children?"

"Yes, I'm sorry to say this is also true in my country," Joan replied.

"I have also heard that in your country," the old woman went on, "your old people are taken away and banished to live isolated with other old people, living far distant from their children. Is this true too?" Joan quietly nodded, "yes."

"Oh, my dear," the old woman said. Eyes brimming over with tears, she reached out and took Joan's hand, "This is what I have heard but I have never been able to ask a Westerner if this was actually so. I want you to know that I pray for you poor people every day."

We have become so inured to the decline of real community in our own culture, that sometimes it takes a vastly different, and more balanced, perspective of another culture's values to wake us out of our insensitivity and forgetfulness. It's sobering to realize that what was viewed as unthinkably tragic in this woman's poor rural village is accepted as commonplace in most modern cities. What will it take for us to look and care deeply enough to appreciate how the social and spiritual poverty in our own lives rivals, or even dwarfs, the material poverty of a people whose dignity and compassion are clothed in tattered saris?

We were talking with a friend recently, who had been on a medical mission that gave immunizations to thousands of children in Africa. "How did that experience touch you?" we asked. "It was amazing," she said, "Those people had nothing. Absolutely nothing. And they were so very happy. Their children had no toys. They barely had enough to eat and hardly any shelter, but they had a sense of heritage, community, and connectedness to their environment. They really knew how to laugh and cry, how to live and love.

"We travel together as passengers on a little spaceship, dependent on its vulnerable reserves of air and soil; all committed for our safety to its security and peace; preserved from annihilation only by the care, the work, and I'll say, the love we give our fragile craft. We cannot maintain it half fortunate, half miserable, half confident, half despairing, half slave to the ancient enemies of man, half free in liberation of resources undreamed of until this day. No craft, no crew can travel safely with such contradictions. On their resolution depends the survival of us all."

—Adlai Stevenson

And they really knew how to sing and dance. They were so very happy and they were the most generous and giving people I have ever met, even though they had so little to give." Returning home after two months away, and after flying sixteen hours to return to the States, her husband picked her up at the airport. It was Monday evening and he had tickets for the football game, so they stopped for fast food and went to the stadium. What a lesson in balance that must have been!

During the course of our lifetimes, the image of a global village is growing from metaphor to reality. Linked by webs of light-speed communication, the diverse people of the planet communicate, travel, and exchange information and energy in countless ways. The following image offers a profound and sobering insight into the relationships among the many people of the earth.

Imagine all of the people of the earth as a village made up of one hundred families. Ninety of these families do not speak English. Sixty-five cannot read or write. About sixty families live on only 10 percent of the land while only seven families own 60 percent of the land. Seven families consume 80 percent of all of the available energy. Only one family has a college education and only twenty families have members who have ever flown in an airplane. Seventy families have no drinking water at their homes. Envision the conditions, the struggles and tensions in this village where there are seven mansions and an airport on one side, and where there is no drinking water, little comfort, and much suffering on the other. Try to comprehend how the activities of both the rich and poor are destroying the life-support systems for the entire planet so that they can survive, feed their families, or profit in this lifetime. Imagine the countless generations of unborn children of all the world's species coming to look down into this world, their voices calling out to us all to seek a more balanced and cooperative way of life upon the earth.

Now imagine that something radical changes. People begin to wake up, to better understand themselves, and to respect and love one another. Can you envision what our world looks like and how we would live if we were to find true balance and harmony among all of

> "Hard material necessity and human evolutionary possibility now seem to converge to create a situation where, in the long run, we will be obliged to do no less than realize our greatest possibilities. We are engaged in a race between self-discovery and self-destruction. The forces that may converge to destroy us are the same forces that may foster societal and self-discovery."
>
> —Duane Elgin

the people of this tiny, fragile world? What courses of development would we continue? Which ones would we change? What new ways of living and learning together in balance would need to emerge?

Then ask yourself, "What choices can I make and what actions can I take to bring greater harmony and balance to all members of our human family? What actions will I take and what investments will I make to build a better world?" If a step toward balance in your life is in the direction of connecting more with your global family, check out the list of suggested references in the Resource Guide for additional guidance and learning.

Remembering Our Biopals

Waking up high on the slopes of Haleakala Crater in Maui, Hawaii, one cold morning, the two of us encounterd our friend Stan, who came over to greet us with a warm cup of chai tea. "Hey, you want to meet my new neighbor?" "Neighbor?" We looked questioningly at each other, and then out across the remote windswept pastures that Stan had homesteaded for twenty years. "We didn't know you had a neighbor," Joel said. Stan smiled, and said somewhat mischievously, "Oh, he's new here and lives just over there." Stan pointed to a hillside with no visible dwelling above an old ranch road. "Follow me. I'll introduce you." We scrambled up the hill behind Stan. Stan's pace slowed to walk very quietly and mindfully through the grass. Raising his finger to his lips, Stan turned and gestured for us to be quiet and to crouch down. He reached gently forward and pulled back a clump of tall grass. Two huge, bright yellow, saucer-shaped eyes peered out from a nest in the hollow.

"And whoooo are you?" the eyes of this baby owl seemed to say. It appeared to have no fear, only a penetrating sense of presence, strength, and objective curiosity. It was clear from the striking presence of this being that someone was home here: balanced, awake, present! We'd seen the look before in the clear presence of wise old elders, or in the deep eyes of some infants, but to encounter such a strong sense of being in a nonhuman was a bit disarming. We've

"One thing to remember is to talk to the animals. If you do, they will talk back to you. But if you don't talk to the animals, they won't talk back to you, then you won't understand, and when you don't understand you will fear and when you fear you will destroy the animals, and if you destroy the animals, you will destroy yourself."

—**Chief Dan George**

"Man has the capacity to love, not just his own species, but life in all its shapes and forms. This empathy with the interknit web of life is the highest spiritual expression I know of."

—**Loren Eiseley**

caught a glimpse of it swimming with the dolphins in Kealakekua Bay, and from time to time in a special cat whose presence calls for attention.

We two-leggeds have incredible influence in assuring or destroying the lives of other beings on this planet. Yet how often do we think about, listen for, and truly hear their voices? Who speaks for wolf, salmon, and the other critters at the policy roundtables of the world?

A recent meeting on the Onodaga Reservation brought together representatives of the Six Nations of New York state. Speaking empassionedly to those gathered, Chief Oren Lyons said, "We see it as our duty to speak as caretakers for the natural world. Government is a process of living together, the principle being that all life is equal, including the four-legged and the winged things. The principle has been lost; the two-legged walks about thinking that he is supreme with his man-made laws. But there are universal laws of all living things. We come here and say they too have rights."

This sensitivity to all the creatures of the earth needs to be a part of each of our lives. Matthew Fox reminds us that when Jesus commanded people to follow the golden rule and to "love your neighbor as yourself," he didn't just say to love your two-legged neighbors. In search of balance, how can we open our hearts and minds to all those living beings who share the earth? According to Jewish *midrash,* both Moses and David were chosen to lead the nation of Israel because of their compassion toward animals. What criteria for choosing a national leader! Saint Francis, it is said, was once so moved with concern for the fate of a lamb that when he met the shepherd on the way to the market he traded the cloak off his back for the sheep so that the lamb might live. It is also said that Saint Francis could listen to and talk to the animals, and he would even preach to them in a way that they could understand. His love for animals was so great that they would follow him everywhere, even going into buildings with him.

If we are to truly learn to live in balance and harmony in this world, we must find room in our hearts and minds for all beings: the

"Our troubles ... arise from the fact that we do not know what we are and cannot agree on what we want to be. The primary cause of this intellectual failure is ignorance of our origins. We did not arrive on this planet as aliens. Humanity is part of nature, a species that evolved among other species. The more closely we identify ourselves with the rest of life, the more quickly we will be able to discover the sources of human sensibility and acquire the knowledge on which an enduring ethic, a sense of preferred direction, can be built."

—Edward O. Wilson

two-legged, the four-legged, the birds of the air, the fish in the seas, the critters that live in the ravines behind our apartment houses, the countless creatures inhabiting the rainforests who may have much to teach us about cooperation and healing, and all the countless beings whom we are unaware of. This life is truly a laboratory to learn about relationships and that includes our relationship to the other beings who inhabit the planet with us. The more conscious and caring we become about all God's creation, the more our lives will reflect that balance.

In our neighborhood, near the heart of Seattle, we have the company of squirrels, raccoons, opossums, eagles, hawks, the seasonal songs of migrating birds, buzzing insects, streams and lakes full of fish—and of coarse various pesky rodents and a herd of domesticated felines and canine friends. When we sleep out on our roof deck, we can hear the voices of the lions, elephants, and monkeys who now live at our local zoo. Keeping an eye out for your neighbors can help you to remember and restore your balance in relationship to the larger web of life in which you live.

Traditionally, Hawaiian families each had three *aumakua* or guardian protectors: one for the earth, such as *mo'o* the lizard, one for the sky, like *pueo* the owl; and one for the sea, the shark or dolphin, for example. Members of that family would show special respect to these protectors, and would consider seeing them as auspicious. They would never kill one of their aumakua. By carefully observing the habits and characteristics of these creatures, the people gained many insights for how to live a balanced life.

People with the roots of deep relationship still intact in their lives regard the four-legged, the winged ones, the swimming beings, and crawling beings as their brothers and sisters, embodying a unique and special gift from the Creator. They honor the swiftness of Hawk, the clear seeing of Eagle, the playfulness of Dolphin, the craftiness of Raccoon. They live with respect for the unique gifts and qualities that each creature offers to the world and to humanity. Each encounter with a moose, or bear, or eagle, or crow, or any other living being is considered a meaningful revelation. And when the

"The ethics of reverence for life makes no distinction between high and low, more precious and less precious lives. It has good reason for this omission ... How can we know what importance other living organisms have in themselves and in terms of the universe?... To the truly ethical man, all life is sacred."

—Albert Schweitzer

medicine gifts of a specific animal are required, the wise ones often fast, pray, and seek guidance from the spirit of these creatures.

Through the ongoing experiment of evolution our planet has seen countless creatures come and go. Yet in the past hundred years, one species—humans—has obliterated tens of thousands of species who will never be known again upon the earth. And each year, millions of creatures are brutally tortured, maimed, or killed in the name of unnecessary research. Millions of others live in intolerable circumstances and are slaughtered for foods that are notoriously deleterious to good health. So even in our modern urban times, our relationship with animals offers many lessons in balance and often opens a doorway into the vital, mythical dimensions of our lives. Take a moment to consider:

"If you listen carefully enough to anything, it will talk to you."

—George Washington Carver

- What animals appear most frequently in your dreams or in your waking visions?
- What qualities or strengths do they represent to you?

When you are driving along the highway and see a moose, or an eagle, or a whale, listen deeply to see if there is a message for you in that unexpected encounter. Joel offers the following insight:

"One day when I was really distraught over how to respond to a particularly complex ethical situation, I went out for a bike ride. On the way back I decided to take a loop around the lake nearby, and as I rounded the north end of the lake, a huge bald eagle swooped down across the path and just narrowly missed me. He was being chased by a hawk. The eagle roosted in the top branch of a tree while I looked on in amazement. In recent years the eagles had begun to return to the city and I had seen them with increasing frequency from a distance, but never up this close, and never being chased by a hawk. This strange encounter shifted something in me and helped me to step back from the unsettling situation I was struggling with. Riding home I had more clarity and perspective on what to do. When I got home, I looked through a bookshelf and checked out some of the qualities and native lore associated with both eagle and hawk. I was amazed to read, "Eagle—*Spirit:* Eagle medicine is

"If I spent enough time with the tiniest creature— even a caterpillar— I would never have to prepare a sermon. So full of God is every creature."

—Meister Eckhart

the power of the Great Spirit, the connection to the Divine. It is the ability to live in the realm of spirit, and yet remain connected and balanced within the realm of the Earth. Eagle soars and is quick to observe expansiveness within the overall pattern of life. From the heights of the clouds, Eagle is close to the heavens where the Great Spirit dwells." And, "Hawk—*Messenger:* Hawk is akin to Mercury, the messenger of the gods. Hawk medicine teaches you to be observant, to look at your surroundings. Observe the obvious in everything you do. Life is sending you signals." Amazingly these two animals were right next to each other in the book I picked up, called *Medicine Cards* by Jamie Sams and David Carson. The juxtaposition and synchronicity of these encounters and their messages gave great comfort and clarity that helped me to find peace of mind and a clear path of action."

In your journey toward balance, remember to keep the animals, our "biopals," in mind as you make choices in the products that you buy, the clothing you wear, and the food you eat. Keep asking yourself, "What would living in balance with all of the creatures of the earth look like for me? And how are my choices creating more balance or imbalance, more joy or sorrow, in the lives of others?"

As we come to a wider, deeper sense of ourselves, we discover a natural connectedness, belonging, and intimacy with all living beings and with all of creation. This naturally expresses itself as living with kindness and relating to others in a nonviolent way. As Gandhi said, "The rock-bottom foundation of the technique for achieving the power of nonviolence is the belief in the essential oneness of all life."

"Ethics is how we behave when we decide that we belong together," Benedictine monk David Steindl-Rast reminds us. It seems clear that any action, however small, that devalues any form of life is a dangerous symptom that we are losing our balance and forgetting our place in the circle of life. For, as Chief Seattle's famous words remind us, "What we do to the animals we do to ourselves."

"We appeal to all the inhabitants of this planet. Each cannot be changed for the better unless the conciousness of individuals is changed. We pledge to work for such transformation in individual and collective conciousness, for the awakening of our spiritual powers through reflection, meditation, prayer, or positive thinking, for a conversion of the heart. Together we can move mountains . . . therefore we commit ourselves to a commom global ethic, to better mutual understanding, and to socially beneficial, peace-fostering, and Earth-friendly way of life."

—From "Toward a Global Ethic," 1993 Parliament of World's Religions

Restoring the World to Wholeness

As the wish for balance not just for ourselves but for all beings awakens in our hearts, we participate in a profound teaching from the Kabbalah on restoring balance. This is called *"tikkun ha-olam"* in Hebrew, which means, "repairing the world." *Tikkun* means to mend or repair. Outwardly, *tikkun* is associated with social action that has the goal of improving the world. But inwardly, in the esoteric traditions, *tikkun* is the sacred innerwork of mending a broken world and restoring it to wholeness and balance through spiritually developing the love that carries us beyond our separate self. *Tikkun* is regarded as the highest, most profound purpose of our life.

This activity to restore balance and harmony in our world is closely akin to the Buddhist notion of *bodhichitta*, "the spirit of awakening," which holds that at the heart/core of every living being is a universal impulse to fully awaken to the wholeness of its potentials and to serve others in their awakening. This is the universal yearning to reduce suffering, cultivate harmonious relations, and find dynamic balance.

The work of repairing, rebalancing, and awakening is an inside-out job. It is said that every tiny bit of restoration of wholeness within ourselves directly contributes to the restoration and awakening of all beings and of the whole world. The impulse of every movement toward healing, every moment of mindfulness, every act of kindness we generate within ourselves, is directly shared or transmitted to support the emergence of that potential within each and every living being.

That's because the more deeply and completely we are balanced within ourselves, the better equipped we are, and the more natural it is, for us to reach out and nurture the emergence of greater harmony in our world. As our awareness and sensitivity increase, we recognize that certain situations in our life or world are intolerably unproductive, toxic, or destructive. This helps to strengthen our resolve to get healthier; resolve conflicts; put a stop to abusive violence in our relationships; and become an advocate, activist, or celebrant of noble

"We are not so different from all the peoples of this world, yet the message which has come through us is special and unique. To discover, express, and expand our uniqueness, as individuals, and as a People, supports tikkun ha-olam, the completion of creation, to which we are called. With gratitude, then, we reach into the heart of our uniqueness. Not to best another, but to better understand ourselves."

—Rabbi Ted Falcon

causes that expand the sphere of balance and harmony to our world and to the lives of others.

Imagine that you are standing on a mountaintop on a still, clear, dark night. In the sky around you are an infinite number of jewels linked together in a subtle network of light. Imagine now that as you light a little candle, instantly its light and warmth is reflected in each and every one of the jewels surrounding you. Not only that, but each of the jewels is also illumined by the light that is reflected in it from all the illuminating jewels. It is a fantastic and inspiring sight. Now imagine that as you light up a moment of mindfulness within you, the light of that mindfulness "lights up" all living beings. Likewise, if within yourself you awaken or light up a moment of love, gratitude, wonder, joy, or forgiveness, that impulse immediately lights up within all others. The transmission is effortless, immediate, heart to heart. Each of the jewels in the net is lighting up all of the other jewels, giving rise to waves of excitement, waves of sympathy, waves of gratitude, love, or blessings.

In each moment that we are awake, we can feel what is reverberating within ourselves and we can respond in a way that lights up the world in either a weird or a wonderful way. Mindful moment to mindful moment, from the very core of our being, we contribute to the balancing and rebuilding of the world in wholeness, or contribute to the fear and confusion. In moments of distraction, when mindlessness sets in and we lose our balance, the momentum of habit and countless impinging forces propels us. In moments of self-remembering, when we awaken to mindfulness, we at least have a choice.

As we learn to recognize and repair the rifts and imbalances in our own life we reestablish wholeness within ourselves. As our internal repair work deepens, we are better able to reach out—inwardly and outwardly—and repair the world around us. As we focus the flow of our dynamic being more into balance, and dissolve the rigid boundaries that separate us from our wholeness, we restore the world to balance. These aren't just nice ideas, this is descriptive of the way things are. Our journey toward balance is one of awakening in order

"The emptying of self and repairing the world with love are two sides of the same spiritual practice. We are not seeking to escape the world, we are seeking to transform it."

—Reb Yerachmiel Ben Yisrael

to bring more lucid, loving, radiant, presence into our world. This is very deep *tikkun*.

The Radiance of Love

A very simple yet potent practice you can do on a daily basis to revitalize your interconnectedness at a deep level is the practice of lovingkindness. We especially like to do this one at the end or start of a day, or to celebrate and share the joy of a job well done or a moment well lived. The essence of this prayer and meditation is the wish that we and all beings enjoy happiness and well-being. Here's how it goes:

> *"Love is that flame that once kindled burns everything, and only the mystery and the journey remain."*
>
> **—Angeles Arrien**

Begin by touching your heart, if you like, breathe deeply, and smile to yourself a smile of tender appreciation and care. Holding the sincere wish to be of benefit to yourself and others, heartfully repeat the following phrases mentally, first to yourself, several times, and then expand the radius of your lovingkindness successively out to wider and wider circles. Go for the meaning and the feeling behind the words:

May I be happy and peaceful.

May I be free from fear and pain.

May I live with love and compassion.

And may I fully Awaken and be free.

Next, reach out with your heart/mind to embrace your loved ones and friends with the energy of lovingkindness in the same way and radiate these thoughts of well-being to them:

May you be happy and peaceful.

May you be free from fear and pain.

May you live with love and compassion.

And may you fully Awaken and be free.

As you hold the image of your beloved ones and repeat these phrases, sense or imagine that they are actually touched by the love radiating out from your heart and that it is truly helpful for them.

Next, hold in mind someone or some group of people toward whom you feel neutral, perhaps some of the neighbors whom you really don't know, or folks you see on the way to work. As you repeat these phrases, bring them into your heart and wish for them:

> *May you be happy and peaceful.*
> *May you be free from fear and pain.*
> *May you live with love and compassion.*
> *And may you fully Awaken and be free.*

Sense or imagine that these wishes and prayers really do support them.

Now, having primed your heart pump, turn your attention toward someone, or ones, toward whom your heart is closed with pain, resentment, or negativity. Remembering that this person or group of people may in the past have actually been kind to you, and that, in their own way, they too are searching for happiness and hoping to avoid suffering in their own lives, let your heart open to them. As best as you are able, wish for them:

> *May you be happy and peaceful.*
> *May you be free from fear and pain.*
> *May you live with love and compassion.*
> *May you fully awaken to your greatest potentials, and be free of any ignorance and confusion that leads you to act in unskillful ways.*
> *May you fully Awaken and be free.*

As you hold them in mind and radiate these thoughts of lovingkindness, be merciful with yourself. Let your own heart open to free you from the prison of imbalance that you may have created for yourself out of your own anger, fear, or resentment toward this person with whom you are having a hard time, or whose relationship you would like to heal.

"Put away all hindrances, let your mind full of love pervade one quarter of the world, and so too the second quarter, and so the third, and so the fourth. And thus the whole wide world, above, below, around and everywhere, altogether continue to pervade with love-filled thought, abounding, sublime, beyond measure, free from hatred and ill-will."

—**The Buddha**

Visualize yourself surrounded now by all your circles of supportive relationships, and invite into your loving awareness, all the networks of support, visible and invisible, known and unknown, near and far, that make up the whole circle of living beings, the web of life. Expand your love and care equally to this larger field as the sun shines its life-giving rays equally to all. In this way, with great equanimity to all living beings, extend the radius of your lovingkindness to all your loved ones and friends, to all the strangers or neutral people in your life, to all the people toward whom your heart has been closed, to all the humans and nonhumans who search for happiness, harmony, and balance on their fleeting journey through life. And, imagining that this vast circle of relations joins you as you open your heart to include and embrace all beings, extend the waves of lovingkindness out now in all directions:

May all beings (or, may we all) be happy and peaceful.

May all beings be free from fear and pain.

May all beings live with love and compassion.

And may all beings fully Awaken to their true nature and potentials and be free!

Let these wishes radiate to all beings to the east. To all beings to the west, to all beings to the south, to all beings to the north. Let these wishes reach out to all beings above you and below you. To all beings in this world, or in all worlds. In this time and in all times.

Then, with your hands, imagine that you can gather the energy and the light you have generated through this series of contemplations. Imagine that you can bring this all to focus as one intensely bright light of love and compassion like a clear shining jewel. Bring this light of lovingkindness and compassion into your heart. Let it shine there like a luminous loving sun that bathes the world and all beings within it in the light of love that radiates through you as a blessing for the world. Carry the natural radiance of this love with you wherever you go. When your awareness of it fades, re-energize it by using the phrases and images offered here, and let the light of your love light up your world.

"Some day, after we have mastered the winds, the waves, the tides, and gravity, we shall harness the energies of love. Then, for a second time in the history of the world man will have discovered fire."

—Pierre Teilhard de Chardin

Reclaiming Our Balance, Embracing the Whole

"Transformation comes from looking deeply within, to a state that exists before fear and isolation arise, the state in which we are inviolably whole just as we are. We connect to ourselves, to our own true experience, and discover there that to be alive means to be whole."

—SHARON SALZBERG

IN THIS FINAL SECTION, WE'D LIKE TO offer a unifying framework in which the synergy of all these different strategies can be seen and understood. You'll learn seven key principles that will give you more leverage for living your life and approaching your work with greater harmony. To celebrate the many paths we've walked to come home to our wholeness and reclaim our essential balance, we'll also take a guided walk in the four directions—north, south, east, and west—where you'll receive some important reminders to help you continue in wholeness on the balancing Way.

We hope you've begun to realize that this search for balance is truly a spiral path—as our inner balance grows, it flows out into the world in ways that improve the harmony and balance in our outer lives and relationships, and this supports the refinement of our inner harmony and balance. The fruit of quality relationships is mind/body harmony and peace of mind. The fruit of peace and clarity of mind is increased mindfulness. The fruit of mindfulness is deeper insight and understanding. The fruit of insight is a wisdom that is inseparable from effectiveness, compassion, and lovingkindness. These, in turn, ripen as the fruits of greater kindness and right relations. The central harvest of all these paths and qualities woven together as a spiral of learning, is confidence in yourself and faith and devotion to the Mystery in which all things and all beings find their wholeness.

Like facets of a jewel-like balanced life, each of these themes is an inseparable aspect of the whole. Wherever you focus steps onto this path, you will find the benefits of your efforts will be reflected in each of the other facets of this jewel. Growing in harmony and health, peace and power, insight and understanding, creativity and compassion, each step along the spiral brings the spirit of balance and wholeness more alive in your life.

THIRTEEN

Seven Principles for
Living in Balance

If you feel that you are living in a time of disintegration, your activities
will be fearful and violent; If you feel that you are living in a time of
reintegration and evolutionary emergence, your activities will be more
open and filled with hope and wonder.

—WILLIAM IRWIN THOMPSON

In this chapter we'd like to present
another set of lenses to illuminate your
pathways toward balance. This frame-
work is drawn from the results of numerous studies, conducted over the past
twenty years, that have searched for clues to the quality of lifestyles most conducive to balance and "optimal health." Research shows that when faced with
major life changes, 5 to 10 percent of the population actually breaks down,
gets sick, or dies. At the other end of the change resilience continuum, however, are a very interesting 5 to 10 percent of people who actually come more
alive and thrive when confronted with significant life changes. Considerable
attention has been given to studying these fortunate people who actually
thrive on change, and this research reveals a number of common factors that
help them to maintain their health and balance.

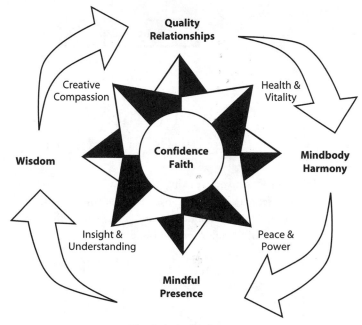

The Spiral of Balance

"Wisdom is the harmony between our mind and the laws of reality.
Morality is the harmony between our convictions and our actions.
Concentration is the harmony between our feelings, our knowledge and our will,
The unity of all our creative forces in the experience of a higher reality."
—Anagarika Govinda

Change Resilience Continuum

Foremost among these studies are the pioneering works of Dr. Krobasa at the City University of New York, and a five-year "Sound-Mind, Sound-Body" research project conducted by Kenneth Pelletier, M.D., director of Stanford University's Corporate Health Program. This groundbreaking research project, funded by the Rockefeller Foundation, identified the central characteristics that are the basis of optimal health.

From these and related studies, seven key principles emerge for living in balance. You'll find that we have touched on these issues throughout the book, for each of these elements reflects a high level of conscious awareness or mindfulness, a more "whole-systems" way of relating to the world, and a spiritually and socially attuned "altruistic" inclination. These seven principles are: attitude, accountability, commitment, supportive relationships, service, personal mastery, and faith.

Attitude

Do you view the stressful changes of your daily lives as a threat, or as a challenge and opportunity? People who are able to take change in stride and respond in a balanced way tend to hold a personally empowered and self-encouraging attitude. They have the confidence and trust that they can handle challenging situations and positively affect the course of their lives. They view change as an opportunity, not as a threat.

A reporter once asked Albert Einstein: "Dr. Einstein, if you could ask the universe a single question and receive a direct reply, what would you ask?" His reply came swiftly, as though he had pondered the question for a long time: "Is the universe friendly?" Pause for a moment to reflect upon Einstein's question. What do you think? How would you live if the universe were truly friendly and supportive of you?

Moment to moment, the attitudinal lenses that you choose to wear color your world for better or for worse. Experience the difference between being appreciative or being critical, or between viewing yourself as a victim or holding a more empowered attitude. Adopting an optimistic attitude toward the universe at large and the immediate challenges you face allows you to tap into a greater reservoir of creative energy potential that helps you maintain an even keel. The first step is to recognize the attitude you are holding, and notice whether it diminishes or enhances your energy and effectiveness. Then, without sacrificing realism, experiment with embodying a more positive outlook that will keep you buoyant and balanced on the sea of constant change.

"We who lived in concentration camps can remember those who walked through the huts comforting others, giving away their last piece of bread. They may have been few in number, but they offer sufficient proof that everything can be take from a person but one thing: the last of human freedoms—to choose one's attitude in any given set of circumstances—to choose one's own way."

—**Victor Frankl**

Accountability

Folks who live generally in balance focus on what they can do and don't lose energy spinning their wheels or getting tied up in knots over what is outside their control. At the same time, they hold a strongly accountable point of view, don't avoid problems, and are willing to own the part they play in a situation.

To get a sense for this, draw three concentric circles on a piece of paper. Label the inner circle "control" and in this circle write or think about all the things in your life that you have direct control over. Next, label the second circle "influence." Here identify all the things in your life that you don't have total control over, but that you can influence by your actions. Now, label the third and largest circle "appreciate" or "learn from." Within this circle, pause to note all the factors and forces in your life that are too large, complex, or distant for you to feel much of a sense of influence over. Many of these forces, such as the powerful realities of the weather, taxes, or organizational bureaucracy are beyond your direct control or even your influence. Yet many people exhaust themselves struggling against, worrying, or complaining about these large and unwieldy forces.

A wiser, more balanced approach is to focus attention on those aspects of our life/work/environment/relationships that we can better learn from, influence, or even control, and allow ourselves to better understand and appreciate the large mysterious forces that are too complex to feel much control over. Saint Francis expressed this balanced awareness in his prayer: "God, Grant me the serenity to accept the things I cannot change, the courage to change the things I can, and the wisdom to know the difference."

In our own work as coaches, facilitators, and trainers with individuals, teams, and organizations, we often remind people to focus on those factors that they can really get some leverage on. Understanding that we can't cover the thorny earth with leather, we concentrate our efforts to make shoes. Realizing that the bureaucracy in our organizations is difficult to change, we mobilize people at a grass roots or team level, and identify ways that we can improve things in the department or area that we do have some control or influence over. Adopting an "accountable" approach to change means being mindful of where we can expand our circle of control and our circle of influence. This also means being mindful of our

"People are always blaming their circumstances for what they are. I don't believe in circumstances. The people who get on in this world are the people who get up and look for the circumstances they want and if they can't find them, make them."

—George Bernard Shaw

often unconscious beliefs, assumptions, or attitudes regarding the larger forces in our lives and finding more balanced, learningful, or appreciative ways to relate to them. "Remember, when we are aware we have a choice. Holding an accountable point of view brings our life more into control and balance by focusing on where we can get leverage and where we can make a difference.

Commitment

Balanced people live and work with a strong and clear sense of purpose. They view themselves as having a meaningful role to fulfill and hold a strong inner belief in its importance.

George Bernard Shaw exemplified the passion and spirit of this when he declared: "This is the true joy in life . . . being used for a purpose recognized by yourself as a mighty one . . . being a force of nature instead of a feverish, selfish little clod of ailments and grievances complaining that the world will not devote itself to making you happy. I am of the opinion that my life belongs to the whole community, and as long as I live it is my privilege to do for it whatever I can. I want to be thoroughly used up when I die. For the harder I work the more I live. I rejoice in life for its own sake. Life is no brief candle to me. It's sort of a splendid torch which I've got to hold up for the moment and I want to make it burn as brightly as possible before handing it on to future generations."

Commitment brings balance by giving more focus and clarity of purpose to your life. It operates like a plumb line, helping you stay tuned to what has meaning and importance, increasing your energy and attention while reducing distraction. When you know what you are committed to, you'll be better able to set and stick to priorities, to recognize and honor limits, and to live with integrity.

"When you are inspired by some great purpose, some extraordinary project, all your thoughts break their bonds; your mind transcends limitations; your consciousness expands in every direction; and you find yourself in a great, new and wonderful world. Dormant forces, faculties and talents become alive and you discover yourself to be a greater person by far than you ever dreamed yourself to be."

—Patanjali

Supportive Relationships

At the core of our being, we are social creatures who thrive on meaningful, caring, and affirming contact with others. Although finding a balance of personal time and social or family time is crucial, the importance of social contact for assuring life balance is a key element not to be overlooked.

One striking example of the importance of supportive relationships in our lives is that the fact that risk factors for a person who is lonely are far greater than for a person who smokes, drinks, eats a poor diet, and doesn't get any exercise! We've already talked about the health-enhancing effects of support networks in chapter ten and community in chapter twelve. The main point here is that people who have supportive networks of close relations and friends do much better in handling life's stresses than those who feel alone, isolated, and unsupported.

Service

We all know how good we feel when we do something to help others. Each time we do, we tap the energy of love and compassion that is fundamental to life. Highly change-resilient people view service as their true mission in life, and hold material wealth and success as secondary to helping others. They have a strong sense of belonging and understand the value of nurturing relationships with family, friends, coworkers, and community.

Many people have discovered that making time in their lives to be of service to others provides a quality of joy and satisfaction that is deeply renewing. We continue to learn more and more about balance by realizing that in serving the needs of others from a selfless place of caring and connectedness, many of our own deepest needs can also be fulfilled.

Personal Mastery

People who understand the importance of personal development and who have cultivated a high degree of self-mastery are the ones most able to sail through challenging times with confident balance. They've learned to deeply listen and respond skillfully to the subtle whispers that warn them when they are drifting out of balance. As a result, they are more likely to eat when they are hungry, and to rest and renew themselves when they are tired. By recognizing and reducing the harmful accumulations of stress, they are able to live in a more balanced and more disease-resistant way. In the process of developing the mindfulness necessary to recognize and master stress, we can also deepen our mind-body-spirit connection as a whole. This allows us to gain the inner strength and understanding necessary to meet every situation in a more balanced, centered way.

One sign of effective personal energy management is that people are able to maintain optimal energy levels throughout the day without dependence upon the use of such stimulants as caffeine, sugar, and nicotine. As we have already discussed, although stimulants appear to offer us free energy, they actually drive the system out of balance at our expense. As a result, the body has to expend more energy to restore the imbalance caused by them. Instead of relying on counterproductive stimulants, "balance masters" choose options such as frequent exercise and practicing self-renewing and revitalizing skills that prevent the accumulation of stress, and bring a higher degree of self-confidence, self-control, self-acceptance, and self-respect. Like skills in any domain, such personal skills are developed gradually over time through discipline, practice, coaching, and proper instruction.

"As human beings, our greatness lies not so much in being able to remake the world ... as in being able to remake ourselves."

—Mahatma Gandhi

Faith

A spiritual outlook toward life is common among people who live in balance. Holding a spiritual frame of reference or reverence develops our faith, confidence, and trust, and reduces the intensity of toxic, worrisome emotions and destructive behaviors. People with a deep spiritual perspective often say that it is their faith that helps them to see their lives within a larger perspective and gives them a sense of belonging to a greater whole. For many, their spirituality is anchored in the fellowship, community, and worship associated with

"Faith is the opening of all sides and every level of one's life to the Divine in-flow."

—Rev. Martin Luther King Jr.

their church, synagogue, temple, mosque, or meditation group. For others, the spiritual grounding of their lives may be found in communion with nature, or through their love for family and friends, or through service to others.

Faith allows us to reach out and take refuge in our connectedness to a larger, deeper reality and Source than our tiny personal selves. By remembering to open our hearts and minds to affirm the link in spirit between our personal identities and our universal nature, we shift the center of gravity in our lives more toward authentic balance.

Compassionate Awareness

These studies on change resilience reveal a number of interesting findings about living in harmony and balance:

- Attention to diet, exercise, rest, and stress management alone will not assure optimal well-being.

- Living with a strong self-centered preoccupation with individualistic and narrowly narcissistic concerns seriously compromises the quality of health, life balance, and performance, and reduces our adaptability and change resilience. The more out of touch or unfeeling we are (regarding ourselves, our relationships, society, or environment), the more dangerously at risk we are.

- Learning to quiet one's body and mind, and to raise or deepen the quality of our mindful awareness, is the essential first step toward living in balance, realizing optimal health, and gaining the deep guiding insights that nourish our lives with inspiration and meaning.

What stands out as we consider these seven elements is that they each speak to living with both a high quality of awareness and a deeper sense of compassion and caring. Under stress we tend to get tense in mind and body. Our awareness narrows and constricts. As

"The whole idea of compassion is based on a keen awareness of the interdependence of all living beings, which are all part of one another and all involved in one another."

—Thomas Merton, speaking hours before his death

"My religion is kindness."

—The Dalai Lama

we tense up, shut down, and narrow our focus we become more ignorant of and oblivious to what is going on around and within us. We implode into self-centered, "me first" thinking and behavior. If we are really in danger, these negative strategies serve only to increase our vulnerability.

However, by recognizing the tendency to implode and constrict, we can choose instead to more quickly relax, center ourselves, and actually expand our thinking and awareness to encompass and see clearly the reality of the whole situation that we are in the midst of.

Reflection

Pause now for a few moments to reflect on the following questions:

- Which of these seven principles of living a balanced life are presently strong in your life?

- Which of these principles would it be wise for you to pay more attention to in order to give you more leverage for living your life and approaching your work in a more balanced way?

It is always heartening to see how deeply impactful these seven principles are when we present them to our corporate clients . People generally recognize their wisdom and feel that their own inner intelligence and their core personal and spiritual values are deeply affirmed and renewed by these findings. With awareness they can begin to shift their priorities to incorporate more of these principles into their lives.

Given that the price we pay for not practicing them is so high, and the benefits are so great, many managers and teams in the organizations we work with have begun to explore how they might practice these principles more conscienciously within the corporate culture. For example, at Travelers-Aetna Insurance and Hewlett-Packard, some of the people on the teams we've worked with started exercising together at lunchtime or bringing in healthy snacks.

"We are accustomed to the phrase Homo sapiens, but our full designation is 'Homo sapiens sapiens.' To be 'sapient' is to be wise or knowing. We humans describe ourselves as being more than sapient or wise, we are sapient sapient and have the unique potential of becoming "doubly wise" or 'doubly knowing.' . . . Our highest potential as a species is our ability to achieve full self-reflective consciousness or 'knowing that we know.'. . . Through humanity's awakening, the universe acquires the ability to look back and reflect upon itself—in wonder, awe, and appreciation."

—Duane Elgin

Others, in various organizations, have launched community service team-building projects, and many take time for prayer or meditation together and discuss how their spiritual life fits in at work. After learning these principles, many people recognize that their network of support has been deteriorating and take a more active role in rebuilding friendships.

Many people also take these principles home to share with their spouses, kids, significant others, church, or community groups. Again and again, we hear that this shared dialogue is a very meaningful forum for helping families come up with strategies to develop a healthier, more balanced lifestyle by clarifying priorities and identifying tangible ways to bring greater harmony and balance alive.

Who are the people in your life with whom you would like to have this conversation? Remember, health, harmony, and balance in our lives is not a solitary pursuit—self-centered and isolated people cope poorly with change and stress, and are in great danger of having the quality of their health, work, families, relationships disintegrate.

Now that you have learned these seven factors, you can use them regularly as reference checkpoints to monitor how you're doing on the course to balance. Like a compass, they will give you reliably clear directions to guide your way home.

"Our deepest fear is not that we are inadequate. Our deepest fear is that we are powerful beyond measure. It is our light, not our darkness that most frightens us. We ask ourselves, 'Who am I to be brilliant, gorgeous, talented, fabulous?' Actually who are you not to be? You are a child of God. Your playing small doesn't serve the world. We were born to make manifest the glory of God...within us. It's not just in some of us; it's in everyone. And when we let our light shine, we unconsciously give other people permission to do the same. As we are liberated from our fear, our presence automatically liberates others."
—**Marianne Williamson**

FOURTEEN

Earthwalk: Essential Reminders For a Balanced Life

Grandfather, Great Spirit ... You have set the powers of the four quarters of the earth to cross each other. You have made me cross the good road, and the road of difficulties, and *where they cross, the place is holy.* Day in, day out, forevermore, you are the life of all things.

—BLACK ELK, OGLALA SIOUX

Each moment and each day of our lives, we are called on to acknowledge and find harmony with a larger sphere of relationships and forces in our world. Living in dynamic interdependence with the world, it is becoming increasingly clear that in order to find happiness, harmony, and balance in our busy, personal lives, it is essential for us to learn to expand our personal concerns to include a more global, whole-systems view.

In this spirit, the elders of the Seneca nation traditionally encouraged their people to reflect on four essential questions in order to determine if they were living in balance with their world. We have found these questions to be helpful in our own lives, and often share them with those with whom we work. These questions are especially relevant for us on our modern-day "earthwalk," as we look at our lives, set our priorities, weigh our choices, and gauge our progress towards our most cherished goals. As you read each of these four questions, pause to reflect and honestly answer each one:

1. Are you happy living how you are living and doing what you are doing?

2. Is what you are doing adding to the confusion?

3. What are you doing to further peace and contentment in your own life and in the world?

4. How will you be remembered after you are gone—either in absence or in death?

If you are happy doing what you are doing, what brings you the greatest joy? What is your next frontier for satisfaction and fulfillment? If you aren't happy living the way you are living, is balance to be found in changing what you are doing, or in changing your mindset or attitude toward what you are doing?

If you find that what you are doing is actually adding to the confusion and creating more problems or imbalances in your life, say "Whoa," and ask yourself, "What is driving me to act in these ways?" Often, the forces that drive us into self-defeating or destructive ways of living are unconscious to us. When we are able to look and listen deeply into our hearts and minds, and to look squarely into the eyes of our own "inner enemies," we are better able to shine the light of our compassion, forgiveness, or wisdom into these aspects of ourself in order to heal our wounds, and restore our balance.

These four essential questions offer us a powerful tool for helping us to bring greater awareness and accountability to creating the quality of life that we want to create for ourselves, for others in our lives, and even for generations to come. If upon reflection you find that you could be doing more to bring greater peace and contentment into your life, listen deeply for what a step in that direction might be for you. Is greater balance for you to be found in taking more time alone, or in spending more quality time with your loved ones and friends, or helping others in your community? Is balance for you at this time in your life to be found in taking on more activity, or creating more quiet time? Listen deeply, pray, reflect, do whatever it takes for you to know what your next step is!

"With beauty before me, may I walk, With beauty behind me, may I walk, With beauty above me, may I walk, With beauty below me, may I walk, With beauty all around me, may I walk, Wandering on a trail of beauty, lively, may I walk."

—Navajo prayer

Compare how you would like to be remembered with the realities of the legacy that you have created thus far. Ask yourself, "If I were to die next week, what would I be most proud of? What wounds would I most like to heal or forgive? What words do I need to speak, and what actions most need to be taken for me to leave this world, or this job, or to complete my watch at this station of my life with integrity, dignity, and balance, as a true pilgrim on the path of wholeness?" Within the laboratory of your own mind body and relationships, experiment with refining and distilling what is most essential, most powerful and most beautiful in your life.

These compelling and poignant reminders call our attention to how much there is to learn from people who for centuries lived in harmony with one another and with the whole of Nature in all of its beauty. On the journey, according to the elders of the Seneca tribe:

- Self-knowledge is the need.

- Self-understanding is the desire.

- Self-discipline is the way.

- Self-realization is the goal.

Take some time to ponder these ideas ... to take them to heart ... and see how these simple but profound principles can help you to live in greater balance.

"The key word is balance. No Navajo believes that if they walk in beauty they will be eternally surrounded by bliss. The idea is to walk the narrow path between the negative and the positive, keeping yourself centered."

—David Chethlahe Paladin

The Pause That Truly Refreshes

Remember, *life is all about learning, and learning brings balance.* Without feedback and self-reflection, there is no learning. In each of our lives it is necessary to regularly take time out to check our bearings and honestly ask ourselves, "Am I living on purpose?" Often we don't make time in our lives for this kind of self-assessment. We are too busy attending to what is urgent, and have little time or attention for what is truly most important. Living in this way, the subtle "whispers" of warning signs are easily overlooked until they become dangerous screams demanding our attention. All too often we wait till a major crisis arises before we pause to look and think deeply about our lives. When we do pause for reflection, often what we find is that, for many reasons, we have strayed from our ideal path. We find that we have neglected people or pastimes that are really important to us and have squandered our precious time with people or activities that are not really so important to us.

In moments of honest self-reflection, there arises a bittersweet sense of three special qualities. One is a quality of profound grief that can shake us to the core, and often leave us sobbing with deep regret. This grief is often mixed with a second quality, that of deep gratitude for what we really cherish in our lives, be it our health, a loved one, or an ability we have or had that we are thankful for. Third is a fierce determination, fueled by both our grief and our gratitude, to live our lives with true integrity in a way that honors what is essential in and to us. This brings about a greater congruence of our innermost beliefs and values with our way of life.

Tumbling on fast-forward, driven by expectations, burdened by responsibilities, and feeling overwhelmed, we are easily distracted and lose our balance. That's why, in your lifelong journey of balance, it's wise to pause often to determine if you have wandered off track. By stopping often to check in with yourself and with those who share the journey with you, you can save valuable time and energy. Remember that each moment of your life is precious and irretrievable. If you are unclear on what direction to go, then take some time to reflect again on these questions, and let your answers offer insight with regard to the next stage of your own journey. Detours can be lengthy, drain you of vital energy, and lead to serious regrets downstream.

Our friend, the poet David Whyte, often tells the story of a woman manager from AT&T who participated in one of his corporate workshops. When invited to reflect upon the ways that her personal life vision and dreams had been sacrificed for career advancement, she wrote, "Ten years ago ... I turned my face for a moment, and it became my life."

How does that resonate for you? Ten years ago I ... launched

"I have come to terms with the future. From this day onward I will walk easy on the earth. Plant trees. Kill no living things. Live in harmony with all creatures. I will restore the earth where I am. Use no more of its resources than I need. And listen, listen to what it is telling me."

—**M.J. Slim Hooey**

onto a career path ... got married ... had kids ... was divorced ... I started a business that grew faster than I would have dreamed.... I went unconscious trying just to cope. Now, richer or poorer, grayer or balder, with or without kids and aging parents, something in you says, "Whoa! Who am I now?" and "How do I want to live the rest of my life?" These fierce moments of awakening to the call for balance are worthy of celebration.

When you wander from your path—as you certainly will—reflect on the forces, inner and outer, that drew you off course, and use those learnings to actually accelerate your progress as the journey continues. What cues did you overlook or misinterpret? What assumptions or expectations blinded you from seeing the actual path? What learning can you take from the last "mistake" to build your wisdom, skills, and confidence as you embark on the next stage of the journey? Mistakes are only mistakes if we don't learn from them. With a learningful attitude we can say to ourselves, "Yep, missed that turn, fell into that trap, crashed and burned, and I have learned a few things along the way. I don't need to invest more time in repeating those mistakes!"

Remember that the word *sin* means literally to "miss the mark." If the mark you are shooting for is to learn greater balance for yourself and your world, then regularly asking yourself the reclarifying questions of the Seneca elders can truly be a lifesaver.

> "The inhabitant or soul of the universe is never seen; its voice alone is heard. All we know is that it has a gentle voice, like a woman, a voice so fine... that even children cannot become afraid. And what it says is 'Sila ersinarsinivdluge,' 'Be not afraid of the universe.'"
>
> —Eskimo teachings

One Step at a Time

In walking a path, the only step you can find balance on is the one on which you are standing. You can work only on yourself, and you can take a step forward only from where you stand on the path. Keeping the whole in mind and being honest with the current state of affairs in your life are the crucial keys to balance. If you are in ill health, make efforts to regain your health. If you are feeling alienated and alone, explore ways to develop more of a sense of belonging and community. If you are resentful or feel guilty about something, explore ways to resolve your situation. If you are stunned by the glory of the universe in which you live, deepen your capacity to commune with the source of life through prayer and meditation. Keeping the whole in mind, knowing where you stand, take one mindful step at a time to deepen and expand your balance.

The Circle of Wholeness

Over the past twenty years, the two of us have studied many systems of higher-order thinking and learning that have been developed in many fields of science and philosophy. These systems invite us to look at the patterns of relationship that weave any system together: beginnings and endings, what is developing and dissolving, what is manifesting and what are the system's potentials. Where is there movement and flexibility? Where is there "stuckness" and resistance to change? This is what is referred to as systems thinking. Weaving together a variety of ancient and modern approaches to systems thinking, we'd like to introduce you here to a physical practice that can help you discover the balance among the many parts of the whole.

Begin by orienting yourself to the four directions: east and west, north and south. (If you're not sure of the directions, simply hold for now that the direction you're facing is the east, and then at a later time when you get your bearings, repeat this technique facing each of the actual directions.)

Turn first to face the east—that place of dawning, sunrise, and new beginnings, the place of inspiration where what was hidden by the night is revealed and becomes clear. The east—where insight crosses the threshold into light that illuminates your world. That place that the earth forever turns and returns to. The east.

Next turn to face the south, that place of the brightest light, that noontime sky when the sun is most high, and the light is warmest and brightest. The south . . . the place where everything is manifest, full blown, and full grown, and, in being in its fullness, is sure to wane from here.

Now turn to face the west. Behold that place of sunsets and

"Grandfather Great Spirit
All over the world the faces of living ones are alike.
With tenderness they have come up out of the ground.
Look upon your children that they may face the winds and walk the good road to the Day of Quiet.
Grandfather Great Spirit
Fill us with the Light.
Give us the strength to understand,
and the eyes to see.
Teach us to walk the soft Earth as relatives to all that live."
—Sioux prayer

completions, the time and place where the last rays of light, the last waves of breath disappear across the threshold into night. The place of transformation and unification of light and darkness, day and night.

Turning again, face the north, home of the North Star—that one still unchanging point in the spinning universe that seems always to be there. That dark place where there is infinite potential for the light of new potentials to emerge.

Returning now to the rising light of a new dawn, face the east, restoring your faith that again out of the deepest darkness, light will surely come, that out of the coldest winter will come a new spring, that out of the darkest night will come a new bright dawn, a new birth, and a new beginning.

"It is only with the heart that one can see clearly,
for what is essential is hidden from the eyes."
—The Fox to the Little Prince (Antoine de Saint Exupéry)

Return again to face the south.

And return again to face the west.

And return again to face the north.

Each breath carries you round this wheel and through every phase of the cycle. Exhaling completely, you arrive at the north, empty, open, receptive. As the inhalation begins, you turn to and through the east to reach your fullness at the top of the inhalation facing the south. Then exhaling, turning toward the west, releasing and letting go of your fullness, trusting to release and let go, returning again and again to the still point of infinite potentials in the north.

Turning again, growing, sprouting, gestating toward a new birth and new beginnings and emergings in the east. Contemplate the meaning of east—spring equinox, inhaling, creativity, blossoming, filling, becoming in your life.

Turning again, reflect upon the meaning of south—summer solstice, full inhalation, ripe fruit on the trees, the prime of life. Growing, strengthening, expanding to the fullness in the south.

Turning again toward the west, contemplate the meanings behind the experience of crossing the threshold into night, autumn equinox, leaves falling from the trees, getting colder, darker, older, endings, deaths, wanings, diminishings, deepenings, dissolvings, exhaling toward the west.

And turning toward the north, ponder midnight, winter solstice, exhalation, receptivity, and emptiness soon to be filled, that plenum void of unmanifest potential waiting . . . to be expressed in a new dawn. North, you old friend, you've been here before, no need for fear of stillness or frozenness, knowing that spring, inspiration, and the seeds of new beginnings are enfolded in potential here. Here you know winter as the womb of spring, darkness as the womb of light, and death as the womb of birth.

You can use this process in your daily life to step into the center of a question or a project in order to see how all the complex forces and phases fit together in search of balance. For example, turning toward the east, metaphorically or in actuality, ask yourself, "What is beginning and emerging here? What has yet to fully emerge into clarity? What is being born that needs to be developed and brought through to fruition? What is the potential for breakthrough in this breakdown?"

To the south ask, "What is clear here? What has reached its peak, fullness, or maximal extension and is about to wane?"

To the west you ask, "What is passing or coming to completion in this process? What seeds are being sowed into the earth now and what is being composted to feed the next cycle?"

And to the north you ask, "What remains unchanged? What are the possibilities that are latent here but have not yet been recognized? Where am I stuck or withdrawn, and what seeds of potential are frozen that must thaw or be released for the next cycle to begin?"

Use the basic truth of the natural cycle to organize your attention and focus your thinking. With each cycle of the process, a clearer and deeper sense of wholeness emerges. With each iteration, you deepen your wisdom of balance by seeing how each part is included in the whole, and how the whole is inseparable from its many parts. Each circle defines a whole: a whole breath, a whole day, a whole lunar cycle or year or lifetime. Understanding this, contemplate how the insights you come to may apply across many

"Everything we do— our discipline, effort, meditation, livelihood, and every single thing we do from the moment we're born until the moment we die—we can use to help us to realize our unity and our completeness with all things."
—**Ane Pema Chodron**

dimensions of wholeness, many cycles of time, many relationships, situations, or projects in which you seek for balance. This quality of multidimensional, whole systems thinking will help you to focus on the many elements of your life and weave them into a balanced whole perspective.

Ultimately, your greatest wisdom is in learning to hold all of these perspectives and points of view simultaneously, to behold a global vision of the whole system in all of its phases and stages at the same time. When you have learned to do this you come to stand in that witnessing wisdom and creative intelligence that is the essence of mindfulness.

As Robert Frost once wrote, "We dance round in a ring and suppose, but the Secret sits in the middle and knows." The great Chinese poet Chuang-tzu shared similar wisdom when he said, "When we understand, we are at the center of the circle and there we sit, while Yes and No chase each other around the circumference."

As you begin to think deeply about the unique aspects of each phase of the cycle, you begin to see a complete view of the whole system. You begin to recognize that the rhythms of energy and change within you and around you are deeply related. In each phase of the cycle, you begin to see every part of the system in its balanced relationship to a larger wholeness, and you begin to feel that the same forces that are alive within you are alive and unfolding in the world around you.

"There are only two ways to live your life. One is as though nothing is a miracle. The other is as though everything is a miracle."

—Albert Einstein

Return to Wholeness

We began this book with the question, "What does it mean to live in balance and wholeness in our world today?" Through the course of the journey you have been making through the many methods and ideas that have been presented here you have, no doubt, been expanding your sense of what this means for you. As you continue to integrate what you've found of value here, you may find that the journey of this book is truly a never-ending story. Each time you return to these pages they will reveal a deeper reflection of the possibilites for balancing your life. And as you grow in balance and wholeness, every-thing else in your life will continue to teach you.

Ultimately, balanced living comes from remembering, affirm-ing, and experiencing in an ongoing way the essential wholeness of your being. The pathway into this experience comes from staying tapped into your connection to a much larger Wholeness whose very nature is always in dynamic balance. Knowing that you are intrinsi-cally, inseparably embedded within the matrix of this fundamental field of Wholeness, that you are intimately a part of it, and it of you, is the most vital wisdom key you can have to access the reservoirs of inner strength and confidence you need to meet life's challenges with balance.

In our own lives, we call this remembrance the practice of "tak-ing refuge." It is something the two of us do on a daily basis, often several times a day, as a way of anchoring ourselves in the ultimate Source of balance, blessing, and guidance. What is it that steadies you? What or who, for you, can be a reliable source of refuge? Here is a meditation you can do to remember.

Receiving and Radiating

As you sit here now, envision yourself sitting at the center of your universe, surrounded by all living beings. Holding this image in mind, pause for a moment to remember, invite, or sense the pres-ence of those who have most deeply inspired you in your life. Reach out now with your heart and hands to these beings whose presence in your life is truly a blessing, a source of renewal, deep information, and inspiration. Imagine that all of them are right here with you now, surrounding you and shining like a constellation of brilliant suns. Or if you like, envision that these many sources of light merge into a single brighter sun that shines a radiance of blessings and inspiration into your life. Imagine that with each breath you reach out to them and hold their hands, and that through your connection with them you can draw strength and inspiration. In fact the stronger and more sincere your own aspiration, the deeper and

"And what does it mean to 'take refuge?' It means we can't do it alone."

—Natalie Goldberg

"With each true friendship, we build more firmly the foundation on which the peace of the whole world rests."

—Mahatma Gandhi

stronger the flow of inspiration becomes. Imagine that each of these inspiring people in turn reaches out to hold the hands of those whom they look to for guidance, strength, and inspiration, and that they in turn reach out to those who have inspired them. Sense your teachers reaching out to their teachers, who reach out to their teachers. Envision yourself balanced within and receiving from this endless cascade of wisdom and love as it flows to you and through you from countless inspired ancestors of the far and distant past.

Envision this inspiration as knowledge and energy, soaking into you now. It energizes the parts of you where your life force is weak. It balances what needs to be balanced. It floods, cleanses, and opens the spaces and places within you that are clogged or congested, and nourishes the seeds of your deepest potentials to blossom beautifully. Like sunlight filtering into a deep clear pool, sense these waves of inspiring grace flooding your body-mind-energy-spirit. Every dimension of your being is illuminated, blessed, and renewed. With each breath you are filled, silently thinking, *receiving*. With each breath you release what you no longer need to hold on to, thinking inwardly *releasing. Receiving... releasing... Receiving... releasing...* Plugging into this renewal circuit, you are revitalized, calmed, and energized, and move toward balance between your inner and outer worlds.

Having cleared your circuits, charged your batteries, and filled your tanks, begin now to radiate and expand this sense of peace and well-being within you. With each inhalation, shift to receive, and then with each exhalation, radiate. Breathing in, imagine the inspiration and blessings converging and spiraling into you, filling your heart. With each out-breath, imagine that your heart is silently radiating like a bright shining star. Effortlessly offer the natural radiance of your innermost being to the world. Allow it to shine through the darkness within or around you. Allow it to light up your inner and outer world effortlessly, immediately. Let this be the light of your love, the light of your peace, the light of your presence, the light of your goodwill and positive regard.

Now, having enhanced and expanded your radiance, begin to

> *"To be truly happy in this world is a revolutionary act because true happiness depends upon a revolution in ourselves. It is a radical change of view that liberates us so that we know who we are most deeply and can acknowledge our enormous ability to love."*
>
> —Sharon Salzberg

direct your attention and energy to the world around you. Reach out now to those who look to you as a source of inspiration, guidance, and support. Reach out to your children, to your students, to your patients, clients, and customers, and to all those who look to you as they seek for balance and belonging in their lives. Receiving inspiration, wisdom, and strength from those you draw guidance from, reach out with your hands and from your heart, and let each exhalation become an inspiring gift that you offer to those who, in turn, look to you.

Envision each person you reach out to taking your gift to heart: feel that it truly inspires and awakens greater wisdom, balance, and strength in their lives. As you reach out to your children, envision them receiving and taking this gift to heart and then passing it on to their children, who pass it on to their children, who pass it on to their children and to all whose lives they touch. Envision your students reaching out to their students who reach out to their students. Imagine that all those whom you reach out to take these gifts to heart, and pass it on to those who will pass it on in an endless cascade of inspiration and blessings that reaches out into the world to help nurture harmony and balance for countless generations to come. In this way, receiving and radiating, sense yourself balanced here reaching out from this fleeting moment where all the experiences of the infinite past and all the potential for the boundless future converge. Viewed in this light, realize that your real life-work is to reach out and realize your connectedness and wholeness, to deepen in balance, to increase your capacity to gather inspiration and wisdom, to take it to heart, and to pass it on as far and wide as you possibly can.

Now, as you breathe, gather the raw energy of any agitation or discomfort into your heart, like raking coal or wood into a furnace, and let it fuel the fire of transformation, giving you more light to radiate. With each breath, breathe in compost, and breathe out flowers and fruit. Breathe in fear, and let its energy be released into the radiance of confidence. Breathe in imbalance, and let it, too, fuel the radiance of your steadiness and resilience. Radiate the power of

"Each time a person stands up for an ideal, or acts to improve the lot of others. . . . he sends forth a tiny ripple of hope, and crossing each other from a million different centers of energy and daring, those ripples build a current that can sweep down the mightiest walls of oppression and resistance."
—Robert F. Kennedy

equanimity out on the waves of your breath as a blessing of balance and peace in the lives of all those who share your world.

In this way, with practice, begin to understand that you can utilize any experience that comes to you as a vehicle to deepen your inner strengths, and tap you into a greater sense of connectedness. If you are faced with fear and suffering, let it fuel the radiance of your love and compassion. Faced with beauty and the sweetness of life, let it intensify the radiance of your gratitude and rejoicing. Imagine yourself as a light bearer, illuminating the world. Imagine the silent light of your innermost being blazing with exquisite clarity and radiating out to fill your body. Imagine it radiating out into the world around you now, as you yourself act as a radiant source of inspiration for the world. Holding your loved ones and friends in mind, radiate this love to them. Bring to heart and mind the leaders of the world, the children of the world, the beleaguered nations and species of the world and radiate your heartfelt care and prayers to them.

"The divine beauty of heaven and earth, All creation, members of one family."

—**Morihei Ueshiba, O'Sensei**

In this way *receiving* . . . *radiating* . . . each breath affirms your deep relationship with the whole of creation, and with all beings in time past, present, and future. In this way, each blessed breath becomes a gesture of balance, a gesture of receiving from and offering to all.

Closing Thoughts

It is humbling for us to reflect on the state of the world and our positions and freedoms within it. Those of us writing or reading this book likely belong to a tiny minority of people who have adequate, or even luxurious, living conditions compared to most of humanity. We live with relative safety and peace of mind, free from much of the frightening unrest and danger in the world. We are educated and have many freedoms that others will never know. Many of us have the privilege and power to affect the lives of thousands of people and to help create the conditions for them to achieve a greater quality of life. We also have the privilege to develop and improve ourselves. If we choose, we can give time and attention to cultivate the paths of transformation, and work with others who share our freedom and inclination to create more balance and a better world for all.

In closing, we ask that you take this good fortune to heart. Utilizing the many methods and principles in this book has saved our life, our health, and our marriage many times, and it has served equally well for thousands of people we've worked with. We have confidence that it can help you in similar ways. Now it's up to you to put these guidelines to the test and make greater balance a living reality in your life.

We hope that your insights in reading this book will continue to ripen over time, and inspire an inquiry that opens you to live and work with greater balance, greater freedom, and a deeper kind of wisdom, caring, and wonder. The closing of this book is an opening into the rest of your life, as the circle of wholeness turns bringing all things into balance. In this spirit, we will end with a beginning—the first verse of Genesis. In the Hebrew language, each letter of the alphabet has a meaning in itself. Understanding this, Stan Tenen's beautiful rendition of this verse translates the original Hebrew words one letter at a time to reveal an inner vision of wholeness. May the deep meaning of these uplifting words remind you of the ever-present wellspring of balancing energies available deep within you and in the heart of all of Creation at all times.

> *"Breaking Open, Inside Outside*
> *Rushing, Radiating, Reaching*
>
> *All Life*
> *Shining Source-Light*
> *In Inner Being*
> *Itself Recurring In Itself*
>
> *Breaking Open, Inside Outside*
> *Rushing, Radiating, Reaching*
> *All-Life*

"As you practice these precious teachings, slowly the clouds of sorrow will melt away, and the sun of wisdom and true joy will be shining in the clear sky of your mind."

—Kalu Rinpoche

All-Life
Blooming, Kindling, Inside Lighting
Looking Open, In with Out
In Inner Being
Golden-Flowing, Moving Outward, In Itself

All-Life
Itself Recurring In Itself

Looking Open, In with Out
Shining Source-Light
Inside Dividing
In Inner Being
Golden-Flowing, Moving Outward, In Itself

Doing, Living, Co-Evolving
All-Life
Itself Recurring In Itself

Looking Open, In with Out
All-Life
Rushing, Radiating, Reaching

Treetop, Upright; Bearing Wholeness, Carrying Light!"

"Blessings and Balance, Balance and Blessings, For from Balance comes all Blessings."

—Grandmother Keewaydinoquay, Ojibway Medicine Woman

ACKNOWLEDGMENTS

Our heartfelt thanks and deepest appreciation to:

Mary Jane Ryan, our inspired editor, whose deep listening to the call for balance was the visionary spark that birthed this book into being. Her wisdom, skillful coaching, and patient faith in us made it all possible.

Everyone else at Conari Press who has shared in weaving these words together into the beautiful book you now hold in your hands. We also want to acknowledge our appreciation to Peris Gumz for her creatively inspired work in so skillfully preparing the index.

Michelle's parents, Ida and Benjamin Gold, who helped her take her first steps in the direction of balance.

Joel's parents, Recia and Alan Millar, for their inspiration, encouragement, and the lessons learned about dynamic balance in relationship over many years.

All of our friends and students in the HumanKind Learning Community, who have inspired and supported us throughout the emergence of this book. Special thanks to: Sheila Hoffman for her creative collaboration in crafting the diagrams for the book; Janis Wignall and Tom Engel, our science advisors, who revealed to us the principles of balance woven in the genetic code, and underlying the equilibrium of living systems; and to Jed and Kaoru Share, for their loving support and for our photograph for this book.

Mahalo to our Hawaiian *aina* and *ohana,* for the gift of balancing our mainland urban road warriors' life with the joyous Island splendor of nature's healing power and beauty. Our appreciation, too, for all the business leaders and change agents, especially Jim Channon and the Arcturus Design Group, who have joined us there in the aloha spirit, and who have demonstrated their commitment to catalyzing sustainability and harmony through their work around the globe.

The many colleagues and clients who have inspired and supported this work including: leaders and teams throughout the

Hewlett-Packard Company, ATL, World Business Academy, Institute of Noetic Sciences, and Performance Edge, the community of the Council Grove Conference, ISSSEEM, and the Dove Health Alliance. In particular, we give thanks to: Peter and Sarah Parks, whose warmth, wisdom, nurturing lovingkindness, and gracious hospitality helped keep balance in our lives and allowed us to meet our writing deadlines while traveling away from home.

Fred Donaldson, whose inspiring example and insights into the vital role of play in dynamic balance has opened up a whole new world of wonder and discovery for us.

Mietek and Margaret Wirkus, whose deep insights and inspirations regarding the healing energies of love and prayer are a blessing to all whose lives they touch.

Peg Jordan, for her enthusiastic support and timely assistance identifying leading health and fitness resources for the Resource Guide.

Lynda and David Chethlahe Paladin, whose enduring love, inspiration, and wisdom glows in our hearts and surrounds us with beauty always.

Our deep respect, appreciation, and admiration to Thich Nhat Hanh, Angeles Arrien, and all our many extraordinary and inspired teachers, living in memory and presence, who have shared with us their wisdom, and the wisdom of their teachers, and teachers' teachers. And, especially, a very deep bow to Nobel Peace Laureate, Tenzin Gyatso, the Dalai Lama, for his kindness in offering the Foreword for this book, and for his inspiring example of balanced living amidst the most challenging of circumstances. Despite the on-going genocide of the Tibetan culture over the past 40 years of Chinese occupation, he has inspired the people and the leaders of the world with the possibility of a wise and nonviolent way of life that actively seeks justice while showing compassion and respect for all. May we all be inspired to seek such a balance in our own lives.

We would also like to acknowledge the trees, the sun, the rain—the countless forces of creation and living beings—who each, in their small, yet necessary ways, have contributed to the flow of resources converging into this book. We honor and give gratitude to all the guiding and supportive forces of the universe that are truly at the heart of this work, and through whose grace the miracle of this book has come into being and into your hands. May we learn to look, listen, and feel ever more deeply, to discover how profoundly interwoven all things and beings are within the mysterious balance of our lives.

Finally, we acknowledge you, the reader, sincere enough in your yearning for balance to invest yourself in reading this book. As you read, we will touch hearts and minds. We invite you to hold this book as a basket containing many seeds and jewels of wisdom that we have gathered through our encounters with many remarkable people. Through your connection with us you will meet many of our friends and teachers, and in meeting them you will encounter their teachers. In this way, may the wisdom stream of our teachers flow into your life. As you read these pages, and as you test or take these ideas to heart, may your own wisdom and faith in the potentials of your life grow. Through your own increasingly balanced way of living, may you, in turn, inspire others, who will inspire others, who will inspire others for generations to come, so that this living source of wisdom and compassion will continue to nourish the spirit of balance in our world in ever more wonderful ways.

RESOURCE GUIDE

The following guide offers a glimpse of some of the many resources that we have found to be helpful in understanding the essential role of balance in our lives. Note that most of these materials relate to more than a single dimension of balance, and although they are assigned to a single category for the purpose of this Guide, their benefits have far-reaching applications that span different realms of living in balance. If you are on-line, the websites offered here are virtual treasuries of resources, insights, and opportunities for further inquiry and discovery.

SECTION ONE: An Inside-Out Approach to Balanced Living

CHAPTER ONE. It's All About Balance, and
CHAPTER TWO. Glimpses of Wholeness

Baraka: A World Beyond Words. MPI World Video, 1995.

Bohm, David and Edwards, W. *Changing Consciousness, Exploring the Hidden Source of the Social, Political, and Environmental Crisis Facing Our World.* N.Y.: HarperCollins, 1991.

Capra, Fritjof. *The Web of Life: A New Scientific Understanding of Living Systems.* N.Y.: Anchor Doubleday, 1996.

Dossey, Larry. *Recovering the Soul: A Scientific and Spiritual Search.* N.Y: Bantam, 1989.

Elgin, Duane. *Awakening Earth: Exploring the Evolution of Human Culture and Consciousness.* N.Y.: William Morrow and Co., 1993.

Gore, Al. *Earth in the Balance: Ecology and the Human Spirit.* N.Y.: Houghton Mifflin Co., 1992.

Harman, Willis. *Global Mind Change.* N.Y.: Warner Books, 1988.

Kelly, Kevin. *Out of Control: The New Biology of Machines, Social Systems, and the Economic World.* N.Y.: Addison Wesley, 1994.

_____. The Home Planet. N.Y.: Addison Wesley, 1992.

Lovelock, James. *Healing Gaia*. N.Y.: Harmony Books, 1991.

Macy, Joanna. *World as Lover, World as Self.* Berkeley: Parallax, 1991.

Mander, Jerry. *In the Absence of the Sacred: The Failure of Technology and the Survival of the Indian Nations.* S.F.: Sierra Club Books, 1991.

Mitchell, Stephen (trans.). *Tao Te Ching.* N.Y.: Harper and Row, 1988.

Russell, Peter. *The Global Brain Awakens.* Palo Alto: Global Brain, Inc. 1995.

Weber, Renee. *Dialogues with Scientists and Sages: The Search for Unity.* N.Y.: Routledge and Paul Kegan, 1986.

Wilber, Ken. *A Brief History of Everything.* Boston: Shambhala, 1996.

CHAPTER THREE. Life as a Learning
Expedition: A Model for Balance

Csikszentmihalyi, Mihaly. Flow: *The Psychology of Optimal Experience.* N.Y.: Harper and Row, 1990.

_____. *Creativity: Flow and the Psychology of Discovery and Invention.* HarperCollins, 1996.

Fletcher, Jerry. *Patterns of High Performance.* S.F.: Berrett-Koehler, 1993.

Murphy, Michael and White, Rhea. *In the Zone: Transcendent Experience in Sports.* N.Y.: Penguin, 1995.

CHAPTER FOUR. Mindfulness:
The Gateway to Balance

Boorstein, Sylvia. *Don't Just Do Something, Sit There: A Mindfulness Retreat.* S.F.: Harper, 1996.

Braza, Jerry. *Moment by Moment: The Art and Practice of Mindfulness.* Boston: Tuttle, 1997.

Goldstein, Joseph. *The Experience of Insight.* Boston: Shambhala., 1983.

Kabat-Zinn, Jon. *Wherever You Go. There You Are: Mindfulness in Everyday Life.* N.Y.: Hyperion, 1994.

Langer, Ellen J. *The Power of Mindful Learning.* N.Y.: Addison Wesley, 1997.

Nhat Hanh, Thich. *The Miracle of Mindfulness.* Boston: Beacon Press, 1987.

Tart, Charles. *Living the Mindful Life: A Handbook for Living in the Present Moment.* Boston: Shambhala, 1994.

Whitmyer, Claude. *Mindfulness and Meaningful Work.* Berkeley: Parallax, 1994.

SECTION TWO: Mind, Body, Spirit Harmony:
Fine-Tuning Our Primary Instrument

Borysenko, Joan. *A Woman's Book of Life: The Biology, Psychology, and Spirituality of the Feminine Life Cycle.* N.Y.: Riverhead, 1996.

_____. *Minding the Body, Mending the Mind.* N.Y.: Bantam,1987.

Domar, Alice. *Healing Mind, Healthy Woman: Using the Mind/Body Connection to Manage Stress and Take Control of Your Health.* New York: Henry Holt, 1996.

Institute of Noetic Sciences. *The Heart of Healing.* Atlanta: Turner Publishing, 1993.

Institute of Noetic Sciences is committed to the development of human consciousness through scientific inquiry, spiritual understanding, and psychological well-being. A highly credible and respected source! 475 Gate Five Road, Suite 300, P.O. Box 909 Sausalito, CA 94966-090. Phone: 800 383-1394. Website: www.noetic.org

Jahnke, Roger. *The Healer Within*. San Francisco: Harper, 1997.

Northrup, Christiane. Health *Wisdom for Women Newsletter*. Phillips Publishing, Inc. 7811 Montrose Road, P.O. Box 60110, Potomac, MD 20897-5924. Phone: 800 804-0935.

Leonard, George and Murphy, Michael. *The Life We Are Given: A Long Term Program for Realizing the Potential of Body, Mind, Heart, and Soul*. L.A.: Tarcher, 1995.

McGarey, Gladys, with Stearn, Jess. *The Physician Within You*. Deerfield Beach, FL: Health Communications, Inc., 1997.

Robbins, John. *Reclaiming Our Health: Exploding the Medical Myth and Embracing the True Source of Healing*. H. J. Kramer, 1996.

New Dimensions Radio. Excellent source of audiotape interviews with leaders in mind-body-spirit research and health. Phone: 800-935-8273. P.O. Box 569, Ukiah, CA 95482. Website: www.new dimensions.org

Sounds True Catalogue. Excellent source of audio recordings related to mind-body-spirit. Phone: 800-333-9185. Email: SoundsTrue@aol.com

Weil, Andrew. *Spontaneous Healing: How to Discover and Enhance Your Body's Natural Ability to Maintain and Heal Itself*. N.Y.: Knopf, 1995.

_____. *Natural Health, Natural Medicine: A Comprehensive Manual for Wellness and Self Care*. Boston: Houghton Mifflin, 1995.

_____. *Eight Weeks to Optimal Health*. N.Y.: Random House, 1997.

CHAPTER FIVE. Physical Balance:
Lessons from and for the Body

Aerobics and Fitness Association. Excellent source of information and training resources. Phone: (800)your-body. Website: www.afaa.com

Albert, Katherine. *Get a Good Night's Sleep*. Fireside, 1997.

Bruun, Ruth and Bertel. *The Human Body: Your Body and How it Works*. N.Y.: Random House, 1982.

Chopra, Deepak. *Restful Sleep*. N.Y.: Random House Audio, 1994.

Douilard, Jim. *Body, Mind and Sport*. N.Y.: Crown Trade, 1994.

Ivker, Robert and Zorensky, Edward. *Thriving: The Complete Mind-Body Guide for Optimal Health and Fitness for Men*. N.Y.: Crown Publishing, 1997.

Jumpin' Productions. A health communications and research firm specializing in current information on total well-being. Phone 510-946-1516. 1493 Paseo Nogales, CA Alamo 94507 Email: flash@flashtrends.com

Levey, Joel. *The Fine Art of Relaxation* (programmable CD). Seattle: Earth View, 1988.

Murphy, Michael. *The Future of the Body: Explorations into the Further Evolution of Human Nature*. L.A.: Tarcher, 1992.

Nhat Hanh, Thich. *The Long Road Turns to Joy: A Guide to Walking Meditation*. Berkeley: Parallax Press, 1996.

Northrup, Christiane. *Women's Bodies, Women's Wisdom*. N.Y.: Bantam, 1994.

O'Shea, Kate. *Finding Your Balance: Caring of Mind, Body, and Soul in Times of Discomfort, Instability, and Surgery— Introducing Orthopedic Psychology*. Sausalito: Institute of Orthopedic Psychology, 1997.

Robbins, John. *May All Be Fed*. (includes great recipes!) N.Y.: William Morrow and Co., 1992.

_____. *Diet for a New America: How Your Food Choices Affect Your Health, Happiness, and the Future of Life on Earth..* Walpole, N.H.: Stillpoint, 1987. Video and information available from: Earthsave 800-DNA-DOIT. 706 Frederick St., Santa Cruz, CA 95062 Website: www.earthsave.org

The Mind, Body, and Soul Network. Excellent source of eclectic
  resources on nutrition, mindbody health, fitness, relationships,
  and so on. Website: www.mindbodysoul.com

The National Wellness Institute. Excellent source of valuable information on health, fitness, wellness, health promotion, and
  national conferences. Phone: 715-342-2969. Website:
  www.wellnessnwi.org

CHAPTER SIX. Emotional Balance:
A Peaceful Heart

Andrews, Frank. *The Art and Practice of Loving.* L.A.: Tarcher,
  1991.

Borysenko, Joan. *Meditations for Overcoming Depression.* Carson:
  Hay House Audio, 1995.

Goleman, Daniel. *Emotional Intelligence: Why It Can Matter More
  Than IQ.* N.Y.: Bantam, 1995.

Salzberg, Sharon. *Lovingkindness: The Revolutionary Art of
  Happiness.* Boston: Shambhala, 1995.

Steindl-Rast, Brother David. *Gratefulness, The Heart of Prayer: An
  Approach to Life in Fullness.* N.Y.: Paulist Press, 1984.

Tavris, Carol. *Anger: The Misunderstood Emotion.* N.Y.: Touchstone,
  1989.

CHAPTER SEVEN. The Balanced Mindstate

Jahn, Robert and Dunne, Brenda. *Margins of Reality: The Role of
  Consciousness in the Physical World.* San Diego: HBJ, 1987.
  (For more information on this exceptional research at
  Princeton University contact: Princeton Engineering
  Anomalies Research, Princeton University, School of
  Engineering and Applied Science. Phone: 609-258-5950.
  Email: pearlab@princeton.edu Website: http//:www.edu/~rdnel-
  son/pear.html.

Levey, Joel. 'Mind Treasure: Intuitive Wisdom and the Dynamics of Mystery and Mastery at Work,' in Frantz, Roger and Pattakos, Alex (eds.) *Intuition at Work*. S.F.: New Leaders Press, 1997.

Levey, Joel and Michelle. *The Fine Art of Relaxation, Concentration, and Meditation: Ancient Skills for Modern Minds*. Boston: Wisdom, 1991.

_____. *Quality of Mind: Tools for Personal Mastery and Enhanced Performance*. Boston: Wisdom, 1991.

_____. *The Focused Mindstate: Maximizing Your Potential Through the Power of Concentration*. (7 tape album with workbook.) Chicago: Nightingale-Conant, 1993.

_____. *Awareness Training Exercises for Mindful Attention*. Chicago: Nightingale-Conant, 1993.

Lhalungpa, Lobsang. *Mahamudra: The Quintessence of Mind & Meditation*. Boston: Shambhala, 1987.

Mitchell, Stephen. *The Enlightened Mind: An Anthology of Sacred Prose*. N.Y.: Harper Perennial, 1991.

Moyers, Bill. *Healing and the Mind*. N.Y.: Doubleday, 1993.

Orloff, Judith. *Second Sight*. N.Y.: Warner, 1996.

Tart, Charles. *Open Mind, Discriminating Mind*. S.F.: Harper and Row, 1989.

Vivekananda, S. *Raga Yoga*. N.Y.: Ramakrishna Vivekananda Center, 1993.

CHAPTER EIGHT. Catching the Waves:
Balancing the Harmonics of Subtle Energy

Becker, Robert O. *Cross Currents: The Perils of Electropollution, The Promise of Electromedicine*. L.A.: Tarcher, 1990.

Becker, Robert O. and Selden, Gary. *The Body Electric: Electromagnetism and the Foundation of Life*. N.Y.: Morrow, 1985.

Brennan, Barbara. *Light Emerging.* N.Y. : Bantam, 1993.

Donden, Yeshi. *Health Through Balance.* Ithaca: Snow Lion, 1986.

Grey, Alex. *Sacred Mirrors: The Visionary Art of Alex Grey.* Rochester, VT: Inner Traditions, 1990. Website: www.alex-grey.com

International Society for the Study of Subtle Energies, and Energy Medicine (ISSSEEM), 356 Goldco Circle, Golden, CO 80403-1347. Phone: 303-425-4625. Fax 303-425-4685. Excellent website: http://vitalenergy.com/issseem/

Krieger, Delores. *Therapeutic Touch Inner Workbook.* Sante Fe: Bear and Company, 1996.

Myss, Carolyn. *Energy Anatomy.* Boulder: Sounds True Audio, 1996.

_____. Anatomy of Spirit: *The Seven Stages of Power and Healing.* N.Y.: Random House, 1996.

Redfield, James. *The Celestine Prophesy.* N.Y.: TimeWarner, 1993.

Stevens, John. *Aikido: The Way of Harmony.* Boston: Shambhala., 1990.

Tiller, Bill. *Science and Human Transformation: Subtle Energies, Intentionality, and Consciousness.* Walnut Creek, CA: Pavior Publishing, 1997.

Ueshiba, Morihei (trans. Stevens, John). *The Art of Peace.* Boston: Shambhala., 1992.

Wirkus, Mietek. *Bioenergy: A Healing Art* (video), available from : Wirkus Bioenergy Foundation, 4803 St. Elmo Ave, Bethesda, MD, 20814. Phone: (301)652-1691. Fax (301)652-3480. Email: 71572.3454@compuserve.com

CHAPTER NINE. Balanced in Spirit

Borysenko, Joan. *Fire in the Soul: A New Psychology of Spiritual Optimism.* N.Y.: Warner Books, 1993.

Dalai Lama. *The Good Heart.* (The World Community for Christian Meditation). Boston: Wisdom, 1996.

Das, Surya. *Awakening the Buddha Within.* New York: Broadway Books, 1997.

De Mello, Father Anthony. *Praying Body and Soul: Principles, Practices, Stories.* N.Y.: Crossroads, 1997.

Dossey, Larry. *Healing Words: The Power of Prayer and the Practice of Medicine.* N.Y.: Harper Collins, 1993.

_____. *Prayer Is Good Medicine.* N.Y.: HarperCollins, 1996.

Fox, Matthew. *A Spirituality Named Compassion.* S.F.: Harper and Row, 1990.

Glassman, Bernard and Fields, Rick. *Instructions to the Cook: A Zen Master's Lessons in Living a Life That Matters.* N.Y.: Random House, 1997.

Jackson, Phil and Delehanty, Hugh. *Sacred Hoops: Spiritual Lessons of a Hardwood Warrior.* N.Y.: Hyperion, 1995.

Keating, Fr. Thomas. *Open Mind, Open Heart.* New York: Continuum Publishing, 1994.

Kelly, Jack and Marcia. *Sanctuaries: The West Coast and Southwest Guide to Lodgings in Monasteries, Abbeys, and Retreats of the United States.* Bell Tower, 1996.

Kornfield, Jack. *A Path With Heart: A Guide Through the Perils and Promises of Spiritual Life.* N.Y.: Bantam, 1993.

Kornfield, Jack and Feldman, Christina. *Soul Food: Stories to Nourish the Spirit and the Heart.* S.F.: Harper, 1996.

Labowitz, Rabbi Shoni. *Miraculous Living.* N.Y.: Simon and Schuster, 1996.

Lhalungpa, Lobsang. *The Life of Milarepa.* Boston: Shambhala, 1997.

Levine, Stephen. *A Gradual Awakening.* N.Y.: Anchor Doubleday, 1978.

Mitchell, Stephen (ed.). *The Enlightened Heart: An Anthology of Sacred Poetry.* N.Y. HarperCollins, 1989.

Moore, Thomas. *Care of the Soul: A Guide for Cultivating Depth and Sacredness in Everyday Life.* N.Y.: HarperCollins, 1992.

_____. *The Re-Enchantment of Everyday Life.* N.Y.: HarperCollins, 1996.

Mueller, Wayne. *How Then Shall We Live? Four Simple Questions That Reveal the Beauty and Meaning of Our Lives.* N.Y.: Bantam, 1996.

Nhat Hanh, Thich. *Living Buddha, Living Christ.* N.Y.: Riverhead, 1996.

Palmer, Parker J. *The Active Life: A Spirituality of Work, Creativity, and Caring.* S.F.: Harper, 1991.

Rinpoche, Sogyal. *The Tibetan Book of Living and Dying.* S.F.: Harper, 1992.

Snow, Kimberley. *Keys to the Open Gate: A Woman's Spirituality Sourcebook.* Berkeley: Conari Press, 1994.

Steindl-Rast, Brother David with Lebell, Sharon. *The Music of Silence: Entering the Sacred Space of Monastic Experience.* S.F.: Harper, 1994.

Yogananda, Paramahansa. *Autobiography of A Yogi.* L.A.: SRF, 1993.

SECTION THREE: Expanding the Circle of Balance:
Home, Play, Work, and World

CHAPTER TEN. All My Relations

Canfield, Jack and Hansen, Mark. The various *Chicken Soup for the Soul* books published by Health Communications.

The Center for Nonviolent Communication (tapes, books, workshops) P.O. Box 2662, Sherman, TX 75091-2662. Phone: 903-893-3886. Email: 104360.1521@compuserve.com. Website: www.cnvc.org

Crum, Thomas. *The Magic of Conflict: Turning a Life of Work into a Work of Art.* N.Y.: Simon and Schuster, 1987.

Dass, Ram and Gorman, Paul. *How Can I Help? Stories and Reflections on Service.* N.Y.: Alfred Knopf, 1990.

Donaldson, O. Fred. *Playing by Heart: The Vision and Practice of Belonging.* Deerfield Beach, FL: Health Communications, Inc., 1993. For information on Fred's pioneering work call 909-652-5625.

Edelman, Joel and Crain, Mary Beth. *The Tao of Negotiation: How You Can Prevent, Resolve, and Transcend Conflict in Work and Everyday Life.* N.Y.: Harper, 1993.

Editors of Conari Press. The various *Random Acts of Kindness* books. Berkeley: Conari, 1995.

Faber, Adele and Mazlish, Elaine. *How to Talk So Kids Will Listen and Listen So Kids Will Talk.* N.Y.: Avon, 1980.

Henderson, Hazel. *Building a Win-Win World: Life Beyond Global Economic Warfare.* S.F.: Berrett-Koehler, 1996.

Kabat-Zinn, Jon and Myla. *Everyday Blessings: The Inner Work of Mindful Parenting.* N.Y.: Hyperion, 1997.

Levine, Stephen and Ondrea. *Embracing the Beloved: Relationship as a Path of Awakening.* N.Y.: Doubleday, 1995.

Nhat Hanh, Thich. *For a Future to Be Possible.* Berkeley: Parallax Press, 1993.

Peck, M. Scott. *A World Waiting to Be Born: Discovering Civility.* N.Y.: Bantam Books, 1993.

Remen, Rachel Naomi. *Kitchen Table Wisdom: Stories That Heal.* Riverhead Books, 1996.

CHAPTER ELEVEN. Life-Work Balance

Barrentine, Pat (ed.). *When the Canary Stops Singing: Women's Perspectives in Transforming Business.* S.F.: Berrett-Koehler, 1993.

Block, Peter. *Stewardship*. S.F.: Berrett-Koehler, 1993.

Business Ethics magazine. Phone: 617-962-4700.

Canfield, Jack, et al. *Chicken Soup for the Soul at Work*. Deerfield Beach, Fl.: Health Communications, Inc., 1996.

Center for a New American Dream. 156 College Street, 2nd Floor, Burlington, VT 05401. Phone: 802-862-6762. Fax: 802-860-1735.

Context Institute. Access to information and networks devoted to cultural change toward a humane and sustainable world. P.O. Box 946, Langely, WA 98260. Phone: 360-221-6044. Email: ci@context.org Website: www.context.org

DeFoore, Bill and Renesch, John (eds.) *Rediscovering the Soul of Business: A Renaissance of Values*. S.F.: New Leaders Press, 1995.

Elgin, Duane. *Voluntary Simplicty: Toward a Way of Life That Is Outwardly Simple, Inwardly Rich*. N.Y.: William Morrow, 1993.

Fox, Matthew. *The Reinvention of Work: A New Vision of Livelihood for Our Time*. S.F.: HarperCollins, 1994.

Garfield, Charles. *Second to None: How the Smartest Companies Put People First*. Homewood, Ill.: Business One Irwin, 1992.

Jaworski, Joseph. *Synchronicity: The Inner Path of Leadership*. S.F.: Berrett-Koehler, 1996.

Land, G. and Jarman, B. *Breakpoint and Beyond: Mastering the Future Today*. N.Y.: Harper Business, 1992.

Levey, Joel. 'Consciousness, Caring, and Commerce: Sustainable Values for the Global Marketplace,' in *The New Bottom Line: Bringing Heart and Soul to Business*. S.F.: New Leaders Press, 1995.

_____. 'The Human Heart and Soul at Work,' in DeFoore, Bill and Renesch, John (eds.) *Rediscovering the Soul of Business: A Renaissance of Values*. S.F.: New Leaders Press, 1995.

Levey, Joel and Michelle. 'Wisdom at Work: An Inquiry into the Dimensions of Higher Order Learning,' in Chawla, Sarita and Renesch, John (eds.) *Learning Organizations: Developing Cultures for Tomorrow's Workplace.* Portland OR: Productivity Press, 1995.

New Road Map Foundation. Books, tapes on simple living including: Dominguez, Joe and Robin, Vicki. *Your Money or Your Life: Transforming Your Relationship With Money and Achieving Financial Independence.* P.O. Box 15981, Seattle, WA 98115. Phone: 206-527-0437. E-mail: newroadmap@igc.apc.org

New Ways to Work. Promotes workplace flexibility through publications, research, and training. 149 9th St., San Francisco, CA 94103.

Osterberg, Rolf. *Corporate Renaissance: Business as an Adventure in Human Development.* Mill Valley: Natara, 1993.

Rechtshaffen, Stephan. *Timeshifting: Creating More Time to Enoy Your Life.* N.Y.: Doubleday, 1996.

Senge, Peter, et al. *The Fifth Discipline Fieldbook: Strategies and Tools for Building a Learning Organization.* N.Y.: Doubleday Currency, 1994.

Simple Living quarterly journal. 1802 N. 54th St. Seattle, WA 98103. Website: www.slnet.com.

Srivasta, Suresh, Cooperrider, David, et al. *Appreciative Management and Leadership: The Power of Positive Thought and Action in Organizations.* S.F.: Jossey-Bass, 1990.

St. James, Elaine. *Simplify Your Life.* N.Y.: Hyperion, 1994.

Wheatley, Margaret. *Leadership and the New Science: Learning About Organization from an Orderly Universe.* S.F.: Berrett-Koehler, 1993.

Wheately, Margaret and Kellner-Rogers, Myron. *A Simpler Way.* S.F.: Berrett-Koehler, 1996.

Whyte, David. *The Heart Aroused: Poetry and the Preservation of the Soul in Corporate America.* N.Y.: Doubleday Currency, 1994.

Yearning for Balance: View of Americans on Consumption, Materialism, and the Environment. Merck Family Fund, 6930 Carroll Ave., Suite 500, Takoma Park, MD 20912. Phone: 301-270-3970. E-mail: merck@ige.apc.org

Weisbord, Marvin, et al. *Discovering Common Ground.* S.F.: Berrett-Koehler, 1992.

World Business Academy. One Market Plaza, 2650 Steuart Tower, S.F., CA 94105-1019. Phone: 415-227-0106. Email: wba@well.com

CHAPTER TWELVE. Finding Yourself in the World

Arrien, Angeles. *The Four Fold Way: Walking the Paths of the Warrior, Teacher, Healer, and Visionary.* S.F.: HarperCollins, 1993.

Cornell, Joseph. *Listening to Nature: How to Deepen Your Awareness of Nature.* Nevada City: Dawn Publications, 1987.

Gozdz, Kazimierz (ed.). *Community Building: Renewing Spirit and Learning in Business.* S.F.: New Leaders Press, 1995.

Institue of Noetic Sciences. *Community Groups Handbook.* Sausalito: IONS, 1995.

Peck, M. Scott. *The Different Drum, Community Making and Peace: A Spiritual Journey Toward Self-Acceptance, True Belonging, and New Hope for the World.* N.Y.: Simon & Schuster, 1987.

Seed, John, Macy, Joanna, Fleming, Pat, and Naess, Arne. *Thinking Like a Mountain: Towards a Council of All Beings.* Santa Cruz: New Society Publishers, 1988.

Shaffer, Carolyn & Anundsen, Kristin. *Creating Community Anywhere: Finding Support & Connection in a Fragmented World.* L.A.: Tarcher, 1993.

Witmyer, Claude (ed.). *In the Company of Others: Making Community in the Modern World.* L.A.: Tarcher, 1993.

Zohar, Dana and Marshall, I. *The Quantum Society.* N.Y.: Morrow, 1994.

SECTION FOUR: Reclaiming Our Balance, Embracing the Whole

CHAPTER THIRTEEN. Seven Principles for Living in Balance

Pelletier, Kenneth. *Sound Mind, Sound Body: A New Model for Lifelong Health.* N.Y. : Simon and Schuster, 1994.

CHAPTER FOURTEEN. Earthwalk: Essential Reminders for a Balanced Life

Beck, Peggy V., Walters, Anna Lee, and Francisco, Nia. *The Sacred: Ways of Knowledge, Sources of Life.* Flagstaff: Northland Publishing Co., and Navajo Community College Press, 1990.

Lawlor, Robert. *Voices of the First Day: Awakening in the Aboriginal Dreamtime.* Rochester, Vt.: Inner Traditions International, 1991.

Paladin, David Chethlahe. *Painting the Dream.* Rochester, Vt.: Park Street Press, 1992.

Tenen, Stan. *Geometric Metaphors of Life.* Meru Foundation, P.O. Box 503, Sharon, MA 02067, Tel. (781)784-8902, or 1-888-422MERU., Email: meru@well.com Website: www.meru.org

Underwood, Paula. *The Walking People: A Native American Oral History.* San Anselmo: Tribe of Two Press & IONS, 1993.

Gandhi, 248, 270
General Motors, 238
Global family, 263-66
Goleman, Daniel, 117
Grace, 192-95. *see also* Flow
Gramps, 189-92
Gratitude, 119-20, 195, 203, 292
Green Berets, 44, 159
Green, Drs. Elmer and Alyce, 72
Gregg, Richard, 248
Grief, 42, 44-45, 202, 292

H

Habit, 22-23, 43, 53-54, 135, 205-06
Hart, Mickey, 77
Harvard Law School, 238
Health, 37, 49, 59; and emotions, 114-16; and gratitude, 119-20; and subtle energy, 155-59; and balance, 156-57; optimal, 280-88. *see also* Exercise; Nutrition
Health care, 156, 236
Heart, 88-89, 102-03, 172, 225; as physical-emotional bridge, 105-07; as bioelectric miracle, 107; practices, 108-10; and toxic emotions, 114-16
Herakleitos, 11
Hershel, Aaron, 138
Hewlett-Packard, 53, 117, 240-41, 243, 287
Hillman, Anne, 263
Hixon, Lex, 177
Homeostasis, 15-18, 38
Huxley, Aldous, 53

I

"Ice field," 98, 140, 145

Illustrations: zones of living and learning, 30; wheel of mindfulness, 66; spiral of balance, 280
Indians of the Six Nations, 241-42
Information and overload, 148-50
Information fatigue syndrome, 149-50
"Inner science," ix, 105, 111
Intention, 22-24, 43, 56, 65-66, 138, 210
Intuition, 148-50

J

Jackson, Phil, 262
Jacobsen, Dr. Stephen E., 186
Jahnke, Roger, 155
Japan, 229, 239
Jesus, 248, 267

K

Kabbalah, 271
Kabir, 192, 195
Kalachakra, 166
Karoshi, 229
Koran, 177
Krobasa, Dr. Suzanne Couellette, 236, 280

L

Lake, Celinda, 231
Lamrimpa, Gen, 54, 126
Lao Tzu, 248
Law of Progressive Simplification, 256
Learning, 6-8, 27-45, 206-07, 291; and zones, 28-43; as lifelong adventure, 39-45; and feedback, 45; and subtle energy, 158

Lebow, Victor, 246
Leverage, 51, 282-83
Lifeforce, *see* Subtle energy
Life-Work balance, 41, 227-257; trends in workplace, 227-34; and women, 230-33, 249-50, 253; three elements for success, 232; and children, 233-34; Wharton study, 234-35; moving toward, 235-41; cultural variation, 241-44; paid vacation, 243; productivity, 244; addictive consumerism and debt, 245-6; satisfaction, 244-47; and simplicity, 248-51, 256-57; "pro-balance" strategies, 250-51; "soulshifters," 252-54
Linquist, Dr. Luann, 232
Listening, 209-13
Lovelock, James, 16
Lovingkindness, 273-75
Lyons, Chief Oren, 267

M

Maynard, Herman, 239
McLuhan, T.C., 241
Meditation, 156, 189, 222, 294. *see also* Practices; Questions
Menninger Clinic, 49
Menninger Foundation, 34, 115, 163, 216
Millman, Dan, 176
Mind, balance of, 125-51; and illusion, 126-27; inner and outer, 127-30; insight into stress response, 130-32; and stories, 132-36; universal, 137-38; active and quiet, 138-43; balanced state, 143-48; being and

doing, 150-51
Mindfulness, 2, 6, 22-24, 36, 45, 47-73; as most crucial tool in balancing, 47-48, 69; and choice, 49-51; and love, 50; benefits of, 50; Tibetan meaning of, 54; and breathing, 55-59, 68-69; of one's body, 59-61, 80; of one's thoughts, 61-66; essence of, 64; wheel of, 64-66; questions, 67; reminders, 68; and exercise, 92; and sleep, 96; and alexythymia, 113-14; and emotional response, 116-23; of thinking, 125-36; and universal mind, 137-38; and active and quiet minds, 138-43; of space, 144; as antidote to information overload, 150; and subtle energy, 156-73; and spiritual path, 179-85, 195-96; and relationship, 201-13; and communication, 209-13; and alone time, 215; and simplicity, 248-57; and restoring world, 271-73; and seven principles of balance, 280-88; and leverage, 282-83; one step at a time, 293-94
Moon Over Morocco, 136
Moses, 267
"Myna birds of mindfulness", 53-55

N

NASA, 165
Nature, and balance, 13-15; as protection, 172; and cycles, 242, 294-97
Neuropeptides, 115
Nostrils, 167-71
Nhat Hanh, Thich, 55, 68-69, 224-25
Nutrition, 80-86

"Theta twitching," 101-02
Thoreau, Henry David, 248
Three realities, 120-21
Tikkun, 271-73
Tohei Sensei, Koichi, 171-72
Touch point, 60
Toynbee, Arnold, 256
Travelers-Aetna Insurance, 287
Tzu, Chuang, 155, 297

U

U.S. West Communications, 228
Ueshiba O'Sensei, Morihei, 28
United Auto Workers, 244
Universal mind, 137-38
Universe, as responsive, 24-25, 180-81, 281
Upanishads, 11
Use of time, 48-49

V

Van Gogh, Vincent, 206
Violence, and play, 216
"Voluntary simplicity, " 248-51

W

Wells Fargo, 237
Wholeness, ix-303!, and especially 71-73, 137-38, 157, 194, 256, 271-73, 294-303
Whyte, David, 292
Wirkus, Mietek, 162-63
Workplace, 185-88; trends in, 227-234; and women, 230-33. *see also* Life-Work balance
Worsley, J.R., 157

X

Xerox, 237

Y

Yin and yang, 157-58. *see also* Subtle energy
Yoga, 156

Z

Zones of comfort, living and learning, 28-44, 192; practice, 41-42

Transcript of a conversation between Lynda and David Chethlahe Paladin. Copyright © 1983 by Lynda Paladin. Reprinted by loving permission of Lynda Paladin.

Psychophysiologic self-awareness and self-regulation training: A data-based assessment of EEG amplitude scores and divergent thinking measures by Dr. Peter Parks. Doctoral dissertation, Saybrook Institute, San Francisco. Copyright ©1996 by Peter Parks. References used by permission of the author.

"A Poetic Interpretation of the Letters of the First Verse of Genesis" by Stan Tenen. Copyright ©1997 by Stan Tenen, Meru Foundation, Sharon, MA. Reprinted by permission of the author. Author's Note to Readers: This translation is only one of dozens of interesting letter level interpretations of Genesis 1:1, and should not be regarded as "the" translation.

"Please Call Me by My True Names" from *Being Peace* by Thich Nhat Hanh. Copyright ©1987 by Thich Nhat Hanh. Reprinted by permission of Parallax Press, Berkeley, CA.

Moon Beach, a collection of original haiku poems by R. Christopher Thorsen. Copyright ©1977 by R. Christopher Thorsen. Reprinted by permission of the author.

Considerable effort has been made to clear all reprint permissions necessary for this book. The process has been complicated and in some cases the source was unknown. If any required acknowledgements have been omitted, it is unintentional. If notified, the author will happily submit those acknowledgements for further editions.

Joel Levey, Ph.D. and Michelle Levey, M.A. have been fortunate to travel extensively and to learn with people of many disciplines, wisdom traditions, and global cultures. Founders of the HumanKind Learning Community, they have been blessed to study and work closely with many of the most respected leaders of our time. The Leveys serve on the National Advisory Board for the National Institute for Health and Productivity Management, and as core-faculty for International Center for Organization Design. Dr. Joel Levey has served as Graduate Faculty at Antioch University, Director of Psychophysiological Therapy and Stress Management for Group Health Cooperative, and Director of MindBody Fitness Training for SportsMind. Michelle Levey has taught stress management and mindbody therapy at Children's Hospital, and is on the Executive Board of the InnerFaith Foundation. Previous publications include: *Quality of Mind; The Fine Arts of Relaxation, Concentration, & Meditation; The Fine Art of Relaxation* CD; and *The Focused Mindstate,* a best selling tape series from Nightingale Conant. Nationally and globally recognized as leaders in their field, their corporate programs and popular workshops are highly acclaimed. They live in Seattle, Washington.

Wisdom at Work

Joel & Michelle Levey are founders of Seattle based InnerWork Technologies, Inc., a firm that specializes in developing and renewing organizational cultures in which team spirit, community, creative intelligence, life-work balance, and inspired leadership can thrive. Over the past 25 years they have worked with over 200 leading organizations including: AT&T, NASA, Advanced Technologies Laboratories, Hewlett-Packard, DuPont, World Bank, NOAA, Petro Canada, Shell, Stanford Research Institute, the U.S. Army Green Berets, many medical centers, professional organizations, world class and Olympic prize winning athletes, and various community service groups.

Joel & Michelle's work offers a unique synthesis of insights woven from contemporary disciplines and enduring wisdom traditions including: systems thinking; social architecture & organization design; community building; peacemaking; quality communications & high performance teamwork; peak performance training; comparative religion and contemplative traditions; mindbody medicine; global travel and cross cultural study.

Joel & Michelle offer workshops, bi-annual week-long retreats, and quarterly gatherings for people committed to deepening the wisdom, balance, creativity and compassion they bring to life-work-world. They also offer executive coaching by special arrangement.

If you would like to learn more about the Leveys' work, or to explore how they may be of service to your organization or community, please let them know of your interest:

Joel & Michelle Levey
InnerWork Technologies, Inc., Seattle
Email: balance@wisdomatwork.com
W e b s i t e:
w i s d o m a t w o r k . c o m

or

c/o Conari Press
2550 Ninth Street, Suite 101
Berkeley, California 94710

Conari Press, established in 1987, publishes books on topics
ranging from spirituality and women's history to sexuality and
personal growth. Our main goal is to publish quality books
that will make a difference in people's lives—both
how we feel about ourselves and how
we relate to one another.

Our readers are our most important resource, and we
value your input, suggestions, and ideas. We'd love to hear
from you—after all, we are publishing
books for you!

For a complete catalog or to be added to our mailing list,
please contact us at:

CONARI PRESS
2550 Ninth Street, Suite 101
Berkeley, California 94710

800-685-9595   Fax 510-649-7190
e-mail Conaripub@aol.com